Melanie Warren

LANCASHIRE FOLK

FOLK

Ghostly Legends and Folklore
from Ancient to Modern

Melanie Warren

LANCASHIRE FOLK

Ghostly Legends and Folklore
from Ancient to Modern

Schiffer Publishing Ltd®

4880 Lower Valley Road • Atglen, PA 19310

Designed by Danielle D. Farmer
Cover design by Brenda McCallum
Type set in ITC American Typewriter/Batik/CasablancaAntique/Benton Sans

ISBN: 978-0-7643-4983-6
Printed in China

Published by Schiffer Publishing, Ltd.
4880 Lower Valley Road
Atglen, PA 19310
Phone: (610) 593-1777; Fax: (610) 593-2002
E-mail: Info@schifferbooks.com

For our complete selection of fine books on this and related subjects, please visit our website at www.schifferbooks.com.
You may also write for a free catalog.
This book may be purchased from the publisher. Please try your bookstore first.

We are always looking for people to write books on new and related subjects. If you have an idea for a book, please contact us at proposals@schifferbooks.com.

Schiffer Publishing's titles are available at special discounts for bulk purchases for sales promotions or premiums. Special editions, including personalized covers, corporate imprints, and excerpts can be created in large quantities for special needs. For more information, contact the publisher.

....

Other Schiffer Books on
Related Subjects:

Haunted London: English Ghosts, Legends, and Lore. Ashley E. Rooney
ISBN: 978-0-7643-3149-7

Fashionable Mourning Jewelry, Clothing, and Customs. Mary Brett.
ISBN: 978-0-7643-2446-8

Scottish Ghosts. Ashley E. Rooney
ISBN: 978-0-7643-3990-5

Ireland's Ghosts, Legends, and Lore. Ashley E. Rooney. ISBN: 978-0-7643-4508-1

Ghosts in the Cemetery: Farther Afield.
Stewart Schneider. ISBN: 978-0-7643-3590-7

CONTENTS

Introduction.................10

A

Accrington...................14
Adlington 17
Anderton 18
Appley Bridge..............19
Arkholme.....................20
Ashton
    (Near Preston).........21

B

Bacup..........................22
Bamber Bridge............23
Barley.........................23
Barnoldswick..............24
Bashall Eaves 25
Bickerstaffe 26
Bispham 26
Blackburn....................27
Blacko 34
Blackpool....................34
Bolton-by-Bowland.....40
Borwick.......................42
Bretherton 42
Briercliffe 43
Brindle 44
Broughton 46
Brunshaw 46
Burnley 46
Burscough 54

C

Carleton 55
Carnforth....................55
Caton 56
Chaigley.....................56
Charnock Richard........57
Chatburn 57

Chipping 58
Chorley 60
Clayton-le-Moors........62
Clayton-le-Woods 64
Clitheroe.....................64
Cliviger.......................69
Clowbridge 70
Cockerham..................71
Colne..........................73
Coppull.......................74
Crawshawbooth...........74
Croston.......................75

D

Darwen 76
Downham 77

E

Eccleston 78
Entwistle 78
Euxton 79
Extwistle 79

F

Fair Snape Fell.............81
Fernyhalgh...................82
Fleetwood 82
Foulridge.....................87
Freckleton...................89
Fulwood 90

G

Galgate........................92
Garstang......................92
Goosnargh...................94
Great Eccleston............97
Great Mitton 97
Greenhalgh..................97
Grindleton...................98

H

Halton 99
Hapton........................99
Hardhorn 99
Haslingden 100
Heskin Green...............101
Heyhouses..................101
Heysham 102
Higher Penwortham... 105
Hoghton......................106
Hornby........................108
Huncoat......................110
Hurst Green.................110
Hurstwood..................112

I

Inglewhite 113

K

Kelbrook 114
Kellamergh 114
Kirkham 115
Knowle Green.............116

L

Lancaster.....................117
Laneshaw Bridge 121
Larbreck......................122
Leyland 122
Longridge....................125
Lostock Hall................126
Lower Bartle................126
Lytham........................127

M

Marton Moss 130
Mawdesley..................132
Medlar-with-Wesham 133
Melling 134

Mellor 135
Mellor Brook 135
Morecambe 136

N

Nelson........................138
Newchurch in
   Pendle.....................139
Newton in Bowland....140

O

Old Langho 141
Ormskirk..................... 141
Osbaldeston 143
Oswaldtwistle............144

P

Padiham.....................145
Pendle 146
Parlick Pike 146
Pilling 151
Pleasington...............153
Poulton-le-Fylde........154
Preesall 155
Preston 155

R

Rawtenstall................ 161
Reedley 161
Ribchester 161
Rivington 162
Rossendale...............163

S

Sabden 164
Salwick......................164
Samlesbury 164
Sawley.......................168
Scotforth 168

Silverdale 169
Simonstone 169
Singleton 171
Slaidburn 171
Slyne 172
St. Annes 172
St. Michael's on
   Wyre 174
Staining 174
Stalmine 175
Stydd..........................176

T

Thornton....................177
Thurnham...................179
Tockholes...................179
Torrisholme 180
Trawden 181
Tunstall 182
Turton 182

U

Ulnes Walton 184
Upholland 185

W

Walton-le-Dale...........187
Warton
   (Near Blackpool) 188
Warton
   (Near Carnforth) 188
Waterfoot...................188
Weeton.......................189
Weir 189
West Bradford 190
Whalley 190
Whitewell 193
Winter Hill 194
Wiswell Moor 195

Withnell......................195
Woodplumpton 196
Worsthorne................198
Wrightington 200
Wycoller 200

Two Last Lancashire
Tales...........................202

Conclusion.................203

Bibliography 204

Topical Index 206

Appendix 223

Photo Gallery 229

INTRODUCTION

In 1899, when Andrew Lang wrote his *Book of Dreams and Ghosts*, he stated that an apparition—a ghost—was simply a hallucination. His book set out much evidence supporting his opinion and perhaps he was correct to suggest that there are no ghosts, there is no such thing as a fairy, and the devil does not pay personal visits. However, Lang's scepticism did not prevent him from enjoying these tales of ghosts in the same way that he loved the folktales that inspired his series of "Fairy" books; many of my generation will fondly remember happy childhood hours engrossed in these lovely books, whose origins are clearly set in British folklore. There is something in the human psyche that loves these tales of ghosts and witches, "boggarts" and fairies.

Additionally, Lancashire has more than enough reason to tell tales of witchcraft, as it saw the execution of many so-called witches in the seventeenth century. There are historical accounts, but there are also many folktales of local witches—elderly Mothers who suddenly became apprised of wisdom and miraculous powers that they used to trick the unwary. In most cases, the unwary often deserved to be tricked, because they were guilty of infidelity or cruelty to those they considered beneath them. These folktales are amusing and even heartening, with their unequivocal message that goodness wins out in the end.

The same can be said of the many tales of the devil in Lancashire. Most of them tell of a common man or woman tricking the creature, or the innate intelligence of the village school teacher or the humble tailor winning out against all the devil's evil thoughts and actions. These stories make it abundantly clear that the devil is not as clever as he thinks—and that he is remarkably clumsy, considering he is a supernatural being. Something about these folktales makes us smile and they persist because people love them.

As for ghost stories, many of them are so old they are folktales themselves, passed down the ages by word of mouth and doubtless elaborated on in the process. But that does not mean such tales should be discarded, for where there is smoke there is fire, and once the smoke has died away, one can often find a real event in local history that is responsible for the tale and is, in itself, just as interesting. For instance, many of the most romantic and tragic stories have their origins in the sixteenth century, when the Reformation led to the persecution and deaths of many Catholic priests and civilians who refused to give up their Popish ways. The stories have been embellished and may not be strictly factual, but they have their basis, at least, in fact. Even very modern stories quickly become embroidered and it can easily be seen how they might become the folktales of the future.

It seems there is hardly a town or a village in Lancashire that does not have a tale or two of a haunted house, a sad spirit grieving for a lost love or a boggart causing trouble. The word "boggart" is a Northern term similar to "bogeyman," used to describe any troublesome invisible being. The locations of these stories vary from houses and farms to great halls and manors, from ancient castles to modern-day factories and shops. There are even ghostly experiences that take place out of doors. Some of the tales are very old indeed; some are very modern. Some are repeated down generations; some are reported quite factually in newspapers and thus preserved for posterity, even if the author of the piece cannot resist adding a line or two of ridicule. Sometimes a later report will triumphantly claim that a natural explanation has been discovered: the White Lady was a scrap of white curtain left in the empty "haunted" house, moving in the breeze, the sound of music simply the wind through a broken window pane. There are quite a few stories amongst these pages that are explained as perfectly natural events, misconstrued by superstitious percipients, but that will not prevent them from entering into local folklore.

The interesting thing about folktales of all kinds is that similar stories can often be found in different locations. The tale of the devil being raised through a floor by unwary schoolboys is told about two separate grammar schools, at Burnley and at Clitheroe, whilst a very similar tale is told about two threshers in Blackburn. (Where such a tale appears in the following pages, reference is made to other occurrences.) Such accounts often can not be claimed as purely Lancastrian, as they also occur in other counties. In some cases, the tales can even be found in other lands far, far away. Asking which story came first is often a useless task—I prefer to believe that they simply have always been.

Folktales often centre around ancient monuments that, before modern excavations, were known about only through folk-memory. Many such sites, with their evocative names, were known as burial places long before archaeologists became involved and pronounced them to be so. Even without excavations, local people always revered them as places of the ancestors and told tales of protective boggarts, or even buried treasure.

The devil himself was given credit for some cairns—although, in the case of stones, he generally dropped them by accident because, as we have heard, he was not as clever as he thought. Standing stones, their real purpose long forgotten, were still regarded with awe and imbued with magical powers by those who spoke of them. Some stones were said to move when no one was there to see; some turned over at midnight; some travelled to a nearby holy well to drink.

In time, legends and folktales also attached themselves to more modern stones: stone crosses, which are truly ancient, their carved illustrations dating from six, seven, or eight centuries ago. They can be seen not only in churchyards, but also in marketplaces and alongside roads, far from either church or market. Those in churchyards did not mark anyone's final resting place, although they did sometimes commemorate a saint; they were used instead for preaching, sometimes before the accompanying church had been built. Roadside crosses were at times boundary markers for Abbey lands, but they also had the purpose of reminding passersby that Christ died on the cross for them. They were often used as resting places for a coffin when the bearers had a particularly long walk to the church and thus became known as "coffin stones." Prayers would be said there while the coffin rested. Market crosses were used for general proclamations, as well as announcements of punishments to be handed out to miscreants of all kinds. Thus the crosses would be in close proximity to whipping posts, pillories, and stocks.

These crosses, with boulders for their bases, have stood in their places since very ancient days and, with a little knowledge, the wonderful carvings upon them can be seen to represent both Pagan and Christian mythology. It is no wonder, then, that legends and stories have grown up around some of the crosses themselves. Many of Lancashire's crosses do not survive, but often their bases do remain and still carry the name of "cross." Even these boulders are regarded as holy, or magical.

Many crosses also marked the sites of holy wells or springs, placed there when these wells were given Christian saints' names in an attempt to move the people away from their Pagan worship of nature. Such wells and springs had always been valued for their miraculous properties: some were reputed never to dry up and so were valuable resources; others had wonderful healing abilities, being known variously for their effects on eyesight, weak limbs, or sickness. Before the saints claimed them, these springs were known to be the haunts of fairies and water-sprites, who could be helpful or harmful, depending upon one's reverence. Gifts would be left: coins, flowers, pins, beads, buttons. Wishes would often be made and some wells were particularly known for their efficacy in granting these wishes.

It is understandable that sources of fresh, clean water were so important to our early ancestors, for water is a necessity for life. Village life often centred around the village well. This was surely also understood by the early Christians who chose to build their churches close to springs and wells already revered in the locality—and also why they chose to use the water to perform Christian baptisms. But the addition of saints' names to these Pagan places did little to halt the Pagan beliefs and rituals, which continued to be observed for centuries after Christianity imagined it had cast them out.

Within these pages I have listed many of Lancashire's ancient monuments, holy wells, and crosses, as long as I could find a legend attached to them. Some of the haunted pubs listed here have changed their names or may no longer exist by the time this book goes to print, as in these fast-moving times, these kinds of changes are common. I've updated them as closely as possible. I have recorded every folktale I've discovered in over thirty years of research. I have also included every ghost story I have heard, whether the detail is rich or scant. Some of you may be able to fill in the details and I will be pleased to hear from you! I am also aware that you may know of other ancient sites and more ghostly tales; often such stories are known only in the immediate locality and are not otherwise recorded. Again, I welcome your comments and stories!

You will find some familiar tales here, but also some new ones that have lain hidden away in dusty books for decades—sometimes, centuries. To you, the reader, I wish the same joy I experienced when finding these particular stories for the first time.

ACCRINGTON

Arndale Shopping Centre

Accrington's Arndale Shopping Centre stands on the site of an old cinema that was long thought to be haunted. There has been a cinema here since 1937, although it has changed its name several times. At first a Regent, it was sold in 1945 to the Odeon group, in 1967 to the Classic chain, and finally, in 1973, it was bought by Unit 4, which turned it into a multi-screen cinema. It is from this last period of conversion that the earliest known stories come.

One workman, described by a workmate as a "pretty hard-boiled, down-to-earth sort of chap," left the building in terror after feeling a ghostly hand settle on the back of his neck and then grab his hair to pull his head backwards. He refused to come back on site after that.

When the cinema manager heard this story, he could not dismiss it as he had also had strange experiences. He reported how he had once watched in disbelief as the stage curtains swept closed in the middle of a film. No one had been in the right place to operate that machinery; it remained a mystery that was never solved. He also said he had seen a ghost—a small, shadowy man. Other staff members had sometimes seen dancing blue lights.

Eventually, the old cinema was demolished to make way for the modern Arndale Centre. Now, shops directly on the site of the old cinema also report their fair share of weird happenings, notably strange noises, and the unexplained triggering of burglar alarms. It has been suggested that there is a natural explanation for these effects. During the construction process of the new shopping centre, a stream had to be culverted and it now runs directly beneath the shops concerned. During heavy storms, the force of water rushing underground may be producing mysterious noises and, who knows, shaking the fabric of the shop-buildings and triggering burglar alarms.

However, that cannot explain the many tales told about the cinema that once stood there...

Black Abbey

The name for this area of the town, Black Abbey, is a misnomer as there was only an abbey grange here, not an abbey, and the monks wore white, not black. It was around 1190 when the monks of Kirkstall Abbey were granted some land here to build a grange—a farm where lay brothers would live and work to supply their abbey with food. Kirkstall Abbey was a Cistercian monastery just outside Leeds and as the grange was so far away from the abbey itself, it is very likely that a Chapel would also have been built on the site, to enable the monks' prayer and, perhaps, encourage local worship. However, this arrangement lasted less than a century, as the land was sold to a local landowner in 1280.

Perhaps the evocative name of Black Abbey stems from the dark story of three hapless monks—named in some sources as Humphrey, Norman, and Robert—who lost their lives when their residence burned to the ground. The fire, it is said, was deliberate, which begs the question: why? The prosaic idea that local villagers set the fire in retribution for the loss of their lands is believable. The chance of it being an accident is even more likely. But, fortunately for mythology, there is a much more romantic story: a legend of love and tragedy.

The story tells of one monk who, despite his sacred vows of chastity, fell in love with a local girl called Ursula. Because of the scandal that would have ensued if the lovers were discovered, they could only meet in secret in the monk's private quarters at the grange. However, their secret was discovered by a local boy who was also in love with Ursula; when she spurned his advances, he took revenge by telling her father about her illicit relationship with the monk.

One night, when Ursula was with her lover, her father came to the grange looking for her. The monk, hearing his angry approach, hid Ursula in a secret room to keep her safe. Confronted by Ursula's father, he refused to admit any knowledge of her, but despite his protestations, he was overpowered, chained up, and locked in his room. After the incensed man had left, Ursula emerged from her hiding place and, as she tried to free her lover, the two of them realised that her father had set fire to the building. Try as she might, Ursula was unable to free the monk from his chains. He begged her to try to escape the fire without him, but she refused, vowing that they would die in each other's arms. And so they both perished.

The Black Abbey area is said to be haunted, not by the monk, but by poor Ursula, who tried so desperately to save the man she loved, only to die with him. It is said that she is beautiful, with long, fair hair, but that her face is full of a great sadness. It is also said that she is sometimes heard to scream, before she disappears.

East Crescent

In 1984, over 300 apples rained from the sky into a garden in East Crescent. The couple who lived there were woken by a horrendous noise, which they thought was a freak hailstorm. They were mystified to discover that the noise was made not by enormous hailstones, but by apples.

It has been suggested that the apples may have fallen from a plane—but the fact is that apples continued to fall for over an hour in the very localised area of this one back garden, so a passing airplane cannot be the answer. It has also been suggested that a tornado may have lifted the fruit and just as suddenly dropped it again. Tornadoes in the UK are more common than one might think—between ten and fifty are reported every year—but they are never very strong and could not transport anything very far. And surely a localised tornado would have been noticed elsewhere and not only affect this one back garden in East Crescent.

Hynd Brook House

Hynd Brook House is a modern block of sheltered accommodation flats, but despite its modernity, residents have become used to catching glimpses of a ghostly man in a brown suit. They are so unconcerned by his presence that they have even given him a nickname: Albert. The flats were built in 1993, so perhaps Albert is a ghost from whatever house stood on that site years ago. He seems friendly enough though, and the atmosphere in the building is peaceful.

Miner's Arms

Regular visitors to the Miner's Arms pub, on Blackburn Road, have reported strange shadows in the bar and the sense that fellow drinkers are "there one minute, gone the next." There have also been physical events such as glasses that smash when no one is near, objects that move on their own, and light bulbs falling out of fittings when no one is near them.

Peel Park

In the Peel Park area of the town, there once were many small cottages. One of these was home to "Old Ailse" who was commonly believed to be a miser with a hidden hoard of wealth. After her death, her hoard could not be found, but the long-held belief that it existed was kept alive by many sightings of Old Ailse's ghost in the area. Surely she must have been hunting for her lost treasure.

In 1889, Accrington Hall was demolished; built in 1800 by Jonathan Peel, this grand house had outlived its usefulness and the land was to be cleared and used for a housing estate. Sadly, this land clearance plan also included Old Ailse's cottage. Legend has it that during the excavations her hoard was finally found. Her ghost has not been seen since.

(See Tasker Street for a very similar story.)

Springhill House

Springhill House is now a care home, but several years ago it belonged to the Sykes family. One night, their eldest daughter awoke and immediately noticed that her bedroom was very cold. She opened her eyes and was startled to see an old man wearing a grey coat standing at the foot of her bed. He vanished after a few moments. Later, her fiancé was staying overnight at the house and woke to see the same man—he was so startled by the "intruder" that he leapt out of bed to confront him, only to realise that he wasn't really there. Over time, everyone in the family came to experience this raincoat-clad ghost.

Soon after moving in, Mrs. Sykes had commissioned a local artist to produce an oil painting of the house and the completed work was given pride of place in the dining room. No one noticed anything odd about the painting at first, but repeated examination revealed a strange anomaly: viewing it from a certain distance gave the impression of a figure standing at a window on the top floor, although this figure disappeared when examined closely. It was Mrs. Sykes' daughter who eventually spotted the resemblance to their ghost. Once pointed out, it was obvious—it was a man, wearing a grey raincoat.

Tasker Street

The tale told about the miser of Tasker Street is very similar to that told about Peel Park. In the miser's day, this street was called Tit-Tat Lane and he lived in an old farmhouse there. It was always said that he had a hoard of wealth hidden somewhere in the old place, and this was the reason for his haunting the area after his death. Eventually, the property was demolished and, according to the legend, the contractor found the treasure...and so the miser's ghost haunts no more.

(See Peel Park for a similar story.)

ADLINGTON

Bridge Inn

At the Bridge Inn on Park Road, many customers and staff have seen the form of an old man wearing a dark coat. He has appeared in many places around the building. Often seen in the cellar, he has just as frequently been spotted in the bar. In 1995, a newspaper report described how a barman, closing up for the night, left his friend alone in the bar for a few minutes. He came back into the room to find his friend frightened out of his wits; he had just watched a man in a dark coat walk quietly past

him and straight through a locked door. Another regular customer returned from a visit to the men's room in a somewhat flustered state, having just seen the ghost standing beside him. Local knowledge says that this unprepossessing ghost is that of ex-landlord Charlie Lamb, who is believed to have died on the premises.

Chaffer's House

A large house at the corner of Church Street and Adlington Street was once known as Chaffer's House after the family who had lived there. It was given an identifying name after a story grew up that there was a secret in its cellar. At the end of the nineteenth century, a small boy was shown the mysterious cellar by the lad who lived there and he never forgot the experience of lifting a large flagstone and seeing, beneath it, a large space.

The boys were forbidden to explore the space but did not need any warning because they were afraid of the ghosts they believed to lurk there. They had been told that the dark space was much larger than could be seen because it was part of an entire passageway that led in one direction to St. Peter's Church and in the other to Towneley Hall. They truly believed that the passageway was peopled by the ghosts of all those who had used it in centuries past.

It cannot be ascertained now whether this secret passageway really existed—except for the fact that over a century ago, one small boy saw it with his own eyes.

Ridgway Arms

No ghost has ever actually been *seen* at the Ridgway Arms, on Chorley Road, but landlord after landlord has claimed that it is haunted. A variety of strange things have been experienced, from glasses going missing to shelves falling off the walls. Customers have often complained about a cold draught, which could be coming from a fireplace, were it not for the fact that it has been bricked up for years. It's assumed that the cause of all these odd occurrences is the presence of a previous landlord—although some people who have experienced the ghost say it is female and have christened her "Betsy."

ANDERTON

Headless Cross

Near the Millstone pub in Anderton, at a crossroads, there is a carved stone a few feet high, known as the Grimeford Cross. It was once at the centre of the village of Grimeford, but the village no longer exists. Some call it the Headless Cross, because there is no actual cross in evidence there now, just the stone that was its base, supporting a waymarker stone of a later date. The original cross may well be that which was found during excavations for the nearby reservoir and now resides in Preston's Harris Museum. The cross has been judged to be a thousand years old and one carving on it shows a figure wearing a horned helmet, so some have said it represents an important Viking chief. However, doubt has lately been cast on the idea that Vikings ever wore helmets bearing horns. It is more likely that the figure represented on the Grimeford Cross is a character from Norse mythology.

The fact that the cross resides in a museum explains why the stone at the crossroads is known as the Headless Cross. It is also said that there was once a chapel here, beneath which was a tunnel. During the sixteenth century, amid the violence of the Reformation, this tunnel was used as a hiding place by a priest escaping the pursuit of the King's men. Unfortunately, when danger had passed, the priest failed to re-emerge. Although his body was never found, it was assumed that he had died—especially when his ghost was repeatedly seen near the Headless Cross.

This ghost may have an alternative explanation, as described several years ago by an elderly Anderton resident, whose great-uncle Joe Hill had been the gamekeeper at Anderton Hall. Joe was cruelly murdered and his body found by his niece, who was taking him some provisions. As she approached Joe's cottage, she saw three men running away, wearing milkmaids' bonnets to shield their faces from view. The men were never caught, their motives never explained. Joe's great-nephew believes that the ghost seen so often by the Headless Cross is Joe himself, still hunting down his murderers.

APPLEY BRIDGE

Skull House

The relic that gives Skull House its name is thought to have once belonged to a martyred priest...or perhaps an Arthurian knight. The latter is not as farfetched as it might seem, because there are many tales linking Lancashire place-names to Arthurian legend. Indeed, Arthur is supposed to have fought one of his most important battles at Wigan, just a few miles away. The story that concerns us here is of Gareth, who fought the Knight of the Skull in his quest to reach Castle Dangerous. The evidence connecting the story with Appley Bridge is that a castle is believed to have once stood on the site of Skull House. Coincidentally, a stretch of road close by has long been known as Dangerous Corner.

Arguably, the alternative tale, of a martyred priest, is more likely, as several similar tales exist in Lancashire and do have their basis in historical fact. We have no name or history for this particular priest, but he is said to have been chased through the house by Roundhead soldiers and caught just as he tried to escape through a skylight window.

Another version of the tale says that he hid up the chimney and was "smoked out" by the soldiers who lit a fire beneath him. When he emerged, he was murdered, like so many other priests at that time.

Whatever the explanation, the skull still resides in Skull House, because if it is removed, awful things happen until it is put back in its rightful place. It has even returned to the house on its own, on occasion! One person threw it into the River Douglas, but the skull mysteriously reappeared in the house—and the offender drowned soon afterwards. Another person who moved it well away from the house almost died when he subsequently fell down the stairs. For a time, it resided in Manchester Museum, but had to be retrieved after a succession of nights disturbed by terrible noises.

Sometime in 1940, a teenage girl brought her friend to stay with her aunt in Skull House. The only bedroom was accessed by an old spiral staircase and the girl and her friend were left alone for the night, the aunt staying with her mother nearby. In the middle of the night, the girl woke to hear a noise like a metallic chain being thrown onto a stone floor, followed by the sound of someone running into the cottage and up the staircase, when the door was thrown open and the sound of panic-stricken breathing filled the room. Terrified, the girl woke her friend, who could hear nothing and was convinced the whole experience had been a dream. Next morning, over breakfast, the girl's aunt listened to the story and apologised for not warning the girls in advance...

Incidentally, this mystery deepens with the knowledge that the Roundheads did not come this far into Lancashire—and that an expert has pronounced the skull to be that of a woman.

ARKHOLME

Redwell Inn

Situated in the beautiful Lune Valley, the Redwell Inn is a seventeenth century coaching inn on Kirkby Lonsdale Road. Long ago, a young stable boy died here, the victim of a fire in the stables. Perhaps it was this young boy who was seen so clearly by the landlord's father-in-law in 1985. The boy appeared to be about ten years old and everything about him seemed very real, although his clothing was unusual: he wore breeches, clogs, and a green-woollen jumper. But then he suddenly disappeared! The father-in-law may not have been the only person to see this young boy—his tiny grandson had sometimes been observed offering biscuits to the empty air, before withdrawing his gift saying, "Gone..."

ASHTON
(NEAR PRESTON)

Preston Castle

At the place known as the Maudlands in Ashton, near Preston, there is an interesting mound. Archaeologists confidently state that this mound was the base for a small observation tower built by the Romans with the purpose of protecting the Friargate entrance to Preston. Local people, however, always had superstitious feelings about the place, because the area was also known to be the site of a medieval leper hospital, St. Mary Magdalene's. The mound was commonly believed to be the site of the hospital's church, now sunken into the earth. On Christmas Eve they say bells can be heard ringing from beneath the ground.

The mound was excavated and found to contain a brick-lined chamber, narrow but about six feet deep, which the archaeologists identified as a powder magazine where gunpowder would have been stored in wooden barrels. However, the local people refused to accept this diagnosis and took the chamber's existence as evidence for their own beliefs, for surely it must be part of the church's steeple.

Interestingly, the story of the subterranean bells of St. Mary Magdalene's is also told about the ground beneath St. Walburge's Church.

St. Walburge's Church was also the scene of a veritable miracle in 1845, when a Preston woman suffered a broken knee that threatened to cripple her. St.Walburge was a Saxon princess whose shrine was known for imparting an oil with healing properties, so a request was sent for a small amount of the magical substance. The woman's knee was entirely healed after using the substance.

Spa Well

Spa Well used to be in the area below Maudlands closer to Preston Marsh, near the river. The well gave forth copious amounts of mineral-rich water that was valued for its health-giving benefits—so much so that late in the sixteenth century, the flow was harnessed into a proper bathing pool that was well-used. The water was said to be extremely cold and was described as "fizzy" and "invigorating," and this is why it became known as Spa Well. Any saint's name the well may once have carried is lost in the mists of time.

BACUP

Hell Clough

Up on the moor near Bacup, Greens Moor has long been an area of stone quarrying and the Greens Moor Quarry was once known as Hell Clough. As you'd expect, there's a legend that explains how this came to be. Somewhere near this rocky area there was once a good-sized natural pool and the devil was fond of using it for bathing. One day a terrific storm swept over the moorland and the devil found that the heavy rain had so overfilled his bathing pool that the edge was about to give way under the weight of the water. If that happened, the pool would empty itself down the hillside. He realised that he needed to construct some sort of dam to prevent this calamity, but how?

The devil looked around for an answer, and down in the valley he saw a hayrick covered with thick sheeting for protection. This gave him an idea. He flew quickly down to the valley, took the sheeting, and wrapped it about his waist like an apron. Then he returned to his pool at a more leisurely pace, gathering boulders as he went along and carrying them in this apron. It was a good plan, but sadly his apron could not hold the weight he expected of it. Before he reached the pool, it gave way and all the boulders tumbled out to land in one huge pile on the moorland. It is this pile that later became known as Hell Clough.

As for the devil's bathing pool...well, as he had feared, the edge of his pool did indeed give way and the whole of the contents poured away down the hillside. The handy bathing pool was gone forever and the devil would have to find somewhere else to wash.

Royal Court Theatre

Bacup Royal Court Theatre on Rochdale Road is housed in a building that has been put to a variety of uses; originally an iron foundry, it became a theatre early in its history, then a cinema, and later a bingo hall, before being remodelled as The Empire Theatre. Now it is known as Bacup Royal Court Theatre, under the ownership of Bacup Amateur Operatic and Dramatic Society.

As well as this interesting history, the theatre also has a resident ghost christened "Norah" by the Society members. She has been seen by members of staff, cast, and crew, as well as unwary visitors. In 2008, the theatre hosted a team of paranormal investigators, who reported hearing the ghostly sights and sounds of an audience settling down for an evening's entertainment. But a psychic amongst them did question the name Norah, saying that she believed the name "Kitty" was more relevant. Later, she was shown a book about the history of the theatre—which mentioned an usher called Kitty...

BAMBER BRIDGE

Baxi Heating

During World War II there was a base in the town of Bamber Bridge for American servicemen—both white and African-American. In June 1943, there were race riots in Detroit and their effects were not lost on the troops in Bamber Bridge, despite the fact that all the soldiers were welcomed by the local residents regardless of their ethnic origin. The news of the Detroit riots eventually led to a riot here, which became known as the Battle of Bamber Bridge. It began as a simple disagreement between some soldiers drinking in the Old Hob Inn, but it quickly led to a fistfight between white and black men, a fight that spilled out onto the road and through the town. It escalated into a battle between the African-American soldiers and the white military police, and in the end shots were fired and one black soldier, William Crossland, suffered a fatal head wound.

Seventy years have passed since then, but at the nearbyBaxi Heating factory all is not well. Some night shift workers have reported feeling very uncomfortable during the darkest hours; they have heard the sound of someone whistling and, at other times, laughing. In recent years, a security officer swore he would not venture into the warehouse again after he saw a ghostly World War II soldier.

St. Saviour's Church

In 2008, two friends decided to spend a night in the churchyard at St. Saviour's Church with the intention of taking photographs that they hoped might show some "orbs"—the mysterious blobs of smoky light that sometimes appear on digital photographs and are commonly supposed to be spirits.

They did take some photographs, but what appeared on them shocked them to the core. Rather than the expected orbs, one of the photographs showed a mist over a grave, out of which a figure was forming. On the next photo, they could make out a misty face. They took no more photographs, preferring instead to head for the safety of their car.

BARLEY

Barley Brow

A pair of poachers from Barley once caught a couple of fairies. One night, they had crept to a rabbit warren, put their sacks over the rabbit holes, and left them there until they could tell by the feel of the sacks that they had caught something. They tied the necks of their sacks, slung them over their backs, and set off for home.

Walking back up the steep hill to Barley, they remarked to each other on the noise their catches were making and then were even more astonished when the squeaking noises coming from their sacks turned into little voices! One voice called out, "Where arta? Where arta?" And the other answered, "Here I am, in a sack, going over Barley Brow!" The poachers dropped their sacks and ran.

(For a very similar story, see Hoghton, Local Legend.)

Lower Black Moss Reservoir

In December 2011, four centuries after the infamous trials of the Lancashire Witches, a grass mound near the Lower Black Moss Reservoir was excavated and found to contain a building. Archaeologists were called in and found a well-preserved cottage, several hundred years old. The area is near the village of Barley, so close to Lancashire Witch territory that conclusions were quickly drawn that this must be the fabled Malkin Tower, scene of the witches' meetings.

The fact that a mummified cat was found bricked up in one of the walls was also given as evidence that this was a place of witchcraft. However, it's very unlikely that this was true, for this common tradition of burying a cat in the walls of a house was believed to keep witches and evil spirits away, rather than encourage them.

The cottage—which was undoubtedly a remarkable archaeological find—was eventually pronounced to date from around 1680, many decades after the time of the Lancashire Witches. The question of why it was buried remains.

BARNOLDSWICK

Lister Well

There is a road on White Moor called Lister Well Road, so this well is relatively easy to locate, although the original stone trough is no longer there. The water from this spring had magical healing properties and was in regular use for at least five centuries. Whether it ever carried a saint's name is unknown; since the sixteenth century, it has been known as Lister Well, named for a farmer who enclosed the land here after the dissolution of the monasteries.

Northern Costume Hire

Northern Costume Hire is a long-established business operating out of a warehouse that holds a vast collection of over 20,000 costumes. The warehouse is frequented by the general public as well as major TV companies—most of the UK's favourite soap-operas have used costumes from this business.

The warehouse is also home to George...who is a ghost. He doesn't cause any problems and the staff is comfortable knowing he's there. They have even learned to treat him as another member of the workforce. If a costume cannot be found, they ask George to find it for them. Next morning, the required outfit will be found hanging on a rail.

BASHALL EAVES

Local Area

The fabled King Arthur is said to have fought an important battle in the local area of Bashall Eaves. Early historians say that Arthur fought twelve major battles against the Saxons and he passed through Lancashire when pursuing Colgrin, following him in his flight to York. The histories mention that he fought a battle at the River Bassas, which is now known as Bashall Brook.

Local Farm

In 1934, farmer John Dawson was on his way home from the local pub when he felt a sharp blow to his shoulder as if someone had thrown a stone at him. He looked around for his assailant but saw no one. His shoulder was painful but he gave it little thought, until the next morning when the pain had increased so much that he asked his sister to have a look at it. She was horrified to realise that her brother's pain was caused not by a stone, but a bullet. She immediately sent John to hospital, but it was too late; he died a few days later in Blackburn Royal Infirmary.

Police spoke to every gun owner in the area and, as the bullet had clearly been handmade, every workshop was examined for evidence, but the killer was never found.

Today, the lane by John Dawson's farm is still avoided at night, as many people have seen the ghost of a figure with a gaping wound in his back passing through the hedge into the farmyard.

BICKERSTAFFE

Mossock Hall

Mossock Hall Golf Club on Liverpool Road is set on 130 acres of beautiful countryside, and the building that now houses the clubhouse is very old—some parts of it date to Elizabethan times. It is an impressive red-brick building adorned with mullioned windows.

For a long time the building was neglected and, during that time, when only a farm labourer was living there, it became known locally as Boggart Hall. There were tales of ghosts walking the narrow road near the barn accompanied by the sound of clanking chains. In the house itself it is said that a ghostly lady in a green dress walked around. When visitors came to the Hall, the lady would follow them, and when they left, she would bang the door shut behind them, before disappearing.

Legend has it that the "Green Lady" walked no more after a substantial hoard of money was found; perhaps it was this treasure that held her to the place. The hoard was found in the hollow staircase or, according to other reports, in a chest on the landing that had commonly been used for hiding valuables and perhaps even accoutrements for celebrating Mass. There was certainly a priest in residence there in the early 1700s.

Another tale speaks of a large stone trough that had been rescued from a field and rehomed near the stables. It seemed to be happy in this spot, for superstition said that if it were ever moved, it would be found back in its original place the next day.

BISPHAM

Robins Lane

Robins Lane extends for several miles, from Bispham to Skippool in one direction, meandering in the other direction to Carleton and beyond the crematorium into Poulton. Only in Carleton is the lane actually lined with houses; the rest is no more than a country path dotted with several old farms. Originally, it linked all the local farms with the agricultural market that used to be held at Carleton.

Late one night, a group of teenagers—including my son—had a strange encounter whilst walking home along Robins Lane. One of the boys had been standing atop a small hillock near one of the many dew ponds, when something white and misty had swept past him before disappearing. None of the other boys had seen anything, but their friend was obviously distressed and they cast about for an explanation for the strange white mist. They found none.

Only a week or so later, another teenager of my acquaintance described his own encounter with "the Robins Lane ghost." A couple of years earlier, he and a friend had been walking home along this popular shortcut, late at night, when suddenly they saw a white shape in front of them. It was only there for a few seconds and so they carried on walking. When they reached the place where the shape had appeared, they saw it again in a field to their left. They walked on and then, to their horror, it appeared once more—in front of them, when it should have been behind them! The idea that some ghostly apparition was playing games with them was too much for these teenage boys; they turned tail and ran back along the path, taking the long route home instead.

Intrigued by these stories, the next Saturday night a friend and I took our dogs for a walk along Robins Lane. We hoped we would see the mysterious light for ourselves. We walked quite a distance, we took several photographs, and the dogs were ecstatic at this midnight adventure, but we saw nothing remotely supernatural—until we developed the photographs. One of them showed a white, misty shape hovering above a field. Had we captured the ghost of Robins Lane on film? Sadly, probably not. We surmised that the strange glow was most likely caused by the camera flash lighting up a patch of marsh-mist. The following day we retraced our steps and sure enough, we found a pond. The boys had probably seen a similar patch of mist, lit up for a second or two by a distant car headlight. How disappointing!

(See also "Local Lane" in Thornton, which may be an earlier example of the same phenomenon. The local lanes may be Robins Lane. Also see Carleton, Crematorium for another Robins Lane ghost.)

BLACKBURN

BBC Radio Lancashire Studios

The Radio Lancashire studios have been the scene of several spooky occurrences. One presenter saw a ghostly figure behind him, reflected in the studio window; another witnessed a speaker moving several inches, in plain sight. Banging noises and strange sounds appearing on recordings are just some of the reported happenings.

The building now housing the radio station was once a bakery and, according to local knowledge, was the scene of an unfortunate death, when an employee toppled into a flour hopper and suffocated. The assumption, of course, is that this is the source of the haunting.

Byrom Street Fire Station

Records show that there has been a fire brigade in Blackburn since at least 1794, based at a variety of locations before finally settling on Byrom Street in 1921. Over thirty cottages in the vicinity were also fire brigade property for the use of firemen, although these cottages are now all privately owned. One former employee's name has passed into legend, as he is believed to have been haunting the Byrom Street Fire Station since his death in 1940. His name was Robert Hodgkinson—commonly referred to as "Bob Ockie."

Arguably the best of these tales about Bob Ockie concerns the experience of one Jim Yates, who was on switchboard duty overnight. In the early hours of the morning, the old-fashioned switchboard indicated a call from the recreation and snooker-room above. Knowing that the room was empty at the time, Jim ignored the call. A short time later, he heard snooker balls rolling across the floor and was forced to investigate. He was mystified to find that over twenty snooker balls were indeed on the floor of the recreation room. There was no one else in the building and no one could have accessed that room without first passing him at the switchboard. Jim later discovered that the house where he was living was the very same one where Bob Ockie had died. It's easy to conclude that this is why he was singled out for such a display of Bob's presence!

CVS Resource Centre

Once the Star and Garter pub, in 2010 this derelict building was renovated and converted into a Community Voluntary Service (CVS) Resource Centre. It came equipped with a ghostly reputation of which the new inhabitants may not be aware.

Many years ago, the Star and Garter gained a haunted history after three successive landlords died within just eight months. Their deaths may have had entirely natural causes, but it would have been surprising if the locals hadn't begun to regard the place with some suspicion. The attic rooms were said to always be cold, no matter how warm the weather; they were unused for many years, but footsteps were heard up there regardless. During a period of renovation, electricians rewiring the upper floors left in haste after one of them found himself having a conversation with his colleague—who was in a different room at the time. Footsteps were also heard on staircases, which were fully carpeted. Regular customers remarked that they had seen an elderly man sitting in the tap room, who was not there the next time they looked. Sometimes he was actually seen to leave the premises—straight through the wall.

Landlords were not immune to these visitations; one even went so far as to have the building blessed, so disturbed was he by the atmosphere. Years later, another landlord's son was tidying up after closing time, when a chap passed him on his way to the men's room. He did not re-emerge and, when the landlord's son finally went to investigate, the room was empty. There was no other possible exit.

Despite the spooky occurrences, one landlady was often amused by her spectral lodger, whom she christened "Dick." One Christmas, frustrated that her Christmas lights refused to work, she commented out loud to her unseen guest, "As you're living here rent free, Dick, do something about the lights." The lights promptly came on.

Duck & Puddle

The Duck & Puddle pub on Dukes Brow used to be called the Quarryman's Arms. The building dates from the eighteenth century and was named for its customers of that time, who were mostly workers from the nearby quarry. Perhaps the ghost haunting there is one of those quarrymen. Whoever it is, it makes its presence known by switching lighting and gas taps off at inopportune moments and sometimes footsteps are heard.

Grimshaw Park

In the Grimshaw Park area of Blackburn, there once stood some old dwellings known as Jack Croft Cottages. The cottages were demolished long ago, but are worthy of mention because of the very musical ghost that once haunted them—it was often heard playing the hornpipes, very capably. In addition, the ghost would playfully tug the bedclothes from sleeping folk and drop them at the other side of the room.

Holy Trinity Church

The stunning Holy Trinity Church in the Mount Pleasant area is no longer used as a church, but the building is cared for by the Church's conservation trust. It is a Grade II listed building. (Grade-listed buildings are those deemed by the Government's Secretary of State to be of special historical interest; rules exist about their preservation, differing according to the building's Grade.) Holy Trinity Church made the news, in February 1887, because of a ghost that was seen in the churchyard. The story was covered by newspapers nationwide, with the headline: "Extraordinary Ghost Scare."

 The story told how a "considerable commotion" had been caused by the sighting of a young and beautiful ghostly woman dressed in modern clothing in the churchyard one Sunday evening. Having heard that a ghost was abroad, some young men camped out in the churchyard in the hope of catching a glimpse of it, but when it eventually did appear—in the midst of a "strange, lurid light"—they were so shocked they didn't know what to do. One of them could think of no better course of action than to throw his bottle of ginger beer at the ghost, and it promptly gave chase! The young men were so frightened that they ran away.

 Two days previously, the same ghost had appeared in the house of a certain Mr. McCann, who lived close by the church. Late on Friday night, McCann's lodger had seen the young woman sitting by the fire, and the next morning he enquired of his landlord about the lovely lady, as he was not aware there were other guests staying in the house. McCann had laughed at him—but on Saturday evening, he saw the woman himself. He spoke to her and, when he received no answer, spoke more crossly. At this point, the woman stood up and McCann, realising that she was a ghost, fainted. He fell so heavily that a doctor had to be called to attend to him.

The ghostly woman was identified by local people as a girl who had tragically died in a fire some years previously, although no mention is made of her possible connection to McCann's house or, for that matter, the churchyard of Holy Trinity Church.

A few days later, a further newspaper report covered the continuing ghost scare, commenting that there were, at that time, around half a dozen houses lying empty because the area had gained such a reputation for being haunted. One woman took a house on Moor Street, but was there for only a matter of days before giving the key back to the landlord, so disturbed had she been by unearthly noises at midnight. The situation was so severe that children living in the area were even being let out of school early, so that on those short winter days they could be sure of being home before dark.

The report ended by saying what a crime it was to have so many houses lying empty on account of such a rash of superstition, which in their view must be down to "some ingenious youth" pretending to be a ghost for reasons of his own. But at the time of writing, the events still remained a mystery.

King George's Hall

The century-old building called King George's Hall is one of Lancashire's top entertainment centres and, with such a theatrical history, it is no surprise that there are stories of ghosts. Running children and a man wearing a top hat are just some of the reported sightings. An older story tells of a man who tragically died after falling into one of the pipes in the organ room—surely one of the most unusual deaths in this book!

Palace Theatre

On Blackburn's Boulevard there is a piece of land now used as a car park that once held a magnificent theatre called the Palace. The ghost of the Palace Theatre was well-known. The tragic story told of an eighteen-year-old girl who visited the theatre one night late in the nineteenth century. Sitting high in the second balcony, she spotted some friends seated below her and, as a joke, tried to attract their attention by aiming peanuts at them. So engrossed was she with her game that she lost her balance and tumbled from the balcony, falling over a hundred feet to the ground. The fall was too much—she hit her head on one of the empty seats and died at once.

The girl's ghost was seen many times, usually when the theatre was empty, apart from drama society members rehearsing their next show. Even when the theatre became a bingo hall, her ghost continued to appear. The building was demolished in 1989—but who knows; this tragic girl may still haunt the prosaic car park on the spot where she died.

Postal Order

In 2001, staff at this town centre pub, which had previously been a post office, reported that the place was haunted. The duty manager explained that strange things had been happening for over twelve months and she had been the first to see, in reflection through a mirror in the bar, a middle-aged lady in a long dress or nightdress. She was so frightened by the experience that she almost quit her job on the spot, but became less worried when other members of the staff also started seeing and hearing things. One colleague saw an unusually well-dressed gentleman in suit and tie enter the kitchen where he was working. He seemed not to be aware of anyone, he did not speak, and after a few moments, he simply turned and left again. Enquiries were made, as it was assumed that the gentleman must have been someone from the head office of the chain operating the pub—but no answers were found. No one of that description had been visiting the pub that day.

Raising the Devil

Blackburn has a story that two men threshing corn in a barn had been discussing the old tale that one could "raise the devil" by drawing a circle on the ground and reciting the Lord's Prayer backwards. They decided to see if the ritual worked and were, naturally, horrified when it did and the devil began to appear, rising between them through the floor of the barn. They had little alternative but to beat him back down with their threshing flails.

(See Burnley and Clitheroe Grammar Schools for very similar stories.)

Telephone Exchange

Blackburn Telephone Exchange has long been regarded as haunted; strange noises have disturbed night-shift workers and the sounds of piano playing and heavy footfalls have been heard.

The site was once occupied by the Grand Theatre, built in 1880 and holding an audience of 3,000. In the early 1930s, management of the theatre was taken over by William Murray, who boasted involvement in launching the career of one Charlie Chaplin. After William died, his son Roy became manager, but like so many theatres, the Grand had to close in 1956, the advent of cinema and TV tolling its death knell.

Even before the building was adapted for use as a telephone exchange, there were rumours that the building was haunted. In addition to the piano playing, sometimes the stage curtains drew across the stage on their own. Demolishing the building and putting a telephone exchange in its place did nothing to dispel the rumours.

Three young men working the night shift in the Telephone Exchange experienced the ghost for themselves. Heavy footsteps were heard upstairs and then they heard the lift in operation, apparently coming up to their floor from the ground floor. The doors opened, but there was no one inside.

The lift was also the scene of a more visible ghost when a cleaner, who had worked at the exchange for over twenty years, saw a rather ill-looking lady go into it. It was full daylight when the cleaner saw the blonde woman dash into the lift as if she was in a hurry to leave. Yet, even though the doors closed, the lift did not move. Concerned about the woman, the cleaner opened the doors again—and the lift was empty. On another occasion, the cleaner's colleague was washing her hands in the ladies' washroom on the fourth floor when she felt someone brush against her—but no one else was in the room. The same ladies' washroom was the scene of another event when two female night-shift workers visited the room and heard the taps gushing water while they were both in the cubicles.

The source of these odd happenings is thought to be the ghost of William Murray, the one-time owner of the theatre that once occupied the plot. However, given the above experiences—the woman in the lift, the taps in the ladies' room—that seems unlikely. Just possibly, there is more than one ghost at the Exchange...

Union Buildings

In 1869, a court in Blackburn pronounced, amazingly, that a boggart had been responsible for breaking numerous windows in the Union buildings. The court heard how windows had been broken by stones every night for several weeks, to the great expense of the residents. The disturbance had been so bad that a reward was offered to anyone who could reveal the assailant, since he had always vanished before he could be spotted.

Finally, a respectable-looking man called George Hindle was arrested by PC Livesey, who had been instructed to keep the buildings under constant watch. His evidence was that he had seen Hindle go into his brother-in-law's house, from where he sent a stone flying at the opposite house. A moment later, Hindle came out of the house and picked up the stone again. However, that was the only point at which the constable could say he had actually seen Hindle with a stone in his hand—not actually in the act of throwing it, but with it in his hand.

Hindle vehemently protested his innocence. He said that the stone had been in his hand because the constable had asked people to collect the offending stones and give them to him as evidence. He said that, despite his innocence, he would rather pay the costs of the broken windows than be standing where he was that day: in court. In his defence, it was pointed out that the reward money had been doubled by the prisoner himself and, moreover, windows in his own house had been broken by the mysterious stone-thrower. Also, since Hindle had been in custody, more windows had been broken. Witnesses were brought forward who said that they had been standing with Hindle when stones had come through their own windows—it could not have been him; it must have been a boggart.

Incredibly, the end result of this court case—which caused much laughter in the courtroom—was that the magistrate had no recourse but to pronounce that a boggart had indeed been responsible for breaking the dozens of windows. George Hindle was released without charge.

Utopia Nightclub

There has been a nightclub at this location for over forty years and many still remember its first incarnation as The Cavendish Club. Now it is known as Utopia. Over the decades there have been many reports of strange happenings that have been blamed on a ghost. It was once suggested that the ghost might be someone who had died when there was a fire at the Cavendish, but news coverage of the time does not contain any reports of deaths.

Reported occurrences include cold atmospheres in particular areas of the club, items going missing only to turn up later, and at least one barman falling over an invisible stool. A cleaner in the late 1970s saw a man in Victorian clothing walk out from the dressing rooms, along the back of the bar area, and then out onto the stage. The entertainments manager saw the ghost, too—it followed her from the building to the nearby cathedral grounds and might have followed her all the way home if she had not said, "Stay here! This is where you belong!"

The most disturbing report comes from a man who was routinely locking up the club one day when his dog suddenly became very distressed. Usually a placid creature, the animal was staring into space and growling, hair on end. The man calmed him and got him into the car, but as he was driving away, he saw that the exit doors—that he had just locked—were wide open. He called the police who could find no intruder. However, the sturdy chain across the doors was now broken—not sawn, but snapped...

Well
(NEAR THE WELLINGTON INN)

Near the Wellington Inn in Livesey, a natural spring flows into a stone trough. In the old days, it was reputed to be good for sore eyes, as are many holy springs that we now know to be rich in healthful minerals. This well does not seem to be dedicated to a saint—if it once was, the dedication is lost in time.

BLACKO

Cross Gaits Inn

It has been said that a concealed cellar at Cross Gaits Inn was used to hold prisoners on their way to Lancaster Castle. There is even speculation that some of these prisoners were witches, maybe even the Pendle witches themselves. A recent landlord was told of this possibility by several of his regulars, who also claimed that there were shackles and chains affixed to the floor of the cellar. Intrigued by this, the landlord used his renovation of the pub as an excuse to examine the building closely. Sadly, he found no such cellar; if it did once exist, it had been completely obliterated by concrete.

The Cross Gaits is also said to be haunted, although this may have nothing at all to do with witches. They say that sometimes a ghostly woman with a dog can be seen sitting close to the fire and, in the spot where she sits, it is cold despite its proximity to the fireplace.

BLACKPOOL

Arnold School

Arnold School on Lytham Road was established in 1896, and the cellars long held a reputation for being haunted. In the 1970s, a group of boys were given permission to spend a night in the cellars by the headmaster, who doubtless thought it would be a harmless game that would put an end to the whole idea of a haunting. Unfortunately, the boys managed to scare themselves witless by using a Ouija® board and getting messages from a lady who claimed she had been murdered and was haunting the school in an attempt to make the truth known. When the room suddenly became icy cold, the séance drew to a hasty conclusion. The boys did not know that, back in time, some previous occupants of the building—which was now the headmaster's house—had been hung for murder.

Blackpool Football Club

Legend has it that the boardroom of Blackpool Football Club is lined with oak panelling taken from Lord Nelson's flagship. Of course, Nelson's flagship HMS *Victory* survives and is safely berthed at Portsmouth Naval Base—but perhaps the panelling was taken from another grand ship that foundered off the Fylde coast. The naval ghost seen in the boardroom, then, may not be Nelson as some have claimed, but possibly he is a long-lost sea captain we will never identify.

Blackpool Tower

In 1848, a ship called the *Ocean Monarch* sank in the seas just off the Blackpool shore and many people drowned. Ever since then, people have claimed to see these poor souls passing through the walls inside Blackpool Tower, some holding hands. Witnesses have reported seeing a White Lady in the ballroom—she plays the piano—and various stars from the Golden Years have also been seen or heard.

Blackpool Zoo

Blackpool Municipal Airport closed in 1945, because the new site at Squires Gate was closer to the coast and thus better placed. The site lay unused and unoccupied for thirty years before Blackpool Zoo was built on the same spot but, despite the time that has elapsed, several keepers have reported that their flats seem to be haunted. The Elephant House is similarly afflicted!

Frenchman's Cove

Frenchman's Cove, a pub on South King Street, was at one time a tobacco warehouse. The cellars were renowned for their spooky atmosphere. The presence was never seen, but it was certainly felt—many of the staff experienced the sensation of being watched, although they knew they were alone in the place. During the building's transformation from warehouse to pub, many different tradesmen were employed, and they all complained of the same feeling: they felt as though they were not alone. The owner of the place eventually had to take them seriously, especially when he went down to spend some time in the cellar—and felt the presence for himself.

Some reports claim that the ghost was the spirit of Laura Schoons, but this is a simple misunderstanding. Laura was, in fact, a clairvoyant from Scarborough who was hired by Leeds United Football Club to exorcise Elland Road football ground and help the team win the league. The manager of Frenchman's Cove had this pointed out to him by his father, who suggested Laura Schoons as an ideal candidate to sort out the cellar in the pub. The manager appealed for her to come forward through newspaper articles, but whether he ever found her, or whether the cellar was indeed exorcised, is uncertain.

Grand Theatre

A former manager of the Grand haunts the theatre—he is recognised by his footsteps, the smell of pipe tobacco, and is thought to be simply popping in to visit a place he loved dearly. Another ghost, Charlie, has a more tragic history. In the 1930s, Charlie developed a crush on the star of a show, even though she wanted little to do with him. When she eventually turned down his advances for good, he was so distraught that he jumped to his death from the dress circle balcony. One producer working at the Grand used to sit in the upper dress circle to watch rehearsals—but stopped after he felt someone tap him on the shoulder, on three occasions, when no one was there but him.

Illuminations Building

The Illuminations are a huge collection of decorative lights that are strung above the road along the famous Golden Mile—which actually stretches for six miles along the coast. Some are purely decorative, but some are in the shape of characters from films, books, and cartoons, and there are also many "tableaux" alongside the road, some of which are interactive. The "Lights," as they are locally known, are lit every evening from August to November and the influx of visitors driving through the exhibition helps to extend this coastal town's summer season and, therefore, the townspeople's livelihoods. For the rest of the year, the Lights are stored in the Illuminations Building on Rigby Road, where they are cleaned, repaired, and refurbished for the next year's display.

The building is haunted by two ghosts: one a drowned boatman, the other a younger man who was killed by a donkey when the site held the donkey stables.

Outside, on the tram tracks, a tram driver was knocked down and killed here by a tram in the early 1960s. He may be the reason why a ghostly tram is sometimes seen quietly progressing along the Prom, very late at night when no earthly trams are in service. Perhaps he is also the reason why people have reported seeing a male ghost walking along the tracks, carrying a lantern.

Old Coach House Hotel

The Old Coach House on Dean Street dates back to 1851 and was formerly a vicarage. It is believed to be the oldest house in the local area of South Shore. Many guests of the hotel have commented that the dining room is home to two ghosts who watch over them at mealtimes: a male figure dressed in a black cloak and cap, and a female, known to the staff as Shirley.

Pleasure Beach

The Pleasure Beach Amusement Park would seem an unlikely home for ghosts, but in fact there are several.

The Ghost Train is haunted by "Cloggy," a clog-wearing ride attendant who died around the end of the 1970s. His footsteps are very distinctive, but some staff have also reported seeing him, too. Other odd things happen as well, such as electrical equipment bursting into life, even though it is disconnected from the power supply. One member of staff witnessed one of the "decorative" skulls on the ride flashing its illuminated eyes as he passed it, but on double-checking found that the power had been switched off.

A ghostly male figure who looks like Karl Marx wanders about in the Star pub; he has been spotted in the cellar, in the old living accommodation, and in the bar. Glasses and bottles—and even pictures on the walls—have been mysteriously moved, lights have been switched on and off, and a woman has been heard singing.

The sound of invisible skaters has been heard in the **Ice Rink**, equipment has been moved by unseen hands, and padlocked doors found open. Perhaps the scariest ghost in the whole Pleasure Beach area is the female ghost haunting the **Arena**, particularly in the area of the tractor bay, where people have felt a terrible chill and a presence they can only describe as "awful." In **Sir Hiram Maxim's Gift Shop**, a ghostly, small girl has been seen and in the **Pleasure Beach Casino**, the ghost of a construction worker named Patrick is sometimes about. He died during the building of the Casino in the 1930s and has haunted the place ever since it opened, especially in the maintenance area. In the **Alice In Wonderland ride**, surely one of the least likely places for ghosts, a phantom hanging man has been seen. This, however, is beaten by the **Tunnel of Love**, which is home to a spectral blood-stained woman.

Raikes Hotel

Raikes Hotel on Liverpool Road was originally Raikes Hall. It was built in the mid-1700s and is now a Grade II listed building. It was originally a private residence surrounded by thirty acres of grounds and remained a family home for a century, until it became home to a Roman Catholic convent school. The school flourished and within fifteen years needed larger premises, which it found in Layton. The new school, St. Mary's High School, still exists. And so, in 1876, Raikes Hall was put up for sale, attracting the attention of local businessmen who saw potential in the Hall's extensive grounds for a park and pleasure gardens.

Now, Raikes Hall is better known as the Raikes Hotel pub and is reputed to be haunted. The ghost is alleged to be one of the nuns who lived at the Hall when it was a convent school and who drowned herself nearby. Her presence is felt today when items in the pub are moved around and when people hear noises emanating from the cellars at times when they are known to be empty.

(See St. Mary's High School in Layton for another ghostly nun.)

Riley's Snooker Hall

The Riley's Snooker Hall building was originally the Regent Cinema. The cinema opened in 1921 and remained so for fifty years, when revenues then declined to the extent that the building was turned into a bingo hall, and latterly the snooker hall. In 2013, the building was auctioned and bought by a company that, happily, intended to restore it as far as possible and use it as an antiques emporium.

Just before the auction, an amateur photographer took advantage of the building's availability and went for a viewing, taking several photographs as he walked around. To his surprise, he later found that one of the photos showed a mist travelling across the area being photographed. On others he saw orbs (balls of light, which ghost hunters commonly believe to be spirit manifestations). One of the photographs showed the shape of a man, sitting in one of the remaining seats in the old cinema's circle. It is hoped that the new owners of the building treat their ghostly resident, who seems to have been there for many decades, with respect.

Ripley's "Believe It Or Not!"

This permanent Ripley exhibition is weird enough all on its own. It is based on the extensive collection of Robert Ripley (1890-1949), an American eccentric who travelled extensively and could not resist acquiring strange objects from wherever he went. He set up several permanent exhibitions all over the world. Blackpool's collection includes shrunken heads and fertility statues. One of the latter has been in the Blackpool exhibit for several years and the museum claims that over a thousand pregnancies can be attributed to its otherworldly powers. Any woman touching it can expect to be pregnant within three months.

Ripley's exhibition was once haunted by the ghost of a woman in the building's cellar area: the "vaults." The ghost was believed to be connected to a skull that had been loaned to the exhibition. The skull was the property of a local man, Mr. Boardman, who had bought it years before in a charity shop and believed it to belong to a sixteenth-century girl who had been buried on the site of the Foxhall Hotel.

Mr. Boardman believed the skull to be the cause of several strange events that followed his purchase of the ancient object. He felt that his home was haunted by ghostly figures connected to the skull, and a run of bad luck led him to think the skull was actually cursed. His own grandmother had begged him to get rid of the object—two days later, she was involved in a car accident that killed her. During the time the skull was on loan to the exhibition, it went missing, and Mr. Boardman warned that if anyone tried to sell or destroy it, they might well suffer similar fates. The skull was found some weeks later, abandoned on a side-street.

Finally, after years of living in fear of the haunted skull and tiring of accusations that he was somehow involved in witchcraft, Mr. Boardman decided to rid himself of the item once and for all; he gave it into the safekeeping of a local priest. Two weeks later, Mr. Boardman was found dead, having apparently died in his sleep.

Saddle Inn

The landlady of the Saddle Inn on Whitegate Drive became so disturbed by supernatural events in her pub that she called in paranormal investigators. Glasses had been smashed when no one was close enough to cause their fall and other objects had been pushed off shelves by invisible hands. These things were puzzling enough, but when one of the barmen saw a ghost in the cellar, the time had come to call for help.

The landlady found the ghost hunt as scary as the events she hoped to cure: a white mist was seen, peculiar smells were experienced, and objects moved on their own. The investigators claimed to have made contact with several spirits including a cleaning lady, a religious father who said the garden of the pub had once been a graveyard, and "Sister Mary," who said very little.

In the cellar, the ghost hunters made contact with one David Cottam, who matched the barman's description of the ghost he had seen, wearing a long jacket and a flat cap. He said he had died many years before and had once been cellarman at the pub. It remains to be seen if anyone can prove David Cottam actually existed...

Sea-Bathing

During the eighteenth century, sea-bathing became popular because of the magical health-giving properties the water was said to impart. Indeed, people advised to partake of the more famous waters at Bath and finding it too far to travel, would come to Blackpool instead. A shoemaker from Lancaster who had lost his sight entirely was brought to Blackpool and stayed for six weeks, during which time he bathed daily and also drank great quantities of the water. It is said that he recovered his sight completely, so that "he could readily distinguish objects at a distance of two miles."

South Shore Hospital

The old South Shore hospital has been demolished to make way for a state-of-the-art, modern primary-care centre. It remains to be seen whether patients of the new hospital experience a ghostly visitation, but it is not unlikely, as demolished buildings do not always mean the end of ghosts. The old South Shore Hospital was often visited by a ghostly nun, walking the wards at night to cast a caring eye on sleeping patients.

St. Mary's High School

St. Mary's High School was once a convent school and there are reports of at least one ghost here: a Grey Lady who is seen walking in an area that was once an orchard. There is talk that she may be one of the nuns who lost her life when she fell from a high window.

(See also Raikes Hall, Blackpool, which is connected with the same order of nuns and similarly has a ghost.)

Superbowl

Blackpool's ten-pin bowling venue, Superbowl, was once the site of the Lobster Pot restaurant, which was well known for being haunted by a former chef who had taken his own life. It seems that the building's change of use has done nothing to lay this spirit to rest—many people have seen a ghostly figure, and bowling machinery has been known to malfunction. Early morning cleaning staff have witnessed machinery running without power. Talking has been heard coming from a passageway, and night staff are never keen on going up to the third floor alone (where the restaurant used to be) because of the strange atmosphere.

Victoria Hospital

Many staff members, from nurses and auxiliary staff to cleaners, have reported that ghostly nurses haunt several wards of Victoria Hospital. Some have even felt an unearthly presence pulling at their clothes.

BOLTON-BY-BOWLAND

Bolton Peel Farm

Bolton Peel Farm on the Bolton-by-Bowland Road is now a dairy and must surely take its name from the fact that there was once a pele tower on the site. Nothing of that fourteenth-century fortification can now be traced, but it is entirely possible that stone from the disintegrating building was used in the construction of the farmhouse and other nearby buildings. There is an ancient story of a boggart in this area and it's likely that this farm was the scene for that tale. Crockery was thrown, milk was spilt, and fires were set. A young girl taken on as a servant was blamed, particularly as the events stopped as soon as she left. Or maybe it really was a boggart who had taken a dislike to her and settled down again once he had frightened her away.

Fooden Spa

A well near Fooden Farm was once well known for its healing properties, although its sulphurous smell would have been rather off-putting.

Rainsber Scar

Now demolished, Bolton Hall was a pleasant building, home to the Pudsay family. Sir Ralph Pudsay was married three times and had twenty-five children, as shown on his monument in the church at Bolton-by-Bowland. He is also remembered for his charity after the Battle of Hexham, when he gave refuge to the defeated King Henry VI. For generations afterwards, the Pudsays treasured the boots, gloves, and spoon the monarch left behind. The king also paid for a spring in the grounds to be properly dug out and a brick enclosure built to collect the water. The resulting pool was large enough to bathe in.

However, another Pudsay concerns us here, one who lived in Elizabethan times. It is said that this Pudsay (we do not know his given name) was once approached by two fairies called Michael and Lob, who wanted to take up residence on his land. To be specific, they wanted to live in Arthur's Cave by the River Ribble, beneath the cliff known as Rainsber Scar. In return, they offered Pudsay a silver coin with magical powers and also told him where a silver mine could be found.

The usual result in such tales is that no one gets rich—but in Pudsay's case, the mine was real enough and the place where he started producing dozens of silver shillings is still called Mint Cottage. Of course, this activity was illegal and before long the authorities came looking for Pudsay, but he evaded them with the help of another gift from the fairies: a bridle with a magic, silver bit that gave his horse the power to outrun his pursuers and even jump off Rainsber Scar and survive. As extra proof that all this really happened— the top of Rainsber Scar is still known as Pudsay's Leap.

In another stroke of luck, which had nothing to do with the fairies, Pudsay's crime of illegally minting coins was set aside by his godmother—who just happened to be Queen Elizabeth.

BORWICK

Borwick Hall

This ancient manor house is a Grade 1 listed building and is now used as an outdoor education centre. A New Year's tradition here is that someone must knock on the door on New Year's Eve and hand over a ripe apple. This practice dates back to the sixteenth century, when one snowy New Year's Eve an old lady knocked on the door looking for shelter. She was taken in by the lord of the manor, who gave her a bed and fed her well. Next day, she gave him a ripe apple and told him to keep it above his fireplace, promising good luck all year, as long as the apple was not removed.

The oldest and most beautiful part of Borwick Hall is the central pele tower, which dates from the fourteenth century. A White Lady haunts the tower; she is young and pretty, but looks sad and distracted. Perhaps she is searching for a way out of the tower, where she was imprisoned by her father when she refused to marry the man he had chosen to be her husband. Her name is commonly thought to be Elizabeth Whittington, daughter of Thomas—although the only Thomas Whittington connected to the hall had no daughter of that name. Whatever her name, the story goes on to tell how she stubbornly refused to marry a man she did not love and, as her father refused to release her from the tower until she agreed, she starved to death.

BRETHERTON

Bank Hall

Well-hidden behind trees, Bank Hall is a gem of Jacobean architecture, its existence given away only by the lodge that sits on the main road. It is a Grade II listed building dating from 1608, and was used as a location for the film *The Haunted House of Horror* in 1969. Only a decade ago the building was close to collapse, until local pressure led to a full restoration programme.

Bank Hall has a White Lady who walks her dog on the grounds—the moment she is seen, she disappears. Also, visitors to the building sometimes hear someone talking to them, when no one is near.

Carr House

Carr House is currently a private residence. It was built in 1613 by two wealthy members of the Stone family, for their brother who was a humble sheep farmer. One of its most famous residents was Jeremiah Horrocks, who may have been tutor to the Stone children and was certainly lodging at the house in 1639, when, whilst practising his interest of astronomy from the room above the porch, he made a ground-breaking observation of the transit of Venus.

More recently, Carr House was, for many years, a doll museum, home to a vast collection belonging to the owner, Barry Elder. It is from that time that most of the tales of strange atmospheres come, and it would be easy to dismiss them as fantasies born of being surrounded by hundreds of dolls with all their tiny glass and ceramic eyes. However, the unsettling atmosphere always seemed centred on a particular area of one particular room, that contained a bolt-hole in the floor. Was it a priest-hole? Did a tragedy befall some priest here?

BRIERCLIFFE
Calf Hey Well

In the Roggerham Gate area of Briercliffe was Calf Hey Well, which was anciently known to be a haunt of fairies. It was a strong spring and as far back as medieval times the water was believed to have healing qualities. It was regarded as a holy well and a veritable market would gather here on holy days, selling jugs of well-water and also food and religious mementos.

Sadly, Calf Hey Well was such a sure source of water that it was redirected to a reservoir to serve the town of Burnley. After this upheaval, the fairies who had so often visited the place were never seen again.

Very close to Roggerham Gate is a place called Brownside. The very name Brownside is locally said to have originated in the many sightings of brownies hereabouts. "Brownie" is simply another name for "fairy"' and many people said they saw the tiny folk in this area. Very early in the nineteenth century, a local woman had cause to travel to Burnley in the middle of the night to fetch a doctor. At the stream by the ford, she saw a brownie smoking a pipe.

Whether these were the same fairies associated with Calf Hey Well, only the fairies know.

BRINDLE

Gregson Lane
THE HOLY HAND

There is a house here whose lintel bears the initials GG (George Gregson) and the date 1700. It was the last shelter of Edmund Arrowsmith, a Catholic priest who is now known as a Saint. Edmund Arrowsmith (whose given name was Brian) was born in Haydock in 1585. He was given his new name when he was confirmed as a Catholic priest on the continent, before he returned to England to fulfil his mission. He settled in Brindle to teach, and the Blue Anchor pub was the centre of his network; the landlord was a sympathiser and those requiring Edmund's services would call for him there.

All was well until Edmund discovered that the landlord's son had married a first cousin and, compounding the heresy, the marriage had been performed by a Protestant. Incensed, Edmund told the boy that the marriage must not be consummated until Rome had pronounced the union valid in the eyes of God. This was enough for the boy to betray Edmund to the authorities, who arrested him at the house on Gregson Lane. Edmund was imprisoned in Lancaster Castle and condemned to death. He was executed in August 1628. In time, Edmund would be beatified and, after his death, many relics of the saint made their way to churches for preservation. It is said that just before his death he begged the attending clergy to preserve his right hand, promising that it would have the power to effect miraculous cures.

The "Holy Hand" was first preserved by Edmund's family, who cared for it for many years at Bryn Hall, and later at Garswood. Pilgrims who came secretly to touch the hand claimed that it had miraculous powers of healing and, as this legend spread, the fame of the Holy Hand grew. People claimed relief from daily ills and, on occasion, impending death, and it was one of these cases that, in 1736, became the Holy Hand's first recorded Miracle. Young Thomas Hawarden had a persistent fever and had gradually lost the use of his limbs, being unable to walk or even stand. His mother drew the Holy Hand up and down Thomas' back, reciting a prayer all the time, until at last Thomas declared he thought he could stand up—and he promptly did so.

Another miracle cure is in the records: Mary Fletcher was cured of convulsions in 1768. She had suffered dreadfully and was confined to bed, her doctor saying there was nothing more to be done for her. The Holy Hand was brought to her bedside by her brother, and Mary prayed to it sincerely whilst it was applied to her body. The very next day, Mary was up and about again, helping her siblings with the housework and the baking.

These cures were formally witnessed by gentry and by priests. One priest, who had witnessed Mary Fletcher's cure, had need of the Holy Hand himself when he had a life-threatening disease of his throat. He was cured with a single touch of the miraculous relic. As late as 1872, miraculous cures were still being reported. A destitute woman from Wigan called Catherine Collins, in the workhouse because she was too sick to make her own way in the world, was cured of paralysis by the Holy Hand. This cure was reported in the *Daily News*.

Edmund Arrowsmith was ratified as a saint in 1929. His Holy Hand now resides in Ashton-in-Makerfield and is still renowned for its powers of healing.

St. Ellen's Well

In Whittle Spinney on Birchin Lane stands a Celtic Cross that is very new, but which marks the site of an ancient well dedicated to St. Helen. It may originally have been called St. Ellen's Well—some local people still refer to it as Stelling or Stellern Well, names that are clearly derived from "St. Helen." It was situated a little above St. Ellen's Chapel and was described two centuries ago as "a spring of very clear water rushing straight upwards into the midst of a fayre fountain, walled square about in stone and flagged in the bottom, very transparent to be seen, and a strong stream issuing out of the same."

As far back as 1657, this well was revered and well-used, visited each year on St. Helen's Day by Catholics who would throw pins into the well to join those of many years gone by, representing the hopes and wishes and prayers of centuries. In the 1940s, all springs and wells in the area were tested for purity and St. Helen's Well was noted as being one of the "most fresh and pure." The water was clear and cold and never ran dry, even when other springs in the area dried up. However, in 1968, none of this history held weight against the imperative of building a new motorway. The precise site of the well is now under the M61 motorway that runs beside the spinney.

In 1990, local residents, including the mayor of Chorley, began to campaign for a plaque or some other memorial to be placed near the site of St. Helen's Well, but naturally their plans were held back by bureaucracy and lack of funding. Eventually, in the spring of 2003, some frustrated (and unnamed) local people took matters into their own hands and erected a stone monument, quite without the permission of the landowners, The Woodland Trust. The monument stands around four feet high, is decorated with a Celtic Cross design, and carries an inscription. Fortunately, the Woodland Trust took kindly to this exhibition of strong local feeling and, at an amicable meeting, agreed that the cross could remain, as long as the local Historical Society took responsibility for its upkeep and future. The Celtic Cross was officially "opened" on May 18, 2004. This is surely a tale which will pass into future folklore!

St. James' Church

At St. James' Church, the devil often made his presence known by hitching rides on carts and wagons. The load of him was so heavy that the horses would not be able to pull their cart any farther and would become very distressed and unsettled. Once, the devil hitched a lift on a coffin being carried to Brindle Church, stopping the funeral procession in its tracks. The vicar was forced to deal with him by reciting a prayer and ordering him to leave—and the funeral continued unhindered.

BROUGHTON

Broughton Tower

At Broughton there was once a fortified tower house, today visible only through crop-marks. One night, in 1646, the master of Broughton Tower awoke from a dream in which he had seen a persecuted priest, Edward Bamber, hiding in a nearby field. A voice in his dream told him firmly that this was reality and so he immediately went out and found the poor priest in the field he had seen in his vision. Bamber had been imprisoned at Preston on his way to Lancaster Castle, and had escaped from his captors through a window, wearing nothing but his long shirt. Bamber was taken to Broughton Tower, where he was given food and shelter—but soon afterwards he was recaptured and taken to meet his fate at Lancaster Castle.

Even in his last moments, Bamber was true to his religious belief. He publicly absolved a fellow captive who was being put to death alongside him and as he climbed to the execution platform he threw coins to the crowd below him, calling out, "God loveth a cheerful giver!"

BRUNSHAW

Turf Moor

Near Burnley football club's ground at Turf Moor is the site of a terrifying boggart attack. The entity known as the Bee Hole Boggart abducted an old woman, "Old Bet." The only clue to Old Bet's disappearance was that the boggart left her skin behind on a thornbush! A tamer version of this tale says that only shreds of the boggart's clothing were found.

BURNLEY

Allen Street

In 1903, the *Burnley Express* investigated the story of a haunting in a house on Allen Street, just off Colne Road in the area of Burnley Lane. Every night for a week, the family living in the house had been tormented by crowds of people gathering outside their property in the hope of catching a glimpse of an otherworldly visitor, who was said to take the shape of a small soldier dressed in khaki. The family was shocked when they opened the door one evening to see a curious crowd outside their house. They were surprised to hear that their house was haunted and claimed they had no knowledge of any such thing. The rumours, however, said differently.

One story claimed that one of the children had awoken one night to hear beautiful music and opened his eyes to find his bedroom illuminated by many small lights on the ceiling. Another story said that two of the children were woken one night by noises emanating from the kitchen, downstairs. The following night, their father stayed awake to catch the intruder and heard footsteps coming towards him, with no visible cause. Still another story said that the father of the family was awoken one night by ghostly noises and when he went to investigate, he was thrown down the stairs by an unseen hand. A friend of the family then volunteered to stay in the house to thoroughly investigate the cause of these upsetting events. Awakened in the early hours by the father of the household, he heard noises coming clearly from the kitchen. Creeping downstairs, he looked into the kitchen and reported seeing all the drawers standing open and, in one of them, a very peculiar little soldier, dressed in khaki and dancing.

The family continued to protest that all these stories were fiction, but nevertheless dozens of people gathered outside their home each night, knocking at the door and asking to see the ghost. One woman simply walked straight in through the front door and into the kitchen, wanting to see for herself the place where the little soldier had danced. One man, on asking if there were a ghost in the house, was told very plainly that there soon would be, if he dared to cross the threshold. One night a shout was heard that the ghost was dancing on the roof of the scullery, resulting in the back of the house being invaded as rudely as the front.

How did these rumours originate? The family continued to insist they had experienced nothing out of the ordinary...although they did admit that the house had been visited by a couple of spiritualists a week or so before. It was suggested that a discussion about this event was overheard by a child at the mill, and so the story had quickly spread. Sometimes, the family admitted, there were knocking sounds in the house, but there was an explanation for this. A steamhammer at an adjacent colliery was often in use in the early hours of the morning and, as there were several subterranean passages in the area; the noise was amplified and could be heard in the cellars of several houses on Allen Street.

The *Burnley Express* report tried its best to explain away this story of a haunting, but the tales were, by now, too deeply believed, and the public refused to listen to reason. It was necessary for policemen to attend the crowds each night, until they finally grew bored of waiting to see the ghostly, tiny soldier dressed in khaki and stayed at home instead.

Barcroft Hall

Barcroft Hall has two legends, the first of which is commonly known as "The Idiot's Curse." The Barcrofts had been an important local family for three centuries, but the male line of the family died out only a few decades after Barcroft Hall was built.

William Barcroft had the hall built and, when he died in 1620, two of his sons began a terrible feud over who would inherit it. Thomas was younger than his brother William and, out of greed, he let it be known that his brother was quite mad—an idiot—and chained him up in the hall's cellar. He then spread the rumour that William was dead, thereby claiming the Barcroft estate for himself. One evening William managed to break out of the cellar and burst in to the party his brother was hosting. Before he was dragged back to his cellar, he lay a curse on Thomas, swearing that the Barcroft line would soon die out and the hall would never be owned by a Barcroft again.

William Barcroft Jr. died in 1641. Thomas's only son died a year later. There would never be another male Barcroft at the hall—the "idiot" had been right.

Later in the hall's history, the home was used as a farmhouse and tales of a boggart were told. The boggart was—at least at first—very helpful around the house and the farm. A tale is told of a night when the farmer called to his sons to bring the sheep into the barn, only to hear a tiny boggart voice calling back, "I'll do it!" A matter of minutes later, the boggart called out again, "I've done it, but I had trouble with the small brown one." When the farmer went to investigate, he found that the "small brown one'" was a large brown hare.

The boggart always did his work in secret, but one night the farmer's son cut a hole in the kitchen ceiling, so he could spy on the boggart at work. What he saw was a tiny, wrinkled, old man, working away in tattered clothes and with no shoes on his tiny feet. Thinking he was doing the boggart a favour, the farmer's son made a little pair of clogs, which he left in the kitchen for the little man to find. The next night he spied through the hole in the ceiling and saw the little man pick up the clogs and say, "New clogs, new wood, T'hob Thurs will never any more do good."

The farmer was dismayed to find that no more good work was done—on the contrary, the boggart became quite a troublemaker, breaking crockery, causing animals to become ill, and generally making a mess. The last straw came one morning when the farmer's bull was found standing on the farmhouse roof! The farmer decided the only way to be rid of the boggart was to move, but even this was not possible. As he drove his loaded cart away, he heard a small voice say, "Stop while I get my clogs and I'll go with you!" Defeated, the farmer went home again!

Burnley Express Offices

The offices of the *Burnley Express* were long believed to be haunted by a deceased printer, one Edward Fishpool. Edward had been a printer all his life and was expert in the handling of the heavy machinery, having transported printing presses all over the world. He came to the Burnley Express in 1910, and spent the next two decades working in the print room. He was due to take retirement in 1928, and his last major task was to prepare some printing machinery for transfer to Nottinghamshire—but he died before the task was completed. This, it is thought, is the reason why he haunted the print room for several years thereafter.

His ghost was first seen a few years after his death by a printer who had learned his art from Edward, knew him very well, and identified him easily. Subsequently, when machinery misbehaved or stalled, the printers knew who to blame. It was just Old Ned, making his presence felt.

Burnley Grammar School

The devil once made an appearance at Burnley Grammar School, a seventeenth-century building next to the parish church. Some boys had discovered that a method of raising the devil was to recite the Lord's Prayer backwards and this they set out to do. The devil dutifully began to appear, rising up through one of the flagstones in the schoolroom where the boys were gathered—but the boys were so scared by their success that they immediately began to beat him back into the earth with a hammer. A black scorch-mark left by the devil on the flagstones remained visible for many years, until the floor was boarded over.

(See Clitheroe for an almost identical story and Blackburn for a very similar one.)

Central Library

Burnley's library ghost plays classical music on the piano in the lecture theatre. The library was built in 1929, so perhaps the ghost is a music lover who inhabited one of the houses that existed there beforehand.

Coal Clough House Hotel

Now a private house, this building is over three centuries old and has had many uses: before it became a hotel, it had been a convent, then a barracks, and it is from that time that the story of a "Grey Lady" originates. According to the legend, the Grey Lady was a humble kitchen maid who allowed herself to be seduced by one of the barrack's resident officers. When she found herself with child, her lover was unwilling to take responsibility. His reputation would have been destroyed by this disgrace and so, to protect his honour, two of his fellow officers murdered the poor girl.

The Grey Lady was often seen in the pub, passing through rooms and disappearing through walls, although reports did decrease over the decades. But she has been seen in modern times and sometimes there is more palpable activity, coinciding with periods of renovation, when the building is disrupted.

An entirely different and much stranger legend attached to this building tells of the ghost of a murdered pedlar. For some reason, this ghost took the form of a bull with golden cherubs on its horns. It would appear on the porch of the building, on the eve of St. John's Day, and stay until dawn. This apparition sounds so disturbing that it's no surprise to learn a priest was eventually summoned to lay it to rest, using the age-old ritual of bell, book, and candle.

Hollin Hey Clough

Near Towneley Hall is a little dell full of holly bushes, giving the place its name of Hollin Hey Clough. The area was once blighted by a boggart who frightened unwary people using the bridge across the River Brun, so that many fell into the river and some were even drowned. The priest from Towneley Hall was entreated to lay the boggart, but he found him a tough customer and was obliged to strike a bargain. He agreed that on one single day every year, the boggart would be free to claim the first living thing to cross the bridge. The boggart promised that he would stick to his side of the bargain "as long as a green leaf grows in the clough."

Every year after that, the villagers took a cockerel to the bridge for the boggart to claim for himself. They made it cross the bridge very early in the morning, before any innocent passer-by could fall foul of the boggart's trickery. They also took note of the boggart's words about green leaves, for what would happen when winter came? And that is why so much holly grows in the clough—the evergreen bush was liberally planted by the villagers, thus preventing the boggart from reverting to his previous mischievous ways.

Keirby Inn

By the usual standard of haunted buildings, the Keirby Inn on Keirby Walk is not terribly old—it was built in the 1950s, taking its name from the Keirby Brewery, which used to stand nearby. Yet it has not just one, but two ghosts. A male ghost dates from a terrible accident during the construction of the lift, when a workman fell to his death down the unguarded shaft. Also, a female ghost has been experienced in the area of the ladies' room and is said to be someone who used to live close by the hotel. Not many reports exist of sightings of these ghosts, but the hotel certainly does sometimes have a cold atmosphere, causing shivers…

Local Legend

Many years ago, there was an old woman living in Burnley who was widely believed to be a witch, so that all her neighbours treated her with great caution. Whenever she requested food or drink it was freely given, for a refusal would elicit a curse from her lips that would undoubtedly come to pass. When people fell ill or their cattle were sick, it was always blamed on the witch and even minor strokes of bad luck were said to be her doing.

Eventually, the old woman fell ill herself. Realising that she was approaching the end of her life, she sent for a friend who lived several miles away. She breathed her dying breath into her friend's mouth and, with it, her trusty familiar spirit who bore responsibility for all the bad things that had happened in years past. Then her friend went back to her own home. And so, the local villagers found their lives improved, their runs of bad luck less frequent—and the witch's friend, miles distant, began to make her own neighbours' lives a misery.

Rowley Hall

Rowley Hall, ancient seat of the Halstead family, was once haunted by a boggart who appeared as a lady in a ball gown. This ghost was blamed for all manner of odd occurrences in the hall: doors that variously would not open, or would not stay shut, and an invisible force that stopped people in their tracks, so that they could walk no farther. The boggart was eventually laid, far from the house, at Netherwood Bridge where two streams met. A headstone marked the place. With distance between the boggart and the house, Rowley Hall was once more trouble-free. Also, by the stream, which runs close to the hall, people have sometimes found pieces of fairy clothes.

Shorey Well

This healing well is thought to be named for St. Audry, today's name of "Shorey" being a derivative. St. Audry was much revered centuries ago. An Anglo-Saxon saint, she was a Northumbrian Queen and founded Ely Abbey in Cambridgeshire. Despite marrying twice for political reasons, she managed to remain virginal, escaping from her second husband with the aid of a miraculously rising tide.

Once, the spring feeding this well issued from the riverbank of the Brun and was a general water supply; when the water was eventually diverted into pipes, the ancient stone basin was carefully preserved, so clearly this was always understood to be more than a simple supply of drinking water. What remains today is little more than a running spring, very near to the church and the Anglo-Saxon Cross at Godly Lane. Incidentally, the Godly Lane Cross is also known as the Paulinus Cross, as some say it marks the place where the Christian missionary Paulinus habitually preached.

Smackwater Jack's

This building on Ormerod Street was once a warehouse for iron and steel, and local legend says that a young warehouse-man once died on the premises. His ghost has never been seen, but he is said to be responsible for footsteps that are heard to this day, on a staircase leading to offices on the upper floor.

St. Peter's Church

If legend is to be believed, St. Peter's Church should have been built on the spot where the Godly Lane Cross now stands and where religious rites were habitually celebrated. However, night after night the stones set out to build the church were moved from that spot by ghostly pigs, so that the builders were forced to give up and build the church on its present site. On the south side of the church and on the ancient font can be seen carvings of pigs, in memory of this tale. (In truth, the pigs were probably representations of the Paschal Lamb.)

This church was also once the home of a ghostly black dog called Trash. He was said to be huge, with enormous eyes, and although he could be seen, he could never be caught because he would disappear in the blink of an eye. Those who saw Trash were certain to hear of the death of someone close to them, very soon—the damned person's distance could be guessed from how clearly the boggart dog appeared. His other name, Skriker, comes from an Anglo-Saxon word for crying or screaming and described the noises the beast was said to make.

St. Peter's was also once home to a ghostly organist, according to a letter printed in the *Burnley Advertiser*, on 1 September 1855:

> Sir some time has elapsed since our friend visited these upper regions, however, here he is again as lively as ever and most musically inclined. At intervals during the past two days all who live within hearing distance have been entertained to a charming variety of most appropriate (ecclesiastical?) music: we may especially mention as performed "con spirits" O Susanna, Merrily Dance The Quaker's Wife, and Coal Black Rose. At the moment of my writing this Willikins and His Dinah is pealing forth in tones more dulcet than Mr Robson ever made pretensions to. By inserting this possibly you may be the means of enlarging the Ghost's audience.

Swan Inn

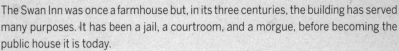

The Swan Inn was once a farmhouse but, in its three centuries, the building has served many purposes. It has been a jail, a courtroom, and a morgue, before becoming the public house it is today.

Many people have reported seeing a shadowy, hooded man in the area of the men's toilets—which used to be the lockup jail cell in the days when the local magistrate lived on the premises. The man is seen going into the room—but he doesn't come out again. A small room next to the main bar was once used as a morgue and, unsurprisingly, a very depressing atmosphere is often reported there. Lastly, a small girl is sometimes seen sitting on some steps that now lead only to a blank wall where once there was a door. In the past, this was the route for coffins to be brought into the morgue.

Towneley Hall

Towneley Hall, a building which incorporates a pele tower, is now the home of Burnley Borough Council's Art Gallery and Museum, but it has a 500-year-long history as the seat of the influential Towneley family. There are one or two stories attached to the house itself, including a spectral lady who is supposed to be seen on the battlements of the ancient tower, but such stories are denied by those who know the house best. There is one story, however, that will not go away.

Sir John Towneley, who lived from 1473 to 1541, inherited Towneley Hall as a child of nine. As a young man, he gained permission from the king to enclose the land around his hall; and, as he grew older, he greedily sought to acquire more and more. In his middle age, the king gave him permission to enclose a further 200 acres of common land, even though this would deprive the villagers of their grazing rights and thereby cause them great hardship. Sir John even evicted some of the villagers entirely, claiming that the land their cottages stood on now belonged to him. The villagers were thrown into homelessness, poverty, and, inevitably, there were deaths.

Sir John did eventually regret the suffering his desire for land had caused. At least, his ghost appears to have been racked by remorse. It is said that he returns every seven years, roaming his ill-gotten lands and calling out to those he mistreated to come and take back their homes. A traditional verse describes his call:

> Be warned, lay out! Be warned, lay out! Around Horelaw
> and Hollin Hey Clough. To her children give back the
> widow's cot. For you and yours there is more than enough!

(Nearby is Hollin Hey Clough, where a boggart was laid—was this boggart Sir John?)

Victoria Hospital

Many years ago, when this was still a coal-mining area, a local pit was the scene of a dreadful disaster and Victoria Hospital received several dozen injured miners. It was a scene of mayhem as wards filled up, and more of the injured were laid in corridors until they could be attended. Inevitably, many of these hapless workers died of their injuries and one, at least, is said to still walk the corridors of the hospital, appearing to the unwary from time to time.

BURSCOUGH

Burscough Airfield

During the Second World War, the land which now houses an industrial estate on the A59 was appropriated by the War Department. A supply depot was built and an airfield constructed. The land was returned to farming after the war, but memories of its wartime use remained in the form of the ghost of a young man, who approached farm workers from time to time. He wore civilian clothes but they appeared to be at least twenty years out of date, as did his hairstyle. His appearance led to the assumption that he may be a young airman who had perished in the war. Smoking a pipe, he would greet witnesses with a polite "Good evening," before vanishing.

Burscough Priory

Burscough Priory was founded in 1190, and a few remnants of the church still survive. A monk is sometimes seen here, but only in reflection through a mirror.

Martin Mere

Manchester historian the Rev. John Whitaker postulated that the Mere, which was once a rather larger lake, is in fact the Lake from which the Arthurian knight Lancelot took his name; Lancelot of the Lake. If this sounds wholly unlikely, bear in mind that tradition does say that Arthur won three battles in the nearby area of Wigan and Blackrod, and other places in Lancashire are said to fit with his legendary history.

Martin Mere is also notable for a monster (believed to be a huge catfish) that attacked several swans and the fact that a mermaid was once sighted here.

CARLETON

Crematorium

Late one night in 1936, a lady hailed Harry Hodges' cab and asked him to take her to Robins Lane in Carleton, requesting that he drop her off at the Crematorium gates. As he turned to take his payment, he looked out of the cab's side window and found himself staring into the face of an old man, "with sunken eyes, long dark hair, a Punch-like nose and prominent chin." His passenger, seeing the face, screamed and ran from the cab down a path to the left of the Crematorium gates. Stunned, Harry continued to watch as the phantom face moved to the front of his cab and then disappeared.

The next day, Harry called the local newspaper, hoping that someone might explain what he had seen or help him find his passenger so she could corroborate his story. The reporter asked around in the area of Robins Lane, in the hope that someone might recognise the woman's description, but without success.

Perhaps it would be surprising if a lane which has been used for hundreds of years, as Robins Lane undoubtedly has, were not haunted. Such an assertion, though, would probably have been of little use to poor Harry Hodges, who lived with his own personal mystery for the rest of his life.

(See also Robins Lane, Bispham.)

CARNFORTH

Moothaw and the
Shrew Tree

There are several hills around Carnforth; indeed the main street of the village is very steep. One hill on the north side of the canal was once known as Moothaw, a derivation of Moot Hall, for it is said that in ancient times it was a meeting place for the local Saxon law court. On this hill there was also a magic tree. It was known as the "Shrew Tree," because shrews and field mice were habitually incarcerated within it as offerings to the spirit of the tree. This sacrificial act imbued the tree with magical properties, so that just a small twig could bring about healing in diseased cattle. It is recorded that the tree was "fed" at regular intervals.

CATON

The Druid's Oak

Standing next to the ancient Fish Stones, on which medieval monks from Cockersand Abbey would sell their catch, is a tree that is, unusually, a protected monument. Its age is all too readily obvious from its battered state and shrunken size, but that is forgivable as the plaque on it says it dates from "the time of the Druids." The place where the Oak stands is the original settlement of Caton, a Norse name from Kati Ton. Modern Caton is on the other side of the Artle Beck.

A White Lady has sometimes been seen on the road approaching this ancient place. Some drivers have been known to believe they have hit the woman, only to jump from their cars to investigate and find no trace of her at all.

CHAIGLEY

Chapel House Farm

There is some doubt as to the identity of a skull that for generations was kept by the Holden family in Chaigley. It was long believed to be a relic of Father Philip Holden, who was murdered in the seventeenth century after being discovered celebrating mass at Chapel House Farm. Roundheads were the murderers: Puritan soldiers, passing through the area with Cromwell on their way to the Battle of Preston.

The story relates that after the murderers left, the priest's severed head was retrieved by his mother and hidden in the chest that held his religious accoutrements: altar cloth, crucifix, chalice, and vestments. This chest was kept in a secret place by the family, who did not want to risk the persecution that would follow if they were known to be harbouring relics of a martyred priest. But local people who heard about it began to come begging for a tooth from the skull, in the belief that it would heal all ailments. Eventually, there were no teeth left in the skull at all.

As generations were born and died, it became tradition in the family that only the eldest of them should be entrusted with the knowledge of the location of the relic chest, passing that wisdom to the next in line when they guessed that their end was near. This chest and its contents, including the martyred priest's skull, stayed at Chapel House Farm until 1823, when it was entrusted to St. Robert's Catholic Church in Catforth. Now that there is no fear of religious persecution, the skull is on display there, resplendent in a glass display case.

This legend was all but destroyed in recent times, when modern forensic tests were applied to the skull and disproved the belief that this was Robert Holden. For one thing, it was of a greater age. It is now thought to have belonged to another priest, Miles Gerard, killed in 1590 in Rochester and also part of the Holden family. Despite the legendary provenance of the skull in St. Robert's Church, what really became of Philip Holden may never be known.

(See Mawdesley for a similar story.)

CHARNOCK RICHARD

Park Hall

In the seventeenth century, Park Hall had a reputation for being a safe-house for priests and monks in the seventeenth century. A ghostly monk has been seen on the grounds and footsteps have been heard in the banqueting hall, but the strangest apparition is that of a lady who rises from the lake on the grounds. It is believed that she drowned herself after a monk, with whom she had fallen in love, rejected her. She has been seen on several occasions in the middle of the lake and is said to be very beautiful.

CHATBURN

Dule Upon Dun

Dule Upon Dun was the name of a legendary old ale-house; the name is Lancashire dialect and means "Devil upon a brown horse." Naturally, there is a story which explains this...

Once upon a time, in Chatburn, there was a tailor who was unhappy with his lot. One day the devil appeared and offered him three wishes. In return, he would visit again in seven years' time and collect the tailor's soul. The tailor agreed, asking immediately for a side of bacon, a delicacy he hadn't tasted for years. His wish was granted at once. Next, the tailor asked to be rid of his nagging wife and, at once, it was done. He was immediately sorry he had made such a silly wish—who would bake his bread now, and knit his stockings? "I wish I had never said that," he said and at once, his wife was returned to her place by the fire.

The tailor, having used all his three wishes, effectively sold his soul for a side of bacon. He had seven years to reconsider what he had done and, by the time the devil came back, he was ready for him. He talked the devil into giving him just one more wish, as he had sold his soul so cheaply. Foolishly, the devil agreed.

"I wish," said the tailor, "that you were on the back of the dun horse in that field over there, riding back to where you came from, and that you're never able to bother me or any other mortals again." At once, the devil was swept out of the house and set upon the dun horse, which galloped away, never to be seen again.

The story of the tailor's great success against the devil spread across the county and people came from far and wide to meet the man who tricked the devil…and the poor tailor finally found a prosperous life by turning his home into an ale-house for the use of his visitors.

(See Sawley for a similar story—but with different wishes.)

CHIPPING

Churchyard

The well by the church wall here is locally believed to be a sure cure for warts.

One past vicar deserves mention here also, for he was locally believed to be a wizard. His name was Wilkinson, and many times he would foretell the death of a person and be proved right. It is probably because of the fear engendered in his congregation that he was able to get away with destroying many of the ancient monuments in the vicinity.

Leagram Hall

When Leagram Hall was demolished in the 1960s, the coffins from the family vault were transferred to the local churchyard. Then began a chain of paranormal phenomena, from passing cars mysteriously breaking down, noises, and strange fogs to ghostly figures stepping out into the road and frightening motorists half to death.

Leagram Mill

There was once a boggart who lived mostly on the fells but who sometimes moved into Leagram Mill to be more comfortable. He could be helpful if he wished, but he was just as often mischievous and troublesome. He would make the horses panic and run. He would bring in the cows for milking, but tether them in the wrong stalls, laughing at their confusion. And sometimes he would drag the servants from their beds to the floor!

Sun Inn

Lizzie Dean was a humble serving girl and she worked at the Sun Inn on Windy Street in the early nineteenth century. She is still fondly thought of, although she died in 1835. People say she was a pretty and good-natured young woman who liked to dress in colourful clothes and have fun. It's too bad, then, that her short life was to end in tragedy.

A young local boy, attracted by Lizzie's looks and good humour, began to court her. He told her he loved her—he even proposed marriage, but only so that he could take liberties with her. Afterwards, when Lizzie discovered that he was not serious about marriage, she was devastated. She also discovered that her lover had really planned to marry her best friend, who had agreed! On the day of their wedding, Lizzie climbed to the attic of the Sun Inn and hanged herself. She left a note, in which she requested that she should be buried next to the path in the churchyard, so that the pair who had betrayed her would have to pass her every time they attended church. Visit St. Bartholomew's Church and you will soon find her grave.

The Sun Inn is haunted by Lizzie's spirit to this day. She was often seen in a long dress with puff sleeves, walking through the pub and straight through an apparently solid wall. Later renovations discovered, under the panelling and plaster-board, a very old door...

Three Lane Ends

One night, three men playing cards in the Three Lane Ends pub were joined by a stranger. They accepted him into their game quite happily, until they began to notice that he wasn't like other men. There seemed to be horns on his head—though he wore a hat to hide them—and when they looked down they saw that his feet were actually cloven hooves. One can only imagine the speed at which the panic-stricken men vacated the pub. A shame for the devil, who only wanted to play a game of cards!

Wolf House

Wolf House was so plagued by numerous boggarts that the local priest was called to turn them all out. The last boggart was laid under a yew tree by the gate of the farm with strict instructions that he should remain there until Chipping Brook ran dry. So seriously did local farmers take these instructions that they redirected field drains into the brook so that it would never run dry, even in the driest seasons. And when the yew tree was felled by a storm, it was replaced by a new yew sapling within hours.

CHORLEY

Astley Hall

Astley Hall was built in 1580 by the Charnock family and remained in their care for many generations. It passed through several other families over the centuries, until the Tattons presented it to Chorley for the purpose of using it as a museum. It is said that Cromwell slept here in 1648 and the bedroom, which was his resting place, is named for him. The hall exhibits a pair of riding boots that Cromwell purportedly left behind and, as you would expect, his ghost has sometimes been seen.

As well as Old Ironsides's ghost, many other strange events are reported at Astley Hall. Members of staff talk of unexplained aromas of baked apples or roasting meat, furniture being moved, taps running, alarms going off, and ethereal piano music. A ghostly serving maid has been seen in the kitchen and once a display of stuffed birds was completely dismantled. Possibly the most common ghost is that of a country gent dressed in 1920s tweeds, who walks in at the main door and proceeds up the stairs. A young girl is often seen with him. It is believed that this may be Reginald Tatton himself, the very man who gave Astley Hall to the town of Chorley.

One of the best-attested tales is that told by a group of old soldiers from Liverpool. They were on a return trip to Astley and made a point of asking about the guide they had met on their first visit—a lady in Elizabethan costume. Costumes have never been employed at the Hall...

The Astley employee responsible for Visitor Services also once saw an Elizabethan lady walking across the courtyard. She has also heard children's laughter, when no children have been present in the hall. Several times she has heard someone playing a Mozart piano piece that stopped the moment she entered the drawing-room, where the piano is situated.

Bagganley Hall

Bagganley Hall was for centuries the home of the Parker family. An interesting note from an ancient document says that, early in the 1500s, the ghost of John Parker had been seen by a John Pilkington. Parker's ghost spoke to Pilkington and asked him to take a message to Parker's son, George. He was to make sure that George then gave this message to two local sisters, Joan and Janet Banastre. It is recorded that George did as he was told. Frustratingly, there is no further information about the content of the message, or its meaning to the Banastre sisters, but it is intriguing that the event was recorded at all.

Botany Bay

This shopping mall is situated in an old mill and there is one area of the building that is referred to as a "hot spot" of ghost sightings, as it is here that a ghostly millworker is seen wearing his customary flat cap and clogs. In 2008, a photographer was called upon to take some press photographs that would be used to publicise a televised ghost hunt planned for some months in the future. The site chosen for the photographs was the hot spot. To the photographer's amazement, when he examined the photographs later, he found that one of them appeared to show the image of a ghostly pair of legs. Was it the ghostly mill-worker?

Chorley Hall

In 1716, Richard Chorley, who then owned the hall, was executed for treason. Weeks later, a mysterious red shower fell on the hall and the gardens, and everyone who saw it was terrified, assuming it to be blood. To add to their superstition, the day was Ash Wednesday, traditionally a very holy day.

Chorley Hospital

Staff still talk about the time in the 1960s when nurses ran to investigate the sounds of footsteps and slamming doors in the maternity wing—the noises alerted them just in time to rescue a baby who was struggling to breathe. They were convinced that a ghost helped save that baby's life.

Hall o' the Hill
CHORLEY GOLF CLUB

The Hall o'the Hill dates from 1727, but the original site of a much older hall was actually somewhere else—it's believed that it originally stood near the twelfth hole, where there is still a moated site. The hall's resident ghost is a lady named Debora, and she is believed to have been the daughter of Bishop Pilkington, whose name appears in connection with the hall in the 1500s. Reports placed her apparition in the area of the cellar or the stairs and she was said to wear a green dress; some reports also mentioning spectacles.

Railway Station

In 1876, newspapers nationwide reported strange phenomena at Chorley's railway station. The disturbances centred around an engine shed where, some months previously, a suicide had taken place. Noises had been heard by engine cleaners—noises that had no apparent natural source and that were accepted by the men as being the work of the suicide's ghost. But then more alarming things began to happen. Night-shift workers complained that large stones had been thrown at them, and some were so disturbed that they actually quit their jobs.

Naturally, the railway's management company assumed that some living person must be responsible, and so they assigned watchmen; but although the watchmen witnessed stones being thrown, they could never find anyone who might have thrown them. The railway company then assigned detectives to the job. One newspaper report commented:

> If the ghost is caught by the detectives, it is to be
> hoped that the magistrates before whom it is brought
> will not remand it on bail, or will, at least, insist
> on the bail being substantial. A small ghost will doubtless
> be leniently dealt with on account of its "extreme youth,"
> but an old ghost who throws stones ought to be severely
> dealt with.

CLAYTON-le-MOORS
Dunkenhalgh Hotel

A few hundred years ago, the Dunkenhalgh was a grand old Hall, the seat of the Walmesley family and the centre of a vast estate covering thousands of acres. Now it's a typically English hotel—a beautiful building surround by fifteen acres of beautiful grounds.

There have been reports of a ghostly woman on the ground floor, and a night porter once witnessed a heavy pair of door-curtains billowing out as if a wind was behind them—but the door was firmly closed. Another employee saw a figure pass through a wall. Next morning she was taken into the Portrait Room for the first time and there she identified the figure she had seen as one of the Walmesley family.

Outside in the grounds there have long been stories about the Dunkenhalgh boggart. There's even a bridge across the river on the grounds that is known as "the Boggart's Bridge," but in this case, the boggart is a beautiful young woman.

Legend says that sometime in the eighteenth century the incumbent family took on a French governess called Lucette to care for their children. One Christmas, Lucette fell in love with a young officer who was staying at the house, and when he proclaimed his love for her, she believed him. She became pregnant and when the time came for the officer to go back to his regiment, he said he would return to marry her. Of course, he was lying.

The months passed, the child would soon be born, and Lucette became distraught at her abandonment. She could not stay in her employment, but neither could she return to her French home for fear of the shame she would bring upon her family. One night she was walking by the River Hyndbum, which flows through the grounds of the Dunkenhalgh and, quite at her wits' end, she threw herself from the bridge into the river. Next morning they found her body caught in reeds and carried her gently back to the house.

Some versions of the story say that the officer did come back a few weeks after Lucette killed herself, but that one of her brothers who had heard of the affair challenged him to a duel and killed him.

Lucette's ghost is said to haunt at Christmastime, dressed in a shroud and drifting silently among the trees. When she reaches the bridge, she disappears. Some say that Lucette's lover carved his initials and hers within a heart in the bark of a particular tree on the grounds. It is to this tree that Lucette is walking. Every Christmas Eve, this carved heart would ooze red blood and, at the same time, the chapel bell would sound. (The chapel and the bell are, sadly, long gone.)

One very old version of the story, told in 1892 by "Old Robin o' Giles of Harwood Cliff," said that Lucette gave birth to a baby boy before jumping into the river, holding the baby in her arms. The baby was cast up by the retreating waters on the doorstep of the old mill, where the miller and his wife found him and brought him up as their own child. The child had a birthmark on his chest, in the shape of a blood-red heart.

The boggart bridge was repaired in the middle of the nineteenth century and a shawl-pin was found in the masonry, the head of which was a red heart-shaped cornelian. It was naturally assumed to have belonged to poor Lucette.

In 1892, the *Blackburn Standard* reported that the "Dungley Boggart" had reappeared at the hall. (Dungley being a fair approximation of the pronunciation of Dunkenhalgh.) This report said that the boggart, who took the form of a Lady in White, was seen in varied locations inside the hall itself. The lady had appeared to several of the servants. By now, the ghost story had taken on more of the traditional details one would expect—it was reported to appear every seven years, and not on just one date, but two: the seventh and fourteenth of May. The servants who had witnessed the White Lady's appearance were, naturally, terrified.

These sightings may well have been the result of young girls' imaginations, but in 1965, another report brought the original story up to date. A young man was walking his dog late at night in the driveway. His dog growled and barked, drawing the man's attention to a woman who was dressed in clothes from a completely different time. He stood very still as the woman approached, and when she was almost upon him, she turned slightly and vanished clean away. She left behind her nothing but a lingering sweet fragrance.

CLAYTON-le-WOODS

Halfway House

The ghost in this pub is well known to regulars and staff alike; they have christened him "Sid." His favourite seat is by the window, but he is more often seen in the cellars. Staff blame him for switching the lights off when they are down there. Occasionally, he has even been heard to say "Excuse me," as if he is moving aside to let staff pass.

Ley Inn

A converted barn next to the Ley Inn, used as a function room, is believed to be haunted. Disturbances there caused the manager to call in paranormal investigators, who claimed to have uncovered a murder mystery connected to the place. In the late 1700s, they believe a wealthy local landowner was having an affair with a young farmer's daughter. When the farmer discovered the affair, he challenged the landowner, who then killed him. The bar may be the site of the murder. Research may prove the story to be true...

CLITHEROE

Bridge

There's a bridge in Clitheroe where bloodstains appear—the relic of a murdered man. It is said that the stains are visible each year on a certain day in March: the day the man died. Sometimes he actually appears to the unwary. In addition, it is said that his body was dragged away from the spot where he died and dumped into a ditch at the other side of a hedge. The hedge stopped growing and nothing has ever grown there again.

Browsholme Hall

Browsholme Hall was built in 1507 by members of the Parker family, who have lived there ever since. The hall is packed with fascinating objects reflecting five centuries of Parker history, including a "cursed skull." It is said to be the relic of a family member who was martyred for his faith after the Pilgrimage of Grace in the 1530s. Like other cursed skulls in Lancashire and around the country, it is perfectly harmless, unless someone attempts to remove it from its home.

In the 1850s, schoolboy Edward Parker took the skull from the locked cabinet where it was kept and, allegedly for a joke, secretly buried it in the garden. In the weeks that followed, a series of disasters befell the hall; the very fabric of the place began to crumble—ceilings began to fall, fires broke out spontaneously, and there were even deaths in the family. Young Edward was horrified by what he assumed were the results of his foolishness and, eventually, he admitted his deed to his parents. The skull was restored to its home and life returned to normal, although Edward's father was left with the enormous costs of restoring the building to its former glory, and the whole family had to move out until the damage was repaired. The skull (which is not on display to the public) has not left the hall since.

Another legend says that Parker family deaths will be foretold by the appearance of a white horse in the mansion's grounds.

Clitheroe Castle

Originally built as a defence, Clitheroe Castle was developed into a comfortable residence for Henry de Lacy in the thirteenth century. Later it became a gaol and a court. The castle was at one time moated, there was a chapel dedicated to St. Michael, and ancient documents mention an orchard below the castle. Several ghosts have been reported in the castle at different times—a White Lady, an entire family, a maid, and a First World War soldier—but no one can say who any of these apparitions were when they lived. Other people have reported strange smells, unexplained noises, and areas of extreme coldness.

The buildings were somewhat damaged by troops in the seventeenth century and it may be this time period that gave rise to a story about the devil. Only the ancient Norman Keep now remains and in the keep is a window that is said to be made by the devil. He was not gentle about it—he threw rocks from nearby Pendle Hill until the hole in the wall was big enough to satisfy him. It was well known that he also once walked the streets of Clitheroe, trying to persuade people to sell him their souls for three wishes. However, he was beaten, defeated by cleverness and trickery, and flew to a bridge, a mile to the south, where he disappeared. Ever since that day, the bridge has been known as Hell Hole Bridge.

(See Cockerham for a very similar tale.)

Grammar School

The Grammar School was demolished in 1830, but that's probably for the best as a hearthstone there was apparently a doorway into another world. One night, some boys at the Grammar School decided to try to raise the devil—they had heard it could be done quite simply by reciting the Lord's Prayer backwards. They must have been terrified when their spell worked; there was a horrible noise beneath the hearthstone and with a rush of fire, the devil stood before them. The boys shouted at him to be gone—but he simply laughed. Fortunately, a schoolmaster discovered the boys were not in their beds and found them in the schoolroom, just in time. This was fortunate, because the schoolmaster knew how to beat the devil. He struck a deal with him that he must complete one task and, if he succeeded, he could stay. The devil agreed and the schoolteacher ordered him to knit a rope of sand—which was, of course, impossible, even for a supernatural being. Furious at being tricked this way, the devil disappeared again, beneath the hearthstone.

(See Burnley Grammar School for an almost identical story, and Cockerham for another story featuring the "rope of sand.")

Methodist Chapel

The Methodist Chapel is said to have been haunted by a lady dressed sometimes in white and sometimes in blue. She was usually accompanied by a child.

Old Hall

There was for many years a boggart who was known for his hideous screeching, a nightly occurrence as he made his way from Old Hall along a circuitous route through the old streets. He would traverse the town right up to the castle and back home to Old Hall again. No one knew what he looked like, for his noise was so terrifying that no one dared look. His regularity and his awfulness was afterwards referred to in a local phrase: "He keeps turning up like t'Old Hall Boggart."

Swan and Royal

The Swan and Royal dates from 1786, but arguably its most interesting story comes from a century later, during the cotton strikes and subsequent riots of 1878. One weekend, a large group of cotton workers from Manchester were coming to the town for a meeting with local workers and, as great trouble was fully expected, the council contacted the War Department with a request for troops.

A group of soldiers from the 24th Regiment of Foot duly arrived and were billeted in the Swan and Royal, which was the only pub allowed to remain open. The others were closed in an attempt to prevent too much alcohol exacerbating the situation. Nevertheless, there was a riot—a terrible one that left many properties in the town damaged and cost several cotton workers their lives.

There was no more trouble after that one dreadful night, but the soldiers stayed in the town to make sure. They remained for the whole of the next month, during which time two of them fell in love with local girls. A double wedding was organised at St. Mary's Church. Sadly, the two soldiers were posted to Zululand before the wedding could take place; their prospective brides were heartbroken. Worse, both of the soldiers died four months later.

Back in Clitheroe, one of the poor girls, a lass of just seventeen named Anne Druce, discovered that she was with child. Disgraced and bereft, she went to the Swan and Royal, shut herself in the room she and the soldier had shared and took her own life.

Many residents of the hotel have reported seeing Anne's ghost and many report more tangible events. One notable news report concerned a gentleman guest who found both sink-taps running one day—he then stood open-mouthed as a bar of soap lifted itself from the dish, turned around, and replaced itself.

One particular room was well known for the sound of a crying baby. It may be just a coincidence that, late in the 1950s, workmen discovered a package in the attic, wrapped in newspaper. The date on the paper was 1879. Inside lay a baby's skeleton.

Waddow Hall

Waddow Hall has an enduring tradition about Peg o' The Well, or Peg O'Nell, as she is variously known. The story is told that Peggy was a servant who died at Waddow Hall, and her angry spirit now demands a living creature as a sacrifice every seven years. Otherwise, she will take a human life for herself by drowning someone in the nearby river. Inside the hall, there is one room that seems unnaturally cold at all times of the year and it is said that this is where Peg slept the night before she died.

The story says that Peg had been quarrelling with her master and mistress, annoying them so much that when she went to fetch water from the well, Mistress Starkie wished she would fall and break her neck. It was winter and the ground was treacherous—Peg slipped on the ice, fell into the river, and broke her neck. Mistress Starkie's wish had come true.

From that moment on, bad luck dogged the Starkie family, despite the fact that they had reverently placed a statue of St. Margaret, in Peg's memory, close to the well that had been her downfall. (Peggy is a common derivative of the name Margaret.) When Master Starkie fell while riding and broke his leg, Peg's spirit was blamed for frightening the horse and causing it to rear up and throw its rider. Later, Starkie had cause to suspect that his young son had been bewitched by Peg and he called for the priest to come and exorcise him. The poor priest fell in the river whilst trying to cross the stepping-stones, near where Peg had died. The priest survived, but when he arrived at the hall, dripping wet, his accident was blamed on Peg, who had clearly tried to drag him into the river. Incensed, Mistress Starkie took an axe, ran outside to where Peg's memorial statue stood, and cut off the statue's head.

After that, it seems that the Starkie family enjoyed peace—although it was said that Peg's spirit continued to live in the river near Brungerley Bridge and that she demanded recompense in the form of a life given to the water every seven years. On "Peg's Night," at the end of every seven years, a bird or other small animal would be deliberately drowned in the river to prevent a human life being taken instead.

One Peg's Night, a young man was travelling to Clitheroe and needed to cross the river at the ford. He broke his journey at the Inn nearby, where the landlord and his maid tried to dissuade him from crossing; the river was uncommonly swollen and, besides, the maid told him, "It's Peg's Night, and she has not yet had her life." The young man ridiculed such superstition and set off to cross the river regardless—but he never reached the other side.

In *The Pictorial History of Lancashire*, written in the 1840s, the author describes stopping by Waddow Hall, intrigued by the stories he had heard of Peg. There he met a servant who clearly gave superstition no quarter and quite happily showed him the statue's head, which she had recently brought down from the attic. "Now she lives in the larder," she told him.

Sometime after that date, reports say that the head was secreted in a wall near Brungerley Bridge.

Well Hall

At Well Hall, on Church Brow, an old woman once lived all alone, apart from a friendly boggart who kept her company. Many people testified to having seen the boggart, who appeared mostly as a man, although some said they had seen a ghostly woman with a child. Whilst friendly to the old woman living there, he was not so friendly towards other people—he once chained a man to the wall and refused to let him go!

In August 1891, the *Sheffield Evening Telegraph* was just one of the newspapers to publish the story of a tremendous upset at Well Hall, which happened when the residents, the Rev. and Mrs. Haslam, were away from home. The hall had temporary residents, a lady and her two daughters, and they and the servants were much alarmed by a succession of events: bedclothes strewn around the floor, all the knives on the dining table collected into a heap, drawers and cupboards found open, window shutters found closed and room bells ringing for no reason. The cause was pronounced to be the well-known ghost, "Peggy Nell." The chief constable, however, thought differently. He sent in a spy to work with the servants, and his spy reported seeing one of the servants go upstairs and throw bedding about the room. Faced with the accusation, the girl at first denied her guilt, but confessed when told she had been watched. She was very sorry, she said.

"Peggy Nell," incidentally, had nothing to do with Well Hall. She rightly belongs to Waddow Hall, not far away, and whose tradition we have just heard in the previous story.

CLIVIGER

Cliviger Gorge

Lady Sybil lived at Bernshaw Tower, a manor house that has long since disappeared. She was loved by Lord William Towneley, but she had little time for him, preferring instead to spend her days in the countryside around Cliviger Gorge, studying the animals and flowers. It is said that she found the atmospheric area around Eagle Crag very affecting, so that she began to long for supernatural powers. The opportunity she longed for came when the devil appeared to her, offering great powers in return for her soul. She signed the deal in her own blood.

Discovering this, Lord William went to see Mother Helston, who was known to be a witch. She assured him that he had no need to worry; she could see that he would gain his lady's hand on All Hallows Eve. However, she did not say how this was to come about.

On All Hallows Eve, Lord William was out hunting around Eagle Crag and came across a milk-white doe. He gave chase but could not catch the animal—who was, in fact, Lady Sybil in disguise. But then a black dog appeared and caught the doe by the neck. The dog (who was Mother Helston in disguise) held on to the doe without harming her until Lord William could tie a cord around her neck and lead her back to his home at Hapton Tower.

That night there was a terrible storm and, in the morning, Lord William discovered that the doe had changed into Lady Sybil. Mother Helston worked spells to counteract the devil's magic, the couple were married, and lived together at Hapton Tower happily ever after.

Some versions of the tale go on to say that this was not the end of Lady Sybil's magical powers. On one occasion, she was suspected of turning herself into a white cat who made mischief in Cliviger Mill. A manservant sent to watch for the cat caught her one day and managed to cut off one of her paws before she slipped from his grasp and ran away. The following day, the manservant called at Hapton Tower carrying a lady's hand... Lady Sybil's hand was miraculously restored to her arm and the proof of this was the red mark that remained around her wrist for ever after.

It is said that Lord William's mad chase after the milk-white doe can still be seen sometimes, repeated in ethereal form at Eagle's Crag. This is an example of "The Spectral Huntsman," a mainstay of folklore in Germanic countries. It is also said that his hounds can be heard howling, and this sound is known as "Gabriel Ratchets"—it is said that anyone hearing them will soon meet death or misfortune.

Gordon Lennox

The Gordon Lennox pub used to be on the other side of the road, but it's believed that when the original centuries-old pub was demolished and resited, the stones were reused. Perhaps that's why the "new" pub looks much older than it should—and perhaps why the place feels haunted. Successive landlords have described strange occurrences here, from odd atmospheres and unusual sounds to heavy glass ashtrays smashing with no help from human hand.

One explanation says that the ghost of an old landlady, Enid, is responsible for the strange events. Enid managed the pub for over fifty years and was a real character. When she left, she said quite definitely that she would never set foot over the doorstep again. But maybe she has changed her mind, because a strong presence is often felt by those left alone at the end of the evening to clean the bar area. Sometimes the feeling is so strong that cleaning up is left until the next morning...

Holme Hall

Holme Hall dates from the fifteenth century, but was rebuilt two centuries later and extended again after that. For centuries, it was the home of the Whitaker family. For a short time it was a retirement home—now it is once again in private hands.

There may be two ghosts here. Adults identify the dim black figure as a monk and indeed the Whitaker ancestry does include a monk: Milo, who was a Cistercian monk at Whalley Abbey. However, children who have experienced a dim black figure say it is a woman. They are not frightened by the meeting.

Even more mysterious is the story about an ancient Whitaker account book, which appeared in the house after it had been completely cleared for its new owners.

CLOWBRIDGE
Clowbridge Reservoir

At Clowbridge Reservoir near Burnley, a young man camping in 1977 met with a very tall, ethereal, bearded man who was dressed in a white robe. The man was quite still, looking out over the water. At the bottom of the reservoir lies the remains of Gambleside, lost to the waters when the valley was flooded to create the reservoir in 1866. Perhaps the ghost was mourning his old home.

COCKERHAM

Invisible Harpist

In 1838, the *Lancaster Gazette* reported that a Cockerham woman had been frightened almost to death by the sound of an Aeolian harp, a musical instrument constructed to be played by the wind. As she did not possess such an instrument, she was naturally worried by the sound, although in broad daylight it was easier to enjoy the ethereal music. However, when nightfall came and the music continued, the woman became more frightened. Her fear was exacerbated when her neighbours, hearing the music, acquainted her with old stories that her house was known to be haunted.

The poor woman sank to her knees and prayed, but no words she spoke could halt the unearthly noise, which continued until two in the morning, when it stopped, apparently of its own accord.

This story might well have passed into the annals of legend, had it not been for the fact that the source of the "music" was eventually traced to a cracked pane of window-glass that vibrated in the wind, producing a sound just like an Aeolian harp.

Local Legends

The devil once took a liking to the pretty village of Cockerham and decided to take up residence there. He delighted in patrolling the lanes of this sleepy village, frightening the villagers and filling their noses with the smell of brimstone. At last they called upon the cleverest amongst them, the schoolmaster, to find some way to be rid of him. One night, at midnight, the schoolmaster consulted an old book of spells and summoned the devil using the time-honoured device of repeating the Lord's Prayer backwards.

When the devil duly appeared, the schoolteacher demanded that he henceforth leave the village, but the devil was not so obedient. He did, however, strike a compromise—he challenged the schoolteacher to set him three tasks, promising that if he could not complete them, he would leave that place forever.

The first task was to count the number of dewdrops on a hedge. This, unfortunately, the devil found too easy, for when he went to the hedge to count, the wild wind caused by his arrival blew the hedge dry and there were only thirteen dewdrops left to count.

The second task thought up by the schoolteacher was to count the number of stalks in a cornfield. Unfortunately, when the devil gave his answer, the schoolteacher realised he had no way of checking whether he was correct!

The third task was to make a rope of sand that would withstand washing in the River Cocker. The devil vanished, but in just a few moments, he proudly reappeared with a beautifully woven rope of sand. His confidence soon faded, however, when he and the schoolteacher went to the river to wash the rope, and it promptly dissolved clean away.

The devil was furious, but a bargain was a bargain and, accepting that he was beaten, the devil flew away to Pilling Moss and was never seen in Cockerham again. In Pilling, it is said that he landed on Broadfleet Bridge—and his footprint can still be seen there, stamped into the stonework.

(See Clitheroe Castle for a similar story about a bridge, and Clitheroe Grammar School for another story featuring a "rope of sand.")

Incidentally, there is another story about the devil in Cockerham—but this time the devil was one unwittingly carved on a rood-screen by a singularly inept craftsman. The church's original rood had been destroyed by order in the reign of Henry VIII, but when Henry's daughter Mary came to the throne, the churchwardens and parishioners were obliged under law to find the money to provide a new one. They employed a man who was alleged to be skilled at carving to decorate the rood-screen with an image of the crucifixion. The image, when it was completed, was just terrible. The churchwardens refused to pay the bill, preferring instead to appear in court at Lancaster to explain their actions.

The mayor of Lancaster, presiding over the case, was told that the image was so ugly and frightening that children were scared to come near it. The mayor dismissed that argument, saying that the man deserved to be paid for his work, whatever their opinion of it. He then advised them to "clap a pair of horns on his head, and so he will make an excellent devil."

Thurnham Hall

Thurnham Hall is seven centuries old and has architecture spanning all the ages. It was owned for over four centuries by the Dalton family and the ghost of Colonel Thomas Dalton, dressed in Cavalier uniform, has sometimes been seen running along the landing. In the chapel there is a chandelier that has been known to swing gently of its own accord. There is also a story about a boggart, one who unhelpfully scattered carefully laid fires across rooms and pulled bedclothes off sleeping servants.

However, Thurnham Hall is perhaps best known for the ghost of Elizabeth Dalton, who was responsible for the addition of the hall's chapel. Locally known as the Green Lady because of the colour of her dress, she has often been seen in her old bedroom. More recently, she has also been seen gathering twigs on the lawns outside, on more than one occasion and by different people.

COLNE
Colne Hall

Colne Hall was originally a manor house, later becoming a pub, before being put to a variety of other uses. Over the years, it has been noticed that dogs do not like the atmosphere in the building; they avoid some areas completely, notably one particular staircase and one particular room. But the only apparition ever to be seen there is that of a harmless little girl in old-fashioned clothes. She has been seen in the boiler room and her footsteps are often heard.

Craven Laithe Farm

At Craven Laithe Farm there is a spa well that is imbued with healing properties. It is said that the waters are beneficial both to humans and animals. The well never runs dry and never freezes over.

Hole In The Wall Inn

At the Hole In The Wall Inn there was once a barn next to the pub that was used as stables. It was haunted by the ghost of an old horse dealer who often visited the pub. One night, when he went out to the stables, he found his best-beloved horse dead. Bereft, the man died of grief the following day. For many years his ghost was seen in the barn and the pub itself was plagued by a worrying atmosphere.

Some say the haunting is more likely to be linked to the fact that several centuries ago there was a monastery and burial ground close by, but this would not explain why, when the barn was demolished in the 1960s, the haunting stopped there and then.

St. Bartholomew's Church

The Emmott Cross, also known as the Touch Cross, now graces St. Bartholomew's churchyard and is Grade II listed. It is seven feet tall and its design and decoration are typical of the medieval Gothic style. Previously, it stood in the grounds of Emmott Hall in Laneshawbridge and was resited when the hall was demolished in 1967. It used to stand close by Hallown Well and was venerated, along with the well, by pilgrims travelling to Whalley Abbey. Hence, its local name of the Touch Cross; because soldiers stationed at Emmott Hall would touch the cross, praying they would survive their battles.

(See also Laneshawbridge. Also, Tockholes for another "Touch Cross.")

St. Helen's Well

St. Helen's Well is located alongside Waterloo Road, but may be difficult to find amidst the undergrowth. There was once a mill here, named after the well. The well itself was apparently named by the Romans. It was generally used as a water supply, but the name indicates quite clearly that it was once venerated as a holy place, long before the Romans came.

COPPULL

Darkland Bridge

Near Darkland Bridge in Coppull there's a ghost-dog known as Pongay. The dog lurks by the bridge looking for opportunities to scare passing travellers. His antics were more effective in the days of horse-drawn vehicles, because of the damage a rearing horse can do. At least one death, that of a young boy in 1836, was blamed on Pongay.

CRAWSHAWBOOTH

Village Green

One Sunday morning, the boys of Crawshawbooth were indulging in a game of football, despite the remonstrations of the vicar who warned of dire consequences resulting from playing such games on the Lord's Day. They paid no heed to his warnings, but perhaps they should have—because the devil himself came along to join in the game. He waited until the ball came in his direction and then he kicked it so high into the sky that it vanished—and so did he, in an explosion of fire. And that was the last time the lads played football on a Sunday!

CROSTON

St. Michael and
All Angels Church

The churchyard here is haunted by a White Lady, said to be the mother of Mary Elizabeth Hudson, a child who died in Croston Industrial Home (the workhouse) in 1890. She was just thirteen years old. Her grave is in a distant corner of the churchyard because, it is said, she died of a virulent fever and it was feared that it would spread. Her mother wanders the churchyard unable to find her tragic little daughter. It seems the child Mary Elizabeth haunts the area as well, because people living near the churchyard have sometimes seen a little girl in a red shawl, which was part of the uniform of the long-gone Industrial Home.

The churchyard is also home to many fairies, according to one elderly resident who has lived for thirty years in a house next to the church. He is always up early to tend to his chickens and has often seen beings made of light, about fifteen inches high, flickering amongst the trees in the ancient church grounds. He first noticed the fairies after he and some other volunteers had placed some wooden, carved statues of a medieval family in the graveyard amongst the trees. He thinks that the fairies approve of the newly installed memorials.

DARWEN

Ashleigh Barrow

This tumulus was excavated and destroyed in the mid-nineteenth century; a number of funerary urns that were found inside can now be seen in Darwen Library. There is a reconstructed tumulus, but it is not exactly on the original site. When the original tumulus still existed, it had such a reputation for being haunted by boggarts that children would take off their shoes before passing it, so the boggarts would be less likely to hear them.

Crown and Thistle

Old Albert was a regular at the pub for years, until his death in the 1960s. A legend grew up that he returned whenever the thirteenth of the month fell on a Friday, and the best way to keep him happy was to leave him a pint of his favourite beer. Hearing this tale over twenty years later, a new landlord followed the instructions of his clientele, and when Friday the thirteenth came around, he left a pint for Old Albert on the bar before he went to bed. To his astonishment, when he came down to the bar the following morning, the tankard was empty!

Darwen Moors

There may still be traces of Lyons' Den here; a hand-built dwelling constructed of boulders and made by local giant John Lyons. Lyons was no mythological giant. He lived in the eighteenth century and, according to local observations, he stood over seven feet tall. He lived in his hand-built home in isolation, working long hours to raise his crops and keep himself alive.

Lower Darwen

In 1663, Lower Darwen was the scene of a prophetic dream that was much publicised at the time, because it led to the solution of a murder mystery.

John Waters was a gardener, murdered by his wife Anne and her lover Gyles Haworth. They hired a hitman, one Mr. Ribchester, who lost his nerve at the last minute and left Haworth to commit the deed himself. Haworth and Anne Waters then buried John under a flagstone in the cowshed and denied all knowledge of his whereabouts, claiming he had simply packed his things and gone.

Unfortunately for them, a neighbour, called Thomas Haworth (no relation), suffered troubling dreams for several weeks following John's disappearance. He dreamed that John's body would be found under a stone in the cowshed. Eventually, Thomas told his dreams to the local constable who, unusually, took this piece of prophecy seriously. A search was mounted and the body discovered. Gyles Haworth and Ribchester both fled, leaving John Waters' wife to take the blame alone. Anne Waters was found guilty of murder and sentenced to death by burning.

Millstone Hotel

The Millstone Hotel has a ghost that has disturbed owners and staff in the middle of the night with the distinct noises of footsteps, knocks on doors, and hand-claps. During the day, chambermaids have found lights on in unused rooms and neatly made beds are later found bare of bedclothes, which are scattered around the rooms. However, the nightly noises are far more worrying.

DOWNHAM
The Great Stone

This stone, not as large as the name suggests, is now set into the wall at the entrance to Downham Hall. Its original site was close by. When it was lifted for use in the wall, human remains were found beneath it. Legend says that it marked the grave of two Roman legionaries killed by the Brigantes who populated this area. Mythology also says that, at midnight, the stone will turn itself over, but given its current secure situation, one assumes this no longer happens.

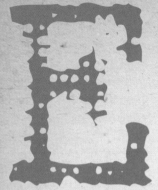

ECCLESTON

Bank House

In 1873, rain poured down at Bank House—not outside, but inside, and in just one room! When the mysterious rain abated, the ceilings were thoroughly inspected, but found to be quite dry. Yet the water was real enough—the furnishings of that room were entirely ruined.

Grove Mill

Grove Mill has housed the antiques centre Bygone Times since the 1980s. It is a centuries-old building that has been home to several different industries, producing wool, corn, calico, and cotton. The site contains a number of separate buildings that were put to a variety of uses. At its height, the mill employed around 300 people.

Ghosts here include a man in 1920s dress, two children noisily playing, and a dalmatian. Less cheerful occurrences include the sounds of children crying or even screaming—perhaps children who had been involved in accidents amongst the lethal machinery in the weaving rooms.

In total, the mill lays claim to over forty different ghosts and phenomena, and the owners have even provided a leaflet for visitors to the buildings, pointing out all the ghostly locations.

ENTWISTLE

Entwistle Halt

In the 1940s, the railway employee in charge of Entwistle Halt, one Mr. Ackroyd, repeatedly saw a small boy playing by himself in the fields near the railway line. He never appeared during winter months, but during the summer, he was there almost every weekend, and Ackroyd never questioned his presence. However, he did sometimes wonder about the boy's home life, as he appeared somewhat thin and pale-faced. Also, he often saw the boy standing at the crossing-gates, looking very sad. It seemed that, for some reason, he was waiting for a particular train to pass before going back to his home, because when the 5.29 train arrived, he would disappear.

In 1945, a terrible accident happened and a local farmer was killed at the crossing, after falling on the line and being unable to get out of the way of the approaching train. Only then did Ackroyd learn that, many years before, a little boy had been killed in a similar manner. In the late afternoons, he would wait at the crossing for his father's horse and cart to come home. One day the lad spotted his father and ran over the crossing, straight into the path of the 5.29. The victim of this latest accident? The first boy's younger brother.

EUXTON

Euxton Mills Hotel

Dating from around 1760, this hotel on Wigan Road has gained quite a reputation for being haunted. In 1999, American parapsychologist Dr. Larry Montz and a team of investigators stayed here and their experiences were filmed as part of a documentary to be aired in the US. In 2008, the UK's popular series *Most Haunted* paid a visit. Both groups of investigators claimed to have found serious evidence of haunting and, in particular, the American group pointed out an area where, they claimed, a lady in grey walks. This was interesting, as it agreed with the experiences of local people. However, despite the TV exposure and the fact that many locals and members of staff had reported strange experiences, the landlord remained unconvinced of the existence of ghosts.

There does not seem to be a legend or story suggesting the identity of the Lady in Grey—but there are countless witnesses to her existence, even with the landlord's opinion.

EXTWISTLE

Extwistle Hall

Now in ruins, this ancient house is situated above Swinden Reservoir. It dates from the late 1500s and was once home to the Parker family. Captain Robert Parker lived here with his family in the seventeenth century and a story tells how he met a fairy funeral one night, on his way home from a Jacobite meeting. To his horror, he saw that the brass plate on the coffin bore his own name. Knowing that this foretold his own death, he took the warning to mean that his end would come because of his involvement with the Jacobites, so he swore that from then on he would never attend another meeting.

As weeks passed, Parker may have come to feel he had been spared the fate of those who had seen fairy funerals in the past. But fate would not be diverted so easily. Perhaps if he had continued to be vigilant, he would not have gone shooting in heavy rain and put his wet coat near the fire to dry. As his children helped him to strip off the rest of his wet clothes, a powder flask in the pocket of the wet coat exploded in the heat of the fire—and the explosion killed him and badly injured two of his daughters.

Lee Green

There is a story here, although only scraps remain. It tells of the local people raising the devil and setting him some tasks, only then realising they were now in grave peril. The priest from Towneley was called for and he laid the devil at the foot of Lee Green. It is to be hoped a promise was extracted from the Old Lad that he would not return.

FAIR SNAPE FELL
Local Legend

Giles Roper was crossing the moor one night, on his way home, when he came to a large boulder that was locally feared as a spot frequented by the devil. Giles gave these rumours no real credence, but when he came to the spot, he looked around carefully, just in case. He saw no devil, but he did see a beautiful golden-haired girl sitting on the boulder. Her beauty was quite entrancing and when she smiled at him and beckoned, Giles moved towards her—only to watch her disappear when he was but a few feet away. Giles could not rid himself of the memory of that lovely girl, so the next night he went back to the boulder, hoping to see her again. Once again, the golden-haired girl appeared and beckoned, only to disappear before Giles could reach her.

It became an obsession. Every night, Giles would return to the spot in the hope of capturing the beautiful creature before she vanished away. But Giles was engaged to the miller's daughter and she soon wanted to know what he was doing every night, when he was supposed to be courting her. Giles told her the truth, but she didn't believe him; she was convinced that he must have found another lover. She engaged some men to follow him and was surprised when they reported that Giles had indeed simply gone for a walk to the lonely spot on Fair Snape Fell. No other woman was involved. They had simply seen him reach a certain spot and then stop, looking disappointed.

The miller's daughter was very relieved by this news, but it did her no good; her entreaties that Giles should spend his evenings with her instead of walking on the Fell had no effect. Night after night, Giles climbed up the Fell to the boulder, just for a glimpse of the golden-haired girl, desperate for her to stay long enough for him to tell her of his love for her.

Eventually, Giles fell ill through his nightly exertions and had not the strength to rise from his bed during the day, let alone go walking on the Fell at night. He was sick with fever, but called repeatedly for the girl to come to him. Then, one night, before he was quite better, he staggered from his bed, out of the house, and up onto Fair Snape Fell.

He was found next morning, lying dead before the boulder. On his face was a look of sheer agony. And around his body, in the peaty ground, were the marks of cloven hooves.

FERNYHALGH

Ladyewell

Ladyewell House is a vocational centre with a small chapel on the upper floor. The well, which is easily accessible, is in the grounds of the house. Once upon a time, when I was a child, the well was positioned deep in the undergrowth of a country lane; one could easily miss it as one walked by. It was a few feet below the road surface and accessible only by descending several steps, where, as a child, I would be surrounded by grass and fern and able to sense the mystery of the place. Now the well has been opened up to the air and surrounded by seating where services take place on summer days. The well is now beautifully maintained, even if some of the magic has disappeared.

There is a lovely legend attached to Lady Well (or Ladyewell). A sailor caught in a storm was so afraid he might die that he prayed earnestly to God, promising that if he and his ship found their way to safety, he would repay God in whatever way He wished. He did indeed survive the storm and landed safely, whereupon he heard a voice telling him to build a chapel in a place called Fernyhalgh, where he would find, close to a spring, a crab-apple tree bearing apples without cores.

The sailor wondered how he would ever find such a spot, because the place where his ship had come ashore was unknown to him. However, soon afterwards, he was taking nourishment at an inn when he overheard a milkmaid describing how she had been forced to follow a stray cow all the way to Fernyhalgh. He asked the milkmaid to show him the place and she promised to do so the next day. In Fernyhalgh, he found the crab-apple tree and the spring, just as the mysterious voice had described. By the spring was a statue of Our Lady. And so he kept his promise and built a chapel there.

The date attached to this legend is 1471 because a small chapel was indeed built there at that date; a new one replaced it in 1796. However, the fact that there was already a statue in place as early as 1471 proves how sacred this spot was always thought to be.

FLEETWOOD

Bourne Hall

A hall at Bourne, near Fleetwood, is mentioned in records as far back as 1345. Naturally, the building underwent rebuilding and remodelling over the centuries, but it remained standing in one form or another until the 1970s, when it was demolished. The land is now home to a recycling plant, but happily the site of the hall itself remains clear. The fact that the hall no longer stands actually made little difference to the ghost, which was a spectral horse. This ghostly mare would roam the environs of Bourne Hall and the

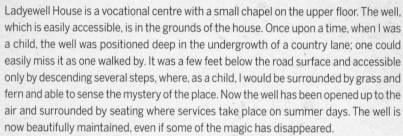

surrounding countryside, most often on moonlit nights. Doubtless it now haunts the recycling plant—the first in the country to have such a reputation?

Fish Market

A 1928 edition of the *Sunday Express* carried an article on the strange phenomena of ghosts on film. The article discussed several photographs that were claimed to show images of people who were no longer alive. One of the photographs discussed was Fleetwood's own "Ghost of Fleetwood Dock."

The photograph showed a group of fish merchants standing together, but the odd thing was that one of the men, Mr. Haig, had died a full year before the photograph was taken. Understandably, the photograph caused quite a stir at the docks and it very quickly became a sensation amongst Fleetwood's spiritualists. Eventually, it came to the attention of Sir Arthur Conan Doyle.

Conan Doyle, a spiritualist as well as a writer, was very interested in such photographs. It must be remembered that photography was a relatively new art, and methods of faking or manipulating pictures were not commonly known at the time. The phrase "the camera does not lie" was seen to be truth. Conan Doyle found these photographs so intriguing that he set up a special investigation group: The Society for the Study of Supernatural Pictures.

His reputation was later damaged by the fact that he accepted as genuine the well-known photographs of the Cottingley Fairies. In 1920, he published an article in which he publicly attested to the authenticity of these photos, which had been taken in a leafy glen in Yorkshire by two young girls. This fact alone, he claimed, was enough to indicate that the photos could not have been faked—how could mere children have manipulated such a newfangled technology? To today's eye, the "fairies" are clearly paper cut-outs; but then, over fifty years ago, they had many people convinced of their reality.

The photograph of the Fleetwood Ghost is different, however. The image of the dead man, standing alongside his colleagues, is no cardboard cut-out.

Fleetwood Hospital

A cottage hospital was first established here in 1890, in a house at Queen's Terrace, donated for the purpose by a wealthy local doctor. Fleetwood had grown to a population of over 9,000 and a hospital was sorely needed. Many years later, two smaller adjoining houses were bought for use as offices, the ground floor being adapted for use as a physiotherapy unit. In fact, the houses were left almost untouched, the only alteration being two new connecting doors to the main house next door.

When I was invited inside one of the old houses in 1996, the friend who took me there refused to accompany me farther than the front door. Inside the house, domestic features survived, such as the bedroom fireplaces and, despite the emptiness of the rooms, the dust, and the slightly musty smell, it was easy to feel that I was trespassing in someone's home. However, I rationalised that it was probably because the fabric of the building had not been touched in many years, so it was easy to feel that I was stepping back in time, into another person's time and space. Perhaps it was this atmosphere alone that inspired the notion that the place was haunted.

Stories were told of a spectral lady in an old-fashioned grey nurse's uniform, who was assumed to be an old matron who once lived in the old building. This last supposition was entirely wrong, as the house had never been used for anything apart from office space and a physiotherapy unit—but there is no doubt that staff members experienced something.

One nurse had been filing when she felt someone tap her on the shoulder—she turned, but no one was there. She was not frightened, for she felt that the place always had a benign atmosphere. However, some years later, the same nurse was again working in the old building when she felt a much stronger sensation, as if something invisible had pushed her heavily in the back and then passed right through her. The experience left her dizzy and confused and she left the place at once, refusing to finish the job she had started there. Her job, incidentally, was to go through all the paperwork in the offices there and collect together anything that needed to be preserved—for the building was about to be demolished.

Whoever haunted that old house in such a disturbing fashion was certainly not the fabled Grey Lady who haunts the main hospital next door—a matron of times past. That Grey Lady is always experienced as a wholly benevolent presence. She has been seen in many locations in the hospital, except for the most recently built wing. Sightings of her always coincide with the moments surrounding a patient's death.

Marine Hall

The Marine Hall is haunted by a very contemporary ghost; that of a middle-aged man in a white shirt. He has been seen walking across the stage and passing from view into an area that has no exit. When followed, he has simply disappeared. It is thought that Old Bill, as he has been christened, is the ghost of a caretaker who died on the premises.

North Euston Hotel

In the 1830s, when the new railway system reached Fleetwood, the North Euston Hotel was built in the full confidence that it would soon be catering to long-distance travellers from London who would then continue their journey to Scotland by ferry. Unfortunately, a couple of years after the hotel was completed, a path for the railway was found over Shap Fell, so the hotel never was quite as lucrative as had been hoped. However, it did survive and is still in business today.

In the 1980s, the North Euston was bought by the Cowpe and Johns families. Before they opened for business, they spent a few months carrying out major renovations. One day, one of the joiners had cause to go down to the cellar—but he came up again quickly, convinced he had seen an apparition of a young man. Nothing could convince him otherwise.

Jim Cowpe was a keen researcher into local history and when he researched the history of the old building, he found that in the 1860s, during the Boer War, the hotel was used as a school of musketry. Whilst the officers lived upstairs, the lowly men in their charge lived and slept below stairs, in the cellars of the building, along with their horses. To his surprise, Jim then came across a story of a young fusilier from Enniskillen, who had become so desperately depressed and homesick that he took his own life, in his little room downstairs. The young man has only been seen twice—but perhaps that's because most people now refuse to go anywhere near the cellars!

Rossall Hall

Old Rossall Hall was long ago swallowed up by the sea and replaced by the more modern buildings of Rossall School, which boasts a well-earned reputation as one of the finest schools on the Fylde. But how many people know that it also boasts a ghostly legend? The legend is similar to those connected to many other old Lancashire Halls, describing a mysterious White Lady who has been seen crossing the grounds outside the school, heading for the shore. A history written in 1895 describes her walks, but doubtless there is a great deal of romance involved, masking what truth there is in the story.

According to some reports, Old Rossall Hall had an underground passage that led from a gazebo on the grounds down to the shoreline. Dug in such sandy earth, it could not have been very safe and, indeed, the legend goes on to describe how one of the ladies of the hall met her death when the passage collapsed. What high drama could have occurred at Rossall to inspire such a story?

Christmas of 1583 was, for many Catholic families in Lancashire, a time of terror. For two years they had heard repeated reports of armed men bursting into the homes of wealthy Catholics, arresting them for their faith and looting their houses for anything of value. The family at Rossall had good reason to be fearful, as they had stronger Catholic connections than most.

Elizabeth Allen, now widowed and so the head of her family, was sister-in-law to Dr. Allen, who would later be Cardinal Allen, founder of the English Catholic colleges at Douai and Rome. She was a redoubtable lady, sheltering priests in her home despite the risk. There was a secret chapel in the roof of the house and, each year, on the anniversary of her husband's death, no fewer than twelve priests were called there to say a mass for his soul.

Elizabeth also had enemies: Edmund Fleetwood was eager to take over as Lord of Rossall and Sheriff Edward Trafford was not above profiting from the misfortune of his neighbours. He had already declared Elizabeth an outlaw because of her refusal to give up the old faith.

News came that the king's men planned to descend on Rossall on the evening of the Epiphany, so Elizabeth entrusted a friend, William Anyon, with 500 pounds to be given to her daughters if she should not survive. She then went to a safe house, but was obliged to leave her daughters in the hall with a sick cousin who could not be moved—she knew that whilst the house might be looted, her daughters would not be harmed or arrested, since only she had been outlawed. Also, the girls were the legal owners of the house since their father's death.

When the soldiers arrived, no one could tell them where Elizabeth was because they honestly did not know. The house was searched, but the soldiers found nothing. Unfortunately, they soon saw that the house was well-stocked with food and drink and so Elizabeth's daughters found themselves with several unwelcome house guests, who clearly had no intention of leaving until the cupboards—and the wine cellars—were bare.

When word came to Elizabeth about this, she persuaded a band of villagers to go to the hall and pretend to volunteer for service, so that they would be invited inside to help eat and drink the provisions. The sooner the cupboards were emptied, the sooner the soldiers would leave. The plan worked and the villagers ate and drank their fill—and were also on hand to watch over Elizabeth's daughters in the meantime.

The girls, however, had decided to escape to find their mother. They hid the keys of the house so the doors could not be locked at night and then slipped away in the darkness, finding their way to the coast where they found a boat and rowed across the estuary. They had no real idea where their mother might be and the story says that it took them almost two weeks to find her.

With the food gone, Elizabeth nowhere to be found, and now her daughters also gone, the soldiers decided the time had come to move on. Knowing that William Anyon was Elizabeth's friend, they paid him a call. They did not find Elizabeth, of course, but they did find and confiscate the 500 pounds she had left in William's safekeeping. The money was given to Sheriff Edward Trafford, who immediately set about trying to prove in court that the money was not legally owned by Elizabeth's daughters. Unfortunately for him, the jury's foreman was Elizabeth's other enemy, Edmund Fleetwood and with both men having a great interest in taking Rossall for themselves, the court battle was long and protracted.

To cut a long story short, as the girls could not be found, the court assumed that they were dead, in which case Rossall and the money would revert to their mother, Elizabeth—but as she had been outlawed, everything she owned was forfeit to the crown. The story ended with Elizabeth and her daughters losing all they had. And surely that's enough drama to justify a ghost story.

Perhaps the fabled passage from the gazebo to the shore did exist, deliberately constructed to provide an escape route for Elizabeth's incumbent priests. Perhaps it was one of her daughters who, running to the shore and freedom, lost her life in the tunnel as it collapsed around her. Or perhaps the White Lady is the ghost of brave Elizabeth herself, making her way to a safe house, but full of fear for her beloved Rossall Hall and the daughters she was leaving behind. Perhaps...that's all that can be said, because like all the best ghost stories, we will never know for sure.

Victoria

The Victoria pub opened for business in 1836 and is one of the oldest pubs in the town. It is believed that odd occurrences on the premises are the work of George, a previous landlord. He has been glimpsed on occasion, but more concrete signs of his presence are banging noises when the place is empty and a handle on an internal door moving up and down all on its own.

FOULRIDGE

Hobstones Farm

As "Hob" is the shortened form of "hobgoblin," it is perhaps no surprise that Hobstones Farm has a reputation for being haunted. Local knowledge avers that the farmhouse is built on an ancient burial ground, a place that was itself associated with mischievous dwarfs and elves.

In the 1950s, the resident farmer was visiting the outside lavatory when, suddenly, the door opened and he saw a small man, dressed as a monk. The man slowly extended the stump of his arm, which had been severed and was still bleeding. Although the vision lasted for only a few seconds, the farmer managed to describe the monk as dwarfish in build, with a weather-beaten and somewhat twisted face.

This one short experience would have been relatively easy to dismiss, but several weeks later, the monk appeared again and this time the farmer's wife also saw him. She watched with astonishment as the diminutive man appeared, took a few steps towards where she stood with her husband, and then vanished in a moment. This distressing experience was enough to make the farmer and his wife move out of Hobstones Farm for good.

Twenty years later, a different family had their own set of experiences—this time of a more material kind. The trouble began with odd noises, as if someone was thumping the walls of the old stone farmhouse. Then, more terrifyingly, objects began to move of their own accord. On one occasion, the washing machine was flung across the kitchen, along with a tray of eggs that had been on top of it. Oddly, whilst all the white eggs in the tray had been broken by the impact, all the brown eggs were intact and positioned in the tray in the shape of a cross. A leaded window was destroyed; on examination it appeared that the window had been pushed from inside the house and the glass had not shattered, but seemed to have been ground into tiny pieces. One day there was an urgent banging on the main door, but there was no one to be seen and yet the banging continued, as if the door was being pounded by a giant, invisible fist.

The family continued to be plagued by uncanny events for four years until, by 1974, they were thoroughly tired of the upheaval. The haunting at Hobstones Farm became well known and the local press added unwelcome fuel to the fire by claiming that the walls and ceilings were shaking so violently that it was feared the house would collapse. They also diagnosed that the house must be possessed by demons.

The mention of devilish works only increased the panic surrounding the case, so the family decided that as a last resort the Reverend Noel Hawthorn should be asked to come and perform an exorcism. He blessed every room with holy water, things began to quieten down and, since then, the farmhouse has been demolished and the land redeveloped.

It is not known whether any residents in the new housing estate now built on the site have ever seen a ghostly monk.

Maiden's Cross

This cross is in the middle of town and is certainly more ancient than the legend to which it owes its name. Margaret Burward was wife to a soldier who went to fight for Cromwell's troops. She swore to wait for him by the cross and, even when she heard he had been killed at Marston Moor, she continued to wait for him there, every day. Eventually, she met her death at the hands of a Royalist soldier and was buried at the cross where she had died.

The cross is also known as Tailor's Cross, from an alternative story that comes from the same period. A tailor who refused to sew uniforms for Cromwell's soldiers was killed and his body laid here as a warning. A pair of tailor's shears is roughly carved onto the cross, which seems to prove the story.

(On the other hand, the "shears" may well be a pair of pincers, one of the instruments of the Passion.)

New Inn

The New Inn on Skipton Old Road has a ghost that has bothered landlords with footsteps and knocks on the door in the dead of night and—most strangely—a luminous cross that is said to have appeared regularly on the ceiling of a small bedroom at the rear of the building. It has been said that the ghost could be a Cavalier, but it is just as likely to be connected with the enclave of Quakers whose gravestones were used to build one of the New Inn's walls.

Standing Stone Lane

Sometimes called the Lark Hill Stone, this is in the vicinity of Standing Stone Lane. The stone itself was too useful to be left alone; it was included in the nearby stone wall and with careful inspection, you can still find it.

FRECKLETON

Road Ghost

A headless lady is said to walk the road somewhere between Freckleton and Kirkham. The exact spot can sometimes be divined by the smell of thyme; legend has it that this lady cried out at the moment of her death: "Give me time!"

(See Staining Hall at Staining for another mention of this phrase.)

Ship Inn

The Ship Inn is reputed to be more than three centuries old. As well as once being a smuggler's watering hole, it also harboured a skull that had its home in the attic of the building. Like other such skulls, it was said locally that it should never be moved or disaster would result. The owners of the pub in the mid-1990s were well aware of the warnings but, one day, the skull was found to have disappeared from its home. This fact was only discovered the day after a restaurant employee saw two ghosts.

Two people wearing "white silk bloomers and red shirts" were seen by the female employee, who said they were apparently deep in conversation. The pub and restaurant had just closed after lunchtime, so she assumed that the oddly dressed people must have been taking part in some sort of fancy dress affair and had unwittingly been locked in. She had a quick word with her manager, who immediately went to assist but found no one. There had been no fancy dress event in the pub that day.

Incidentally, no one can explain how the skull disappeared, or where it is today.

FULWOOD

Black Bull Lane

A cottage on Black Bull Lane that dates from 1780 is reputed to be the oldest building in Fulwood. It is also haunted. Stories of the ghostly lady, who has been christened Dorothy, have been passed from owner to owner, and they all have their tales to tell. Dorothy has been seen sitting in a chair in the lounge and sometimes a smell of tobacco has been noticed, but mostly she is responsible for the atmosphere of the cottage, which is full of harmony.

Fulwood Barracks

The garrison church at Fulwood Barracks dates from 1847. It is haunted by a soldier, thought to be a former chaplain who lost his life in the First World War. He was seen quite clearly in full light of day by the verger of thirteen years, who turned from her work to see "a soldier in full dress uniform" standing quite still, his hands resting on his sword. The Padre, to her surprise, believed her without question. He explained that a soldier guarding a coffin in the church would quite naturally be wearing full uniform and would be leaning on his drawn sword, just as she had seen.

In recent years, a TV crew came to investigate the story of the haunted church and their sophisticated camera panned around until the pulpit area came into view—the spot where the ghostly soldier had been seen. The camera promptly malfunctioned. Several times.

The old Officers' Mess also has its own ghost, which is well-documented. An officer stationed there in 1910 wrote his own account. His room was on the ground floor of the mess and was clearly an original part of the building, as it still boasted a marble mantelpiece. One night, the officer retired to bed as usual, but was much disturbed by a gale and, later, a single clap of thunder. He opened his eyes and saw, to his surprise, a luminous figure between the bed and the fireplace. He spent the rest of the night in another officer's room.

The officer was teased about his experience for days, but was vindicated about three weeks later, when a certain Lieutenant Walmsley, newly arrived at the barracks, mentioned in conversation that a friend had told him of his experience there. The soldier had slept in a room with a marble mantelpiece, he said, on the ground floor. He had seen something, he said, in that room.

A couple of years later, another officer, Lieutenant James, was returning to his room in the same block when he saw something in the passage so clearly that he instinctively drew his sword and took a swipe at the shape, hitting only the wall.

Legend has it that the ghost is that of a cavalry man, stationed at the barracks in the early days, who had inhabited that very room, the one with the marble mantelpiece. Private McCaffery had been sentenced by Captain Hanham to a fortnight's confinement after the relatively minor offence of failing to apprehend some stone-throwing children. McCaffrey was furious at this sentence and furious with Hanham, who had a long reputation for bullying. One day, he saw Captain Hanham walking across the parade ground with Colonel Crofton and he raised his gun and fired, killing both the Captain and the Colonel with a single bullet.

Private McCaffrey was sentenced to death by hanging.

Finally… the old Roman Road, Watling Street, passes through the parade ground at the barracks. It is said that a legion of Roman soldiers can sometimes be seen marching along this road.

Preston Workhouse Hospital

The Workhouse Hospital, a beautiful building, was for a greater part of its life a mental health hospital and latterly housed a maternity wing. It is now home to several businesses and one wonders if any of their employees have ever come across the Grey Lady who used to haunt there. She would visit bedsides in the dead of night, always a benign presence, clearly intending only to look after the sick people who might need her care.

Withy Trees

Two Roman roads cross each other at Fulwood, one being Watling Street, and it was said that these roads stretched from sea to sea in every direction: north, south, east, and west. The crossroads might well be at the place known locally as Withy Trees—a very old name that indicates that here was once a grove of willows. Here, Watling Street Road crosses Garstang Road. The former leads to Ribchester, the latter to Lancaster, both of which are Roman sites.

Locally, however, the Romans were given no credit for these fantastic roads. Instead, it was said that the devil himself made them and, what's more, he made them in just one night.

GALGATE
Green Lane

On the evening of January 11, 1866, a thirty-one year old spinster called Elizabeth Nelson was brutally murdered on Green Lane, a rural lane, just a little too far from any houses for anyone to hear her screams. Her body was discovered, shrouded in snow, the next morning. The place where she lay is now the site of the War Memorial and it is said that snow falls there each year on the anniversary of her death.

Hampson Green

The ancient hamlet of Hampson Green, close to Ellel Grange, was once well known for a great fight between a Dobbie and a Hobbie. Both creatures were common to Lancashire—otherworldly sprites who offered help in the house and assistance on the farm, as long as their rules were followed. The Hampson Green Dobbie was an unseen farmhand who would helpfully pen the cattle at night—once he is said to have penned up a large brown hare as well, a motif which appears in many similar tales. It is said that a lady left him a suit of clothes and anyone familiar with boggart stories will guess that he was never seen again at the farm.

  The Dobbie's final end came when he entered into a fierce fight with a Hobbie from Brunshaw, and both lost their lives. The place where they were buried was known ever after as Dobb's Field.

GARSTANG
Garstang Church

In the churchyard here is a stone known as the Church Stone—or sometimes Grappentop—which is supposed to have been thrown from the steeple by a mysterious force.

Local Legend

A folktale set in Garstang concerns a "poor idiot" named Gregory, who was simple-minded but kind. His mother understood how kindhearted he was, but the village children were cruel and made fun of him whenever they could. One night a group of boys decided to played a trick on him by dressing one of their party in a white sheet and frightening poor Gregory into thinking he had seen a ghost. The pretend ghost hid in a tree and his friends crouched in the ditch by the hedge, to watch the fun.

Along the lane came Gregory and out stepped the pretend ghost to the accompaniment of wailings and moanings from his friends in the ditch—but it seemed that Gregory was not such an idiot after all, for he simply laughed at the white "ghost" in front of him. Then, suddenly, his expression changed to one of horror and he shouted out, "Oh, oh! A black one! A black one!"'

His tormentors looked around and there, next to their white-sheeted friend, stood a terrifying black shape who could only be the devil. Away they all ran with the devil chasing after them and Gregory shouting, "Run, black devil! Catch white devil!"

The boys soon reached the village and ran into the inn to find their fathers, but their white-sheeted friend continued to race down the street pursued by the devil, with Gregory behind him. Suddenly the devil vanished, but Gregory kept up the chase until finally he caught the pretend ghost, who fell into the ditch at the side of the lane. Close behind the two of them were men from the village, summoned by the rest of the boys. They found Gregory easily enough for he was still triumphantly shouting, "Catch white devil! Catch white devil!" But they found the pretend ghost in the ditch, quite still and silent.

The boy in the white sheet was carried home and was ill in bed for some time. As his parents were too poor to afford a doctor, Gregory's kind mother called on them every day to give them all they needed to make the poor lad well again. With her went Gregory, her simple, kindhearted boy. And what should happen but that the two boys became great friends and stayed that way forever.

Now that Gregory had a protector in the form of his new friend, the other boys thought twice before making fun of him—they had only to remember the time they had tried to frighten him with a white sheet and that it had been the devil himself who had come to his aid.

Curiously, the newspapers of September 1881 reported a story that may have been the source of the legend above. The report said that villagers had for some days been concerned about a "white ghost" who walked at night along the lane between the railway station and the village. A servant girl was so scared by the apparition that she had taken to her bed with the shock. A postman whose job it was to meet the night train delivering the post could no longer make that journey, because of what he had seen.

Most people—and the police—believed that the ghost was in fact "some young fellow" wrapped in a sheet and a group of young men had begun walking the lane every night, armed with cudgels, determined to catch the "ghost." We are not told if they succeeded. It would be nice to think that the solution of this troublesome mystery of the "white ghost" was, in fact, truly down to Gregory and his friend, the black devil.

GOOSNARGH

Chingle Hall

Chingle Hall dates from 1260 when it was built by Adam de Singleton. Legend has it that the hall passed into the Wall family, one of whom was the Blessed Saint John Wall, Franciscan priest, hanged for his faith in 1679. His head was supposed to be secreted somewhere in the walls of this old place but, sadly, scholarly research has shown that whilst a Wall family did live there, St. John was not part of that family.

However, it cannot be denied that the hall harbours numerous priest-holes, including one in the huge chimney. A pre-Reformation cross was also found inside a wall in a downstairs room that was believed to have once been used as a chapel. Over the years, a grand variety of stories have given Chingle Hall the reputation of being the most haunted house in Lancashire, if not the country.

In the beginning, the hall was reputed to have only a single ghost: that of the priest, who was assumed to be St. John Wall. By the 1970s, the number of entities had risen to eleven, and by the end of the 1990s, the tally had risen to seventeen! These apparitions include: a cavalier seated on a horse and knocking at the door, a Roman soldier walking down the stairs, a teenage girl sitting in a room known as the Priest's Room, a lady nicknamed Mad Eleanor, and a child playing outside the house. There are smells of burning lavender and incense, as well as sounds of a harmonium, a child crying, and, in the lane outside, galloping horses.

Upstairs in the hall, one room is known as the Priest's Room because it has an evident priest-hide. It is this room that is alleged to be the most haunted of all. Once, when a party of visitors was being shown around, one of them fainted on seeing a spectral hand withdrawing back into the priest-hide. Another visitor who wanted to take photographs couldn't get his camera to work until he apologised to the ghost for being there.

In 1980, when Chingle Hall was still a private residence, a group of three young men were some of the first people to stay overnight, to raise money for a local hospital. The evening started quietly enough, but by midnight, they had all fled the building.

Phil, Alan, and Martin were shown into the Priest's Room, which was uncarpeted and bare apart from a deck chair and a very old desk in the corner in front of the priest-hide. Phil settled in that corner and the other two men sat on the floor across the room. Alan set up his tape recorder so that if something dramatic did happen, he could record it for posterity.

By ten o'clock, the men had been in the Priest's Room for three hours and nothing had happened. Phil started to doze from boredom, but was suddenly awakened by a loud bang as if the desk beside him had been struck. Some minutes later, there was another bang—this time on the door. Alan called out, "If there's anybody there, come in!" The door didn't open, but it seemed as if someone had indeed entered the room, as the uncarpeted wooden floor reverberated with heavy footsteps. The footsteps headed towards Phil, who was still sitting in front of the priest-hide. The three men could feel the floor moving with every step. After a few seconds, the footsteps moved around the room to the third corner and stopped again. Nothing further happened, there were no more footsteps, but the three men had experienced quite enough. They packed up their things and left.

Back at Phil's house, they listened to Alan's tapes. The bang on the door was certainly recorded. So was Alan's voice, inviting whatever-it-was to come into the room. Then, as the footsteps came into the room, there was the noise of an unearthly wind...

Dun Cow Rib Farm

A lovely old cottage on Halfpenny Lane was once known as Dun Cow Rib Farm, because of a huge, curved bone that hung proudly above the lintel. It was, allegedly, all that remained of an enormous cow. The cow, a rich dun-red colour, had been loved by everyone in the area, for she would give of her milk to anyone who asked kindly. Because of her huge size, her milk never ran dry. In addition, it was well known that milk from a red cow had different qualities from any other. It was valued for its curative properties, especially against consumption (tuberculosis).

The only person who did not love the Dun Cow was an old witch, who could not sell the milk from her own cow as long as the Dun Cow, who was giving her milk for free, still lived on Parlick Fell. So she decided that something must be done.

One morning, the witch found the Dun Cow and asked her if she would kindly fill her jug. The cow agreed, but as the witch settled by her side to milk her, she changed her jug into a sieve. She did this quietly, so that the Dun Cow did not see her trick, and all the milk she gave simply ran through the sieve and away. At length, the Dun Cow became so exhausted from trying to fill the witch's "jug" that she died.

The great Dun Cow was buried on nearby Cow Hill and her grave was visited often by the local people. The story of the great Dun Cow was told many times, but as the years passed, those who heard the stories believed it less and less, until at last some of them explored the grave of the old Dun Cow to see what was really there. They did, indeed, find an enormous skeleton and one of the men took away a rib as proof and fixed it to the wall of his house on Halfpenny Lane, above the lintel.

Once, the rib disappeared, but not for long. It was stolen as a prank and hidden in a nearby brook, but the prankster suffered so much bad luck so quickly that he was forced to return the rib to its rightful place.

Interestingly, at Warwick, Bristol, Chesterfield, and Lincoln there are also ribs or other bones that are claimed as being from an old Dun Cow. The cow in Bristol was said to have given enough milk for the whole of the city.

The Hill Presbytery

St. Francis' Church in Goosnargh is known locally as Hill Chapel. The Presbytery standing nearby is older than the church by well over a century, having originated as a humble farmhouse in the late 1600s. A resident priest was quite certain the place was haunted. He described the ghost as a monk wearing a brown habit, who would appear only in the living-room, which was the oldest part of the house. He would walk the same route every time, crossing the room before disappearing.

Local Legend

One night, long ago, a happy band of fairies was seen in a field here. They were dressed in full hunting gear, dancing and clapping and having fun.

Whittingham Hospital

In 1927, the *Aberdeen Journal* carried a syndicated story about a ghost at Whittingham Hospital, an asylum for the mentally ill. The ghost had been seen, on two consecutive evenings, on the roof of one of the hospital buildings, moving so smoothly that it was later described as "gliding." Thorough searches on both occasions found nothing. A few nights later, a nurse came face-to-face with the ghost as she walked through the hospital grounds, and when the ghost reached out to her, she fainted.

The main hospital was a typical roomy Victorian red-brick building with large wards, wide corridors, and expanses of grounds outside. In later years, reports of hauntings also came from inside the building, with one particular corridor being renowned for its spooky atmosphere. Staff walking along it alone would feel they were being watched, even when the wards lining it were empty of patients. One young woman was terrified when, as she walked down the corridor, all the lights went off.

Whittingham Hospital closed in 1995, and the abandoned buildings have been haunted ever since by ghost-hunters and others engaging in the modern hobby of "urban exploration"—but all that will end soon as the whole complex is being demolished to make way for a new estate of houses.

GREAT ECCLESTON

Cross House

Cross House was once well known for its ghost, a White Lady who was sometimes seen at an attic window looking out. She was held responsible for noises heard in the house for which no natural cause could be found.

GREAT MITTON

All Hallows Church

A curious tale is told about All Hallows Church. The legend says that it once stood somewhere else entirely. The devil, or the fairies, or some other supernatural agency felt that it was in quite the wrong spot, and so they moved it, stone by stone, to Mitton where it now stands. The task was completed in a single night.

The cross in the churchyard here has carvings of the crucifixion on both sides, but they are thought to date from different times, as much as two centuries apart. The oldest is from the thirteenth century.

A Green Man can also be found in this church, hidden away on a centuries-old screen that was brought here from Sawley Abbey. The screen is said to date from the fifteenth century.

GREENHALGH

Greenhalgh Castle

Greenhalgh Castle was built in 1490 by the Earl of Derby. It is clear he felt the need of a fortified home as he sought permission from the king to crenelate and "embattle" the building. It originally had four towers and was described as "pretty."

The castle was severely damaged in 1645 during the Civil War, after resisting Cromwell's followers for several months. Local people were called upon to protect the castle, but in the end, they gave it up on the promise that they would be allowed to return to their own homes unharmed. The castle was virtually destroyed. Much of the rubble was used to build nearby farms and dwellings, and all that now remains is one tower—and that is a ruin. This is still a picturesque and evocative spot; however, it is now private farmland.

During the Siege of Greenhalgh Castle, a soldier killed his wife, from whom he was estranged, at Gubberford Bridge. It is said that this bridge is known for its boggart— the ghost of the murdered woman. In years gone by, she would appear to unwary horsemen as a cloaked woman looking for a lift. Only when mounted behind a rider would she reveal herself to be nothing but a skeleton. She was said to be responsible for the deaths and injuries of several terrified riders.

GRINDLETON

Cat Steps

Many years ago, the verger of Grindleton Church told how two boys had reported hearing fairy music in West Clough Woods, near Cat Steps, and had then seen little people dancing amongst the trees. The verger believed them because he had seen the fairies himself. Their coats had been green, their caps red.

Dinkling Green

Dinkling Green is such a charming name, and the area such a charming place, it comes as no surprise to hear that fairies were often seen here—particularly on a spot known as White Stone.

HALTON

St.Wilfrid's Church

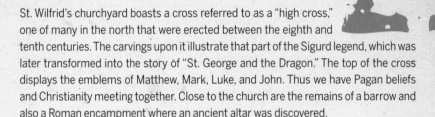

St. Wilfrid's churchyard boasts a cross referred to as a "high cross," one of many in the north that were erected between the eighth and tenth centuries. The carvings upon it illustrate that part of the Sigurd legend, which was later transformed into the story of "St. George and the Dragon." The top of the cross displays the emblems of Matthew, Mark, Luke, and John. Thus we have Pagan beliefs and Christianity meeting together. Close to the church are the remains of a barrow and also a Roman encampment where an ancient altar was discovered.

HAPTON

Bridge House Inn

To the rear of the Bridge House Inn on Manchester Road, there are several stables, one of which was often used as a temporary mortuary for unfortunates who drowned in the canal that runs alongside the pub. Many years ago, a young girl who worked as a servant at the Bridge House killed herself by jumping from the bridge over the canal, and it is likely that her body was brought back to the stables to rest overnight before proper arrangements could be made. As a suicide, she may never have been given a proper Christian burial. Perhaps that's why she is said to haunt the Bridge House still, walking the stairs to the room that was once the pantry.

HARDHORN

Local Legend

Between Hardhorn and Staining, there is a small spring that is still known to this day as Fairies Well. It was well known in its time for its miraculous healing powers and often visited by people from far and near seeking relief from their ailments. Many tales are also told of the fairies that frequented this place.

One story tells of a Preston woman. She was a poor widow who came here one day to collect water to bathe her baby's eyes, for the water was known for its curative properties and her child was losing its sight. While she was thus engaged, she was disturbed by a good-looking little man in green who gave her some ointment that he said was a sure cure for what ailed her child. The woman may have been poor, but she was not stupid, for when she had returned to her home that evening, she first applied the ointment to one of her own eyes to make sure there was no danger. No ill befell her and so she went ahead and anointed her baby's eyes with the ointment. She was delighted to find that her baby's eyes healed well and her sight was restored.

Some time later, when this strange event was just a memory, the woman saw the same little man dressed in green—this time in Preston Market. There he was, clear as day, helping himself to corn from an open sack. The woman approached him; she did not mean to accuse him, but merely wanted to thank him for the magical ointment, but the little man was shocked that she could see him. He was in fact a fairy and was certain of being invisible to everyone else. When he questioned her, she confessed that she had used some of the ointment on herself, just to make sure it was safe. As she spoke, she pointed to the eye she had anointed. The fairy was very angry at what she had done, for it was the ointment that had allowed the woman to see him. He jumped up and hit her on that eye with all his might. The poor woman found she was now half-blind and her sight in that eye never returned.

The woman's daughter, however, could see the fairies all her life—but she never spoke to them, for fear of what might happen.

HASLINGDEN

Griffin Hotel

The Griffin Hotel's ghost is believed to be an old lady with a sense of humour and, judging from her actions, someone who likes to have fun. She has been known to turn on the jukebox—Shirley Bassey being favoured—and one day a poor customer standing at the bar was soaked in beer when his glass disintegrated in his hand!

Haslingden Grains

One day some local men were playing a gambling game at a disused church here—on a Sunday! One of them threw a halfpenny up in the air and all were puzzled when it did not come down again. All was explained, though, when they looked up to see the devil smiling at them from the beams.

HESKIN GREEN

Heskin Hall

This sixteenth-century building is now a modern conference centre, but its ancient origins can still be seen. During the Civil War, Heskin Hall was a Royalist house, well known for harbouring priests. One of these priests was discovered here by Roundhead leader Colonel Rigby and was so afraid of his impending death that he denied his faith entirely. He tried to distract attention by naming the sixteen-year-old daughter of the house as a Catholic, but this backfired when Rigby demanded he prove that he was truly a Parliamentarian supporter by putting the girl to death. Terrified, the priest did as he was asked and hanged the girl from a beam in what is now known as the Scarlet Room. This act did not save the priest; he was killed anyway.

The Scarlet Room is known for its chilly atmosphere and those who have slept there over the years have complained of mysterious noises: raps and bangs. Some have even seen the White Lady herself. It is traditional to touch the beam where the girl was hanged, for luck.

Stories of the White Lady tell of her being seen in the Scarlet Room, or running along a corridor pursued by the priest. At other times, she appears downstairs in the kitchen. At least one sighting tells of a girl who looked very real indeed—so real that the person who saw her spoke to her and was disconcerted when she did not reply.

One of the owners of Heskin Hall, Lady Lilford, has told repeated accounts of seeing a ghostly girl standing beside a large chest in the hall of the house. It is thought that she is the ghost of a newly married young woman who had hidden herself in the chest as a joke, holding a bunch of mistletoe, expecting that her new husband would soon find her and give her a traditional kiss. Sadly, the cover of the chest locked itself and she could not loosen it. She died there of suffocation before anyone realised where she might be. When she was discovered, she was still holding the bunch of mistletoe. However, this charmingly tragic tale, known as "The Mistletoe Bough," has been told about many other chests, in many other ancient halls throughout England.

HEYHOUSES

Fancy Lodge

Heyhouses, now an area of St. Annes, was once a tranquil country village in its own right. Fancy Lodge has made way for a new block of flats, but in the days when this area was open fields and country lanes, it was a seventeenth-century thatched cottage—and the lane outside its door was haunted.

The ghost may have been Mrs. Eastham, resident of a cottage just up the lane, for the first recorded story states that the White Lady was seen just a few days after her death. She was seen by the tenant of Fancy Lodge—in fact, she followed him home. The sighting was remarked upon by his family who were convinced of the tale because he couldn't eat his evening meal! Another man, Will Cross, was visiting his father on the farm across the road from Fancy Lodge one night, when the woman in white appeared before him. He spoke to her, but she did not answer, and he froze in shock when she disappeared in an instant. Other sightings were also reported and at least two of them stated that the lady wore spectacles—which is unusual.

HEYSHAM

The Barrows

Halfway up the cliff behind Heysham Rectory, in the area known as The Barrows, there is a very large stone known locally as the Druid's Stone. It may simply be a natural feature, but it may be far more important. If it is the one I discovered recently, it has a rectangular recess cut into its flat surface, measuring about two by four feet. The recess is only a couple of inches deep, so its possible use is not immediately apparent. It seems too large to have been the base for a cross. The area around it has given up evidence of a Mesolithic encampment, so the carved stone may well have had some ritual use.

Converted Barn

Many years ago, a family bought a dilapidated building in the centre of Heysham Village. The building was a traditional Lancashire long-house, with living accommodation at one end and a barn for animals at the other. The last resident of the cottage was an elderly lady, who had recently died. Her family lived next door, and so, when strange things started happening in the old house, they were able to explain that it was probably Aunty Nelly, just going about her business as usual.

One of the most common occurrences would happen in the evenings, when the family would go up to bed and find the landing light already on. In the mornings, the back door would be found wide open, although it had been securely locked the night before. This made complete sense to the family next door, who explained that Aunty Nelly was always early to bed—and it was her habit to get up at 5:30 a.m. and go outside to feed the birds.

Crime Well

Crime Well Lane in Lower Heysham is named for the holy well near the church. The origin of this well's incongruous name is a mystery.

Heysham Chapel

St. Patrick's Chapel, on the headland at Heysham, is over a thousand years old and boasts a series of graves cut into the solid stone at the very edge of the cliff. The excavations in the rock are of differing sizes and so a romantic story has grown up about a whole family who lost their lives in a storm. The chapel beside them is said to have been a monument to their lives. Whatever the truth of this story, there is no doubt that whoever lay here must have had enormous importance to the community, as great effort was expended in preparing their final resting place.

The chapel, dedicated to St. Patrick, was visited on that saint's day for centuries. Just off the coast, at low tide, a bank of stones can be seen that is known as St. Patrick's Skeer. A little way up the coast, at Hest Bank, a holy well also bears the saint's name. St. Patrick, who was in fact English, is said to have been born near Carlisle and the story of his years in Ireland is well documented, as is the tale of his escape and the fact that he was shipwrecked on the English coast. It has been suggested that Heysham was the site of that shipwreck and the evidence would seem to support that theory.

Heysham Library

One day, a librarian at Heysham Library heard a child crying. It was early in the morning and the doors had not yet opened to the public. She and her colleague, who had heard nothing, looked all around the building but could not find the source of this odd sound. Half an hour after opening the doors, the sound of crying was heard again by the first librarian—and once more, later in the day. No explanation was ever found. On another occasion, the two librarians went to warn a man in the reading room that they were about to close for the day, but he was no longer there. Yet neither of them had seen him leave and he would certainly have had to pass them on his way out. This may have been the same old gent in a tweed suit who was sometimes seen outside the building's small kitchen.

No explanations were ever suggested for any of these strange happenings. The building was eighty years old when it was demolished in 2008. The brand-new library that was built on the site has remained unaffected—so far.

Old Hall Hotel

The Old Hall at Heysham is an imposing building. It is around four centuries old and was clearly built as a private dwelling. There are several secret passages and priest-holes. As one landlord put it, "At the time this place was built, if you were building a house and you had plenty of money, with all the religious instability of that time, you'd put in secret passages. You'd be mad not to."

One priest-hide was rumoured to be the entrance to a tunnel that led to the village and thence to the sea. Behind a bedroom wall, a passage has been found that extends along the top of the hall and then down to the kitchens. The main chimney at the centre of the pub is interesting—beside it is a "draught," or second chimney, which would have been used to feed the fire with air and keep it blazing. It is several feet square and would have been an ideal hiding place. Noises caused by wind in this now-unused chimney may well have led to tales of ghosts.

Whilst there are no legends about this fascinating building, there are several reports of ghosts, both male and female. Strange sounds come from the disused third floor and visitors sitting in the beer garden frequently report seeing shadowy figures at the third-floor windows. A Grey Lady has been seen in a room that is now unused, but was once a ladies restroom. Women would find themselves chatting to a lady, only to turn and find no one there. Old stables at the back of the house are now storerooms and, on occasion, a young fellow with a pitchfork has been seen, engaged in his task of mucking-out. And where there was once an internal well, a monk has been seen, apparently going to draw water.

One landlord reported that whilst he had never seen anything in the Old Hall, he was less sceptical than he had been when he moved in. He had been forced to admit that the place sometimes had a very strange atmosphere. He was most perturbed by his dog's erratic behaviour; on occasion he would stand barking at the door of their flat (upstairs) even though everything was secure and any intruder would have triggered the alarms. More mysteriously still, there was a whole period of time when the dog would simply stand in the pub and bark at the wall—behind which it is now known there are passages. He kept up his noisy vigil every night for two weeks!

Royal Oak

On enquiry, I was told that the Royal Oak pub is not haunted—unless, of course, you count old Mary, who used to work here as a barmaid. Customers have said they still see her, at work behind the bar.

Sainty Well

Unusually, Heysham boasts two holy wells; this one is more appropriately named Sainty Well.

St. Peter's Church

Inside the Anglo-Saxon porch of this lovely little church there is a carving of a Green Man. He is, naturally, very weathered on account of his age, but look closely and you will see him.

HIGHER PENWORTHAM

Church Avenue

Near St. Mary's Church, be wary of laying eyes on the Fairy Funeral, for such a sighting forecasts your death!

One night, two men were walking this way at the dangerous hour of midnight. One was old and one was young, but neither was happy to hear the church clock chime twelve times. They were even less happy to then hear another bell tolling, a bell that they recognised as the passing-bell. Neither man had heard the passing-bell at that time of night before, but out of habit they stopped and counted the number of times the bell rang out, for they knew it would toll once for each year of the life of the poor departed. The poor departed, it turned out, was exactly the same age as the younger man and this saddened them, for the younger man was no great age at all. But as there was nothing to be done at that hour, they set off again on their journey home.

They had not walked far before they saw a tiny man dressed in blue coming towards them, chanting as he walked. The older man immediately recognised that this was a fairy and he guessed he must be leading a fairy funeral. He told the younger man to hide against the hedge with him, for if they were not seen, no harm would come to them. They stood quietly, watching a procession of tiny fairies pass by, bearing with them a coffin that was open. They caught a glimpse of the coffin as it passed and, to their horror, they saw that the face on the corpse was that of the younger man! The younger man ran forward, calling to the fairies to tell him how long he had left to live, but he received no answer, for as soon as they heard his voice, they vanished away.

Every day after that, the younger man grew more and more morose, expecting that his life would soon end, as indeed it did, about a month later when he fell hard from a haystack. His funeral passed along the same route where the two men had seen the fairy funeral that night, and the older man was one of his pallbearers.

St. Mary's Well

A little distance from St. Mary's Church, there was once a well dedicated to St. Mary that had miraculous healing properties. It was paved over in the middle of the nineteenth century, however, as too many travellers were polluting it by using it to bathe themselves. The stone trough in which the water gathered was removed and access to the water was reduced to an unremarkable pipe. It was situated on Penwortham Brow, by the side of the road, and its position can possibly still be seen today as there is a depression in the ground, which is almost always full of water. It has been reported that in the area of the well, Roman soldiers have sometimes been seen.

HOGHTON

Hoghton Tower

Once Hoghton Tower was a simple pele tower; centuries passed before it was replaced with the building we see today. Hoghton Tower has had an eventful history and it would be surprising if there were no tales of ghosts in such an ancient place.

The story is often told of Ann, a daughter of this Protestant household centuries ago, who fell in love with the son of the Catholic family at Samlesbury Hall. Knowing that their union would never be accepted, their only recourse was elopement and so, one night, the young man came on horseback to collect his love. Unfortunately, their plan had been discovered and, as Ann came out of the house, her lover was killed in front of her eyes. She never recovered from the shock and spent the rest of her life in a nunnery.

(See Samlesbury Hall for a similar story.)

Ann is known to haunt Hoghton Tower, but there are also other ghosts attested to by family members and visitors touring the building. A Green Lady, so-called because of the colour of her velvet dress, is sometimes seen around the minstrel's gallery. A woman in Tudor dress has been seen crossing the courtyard outside. A little girl has been seen inside the house and there are reports of a ghostly monk at the north entrance to the building. On occasion, a man is seen apparently searching for something in the area of the staircase. It is said that during the Civil War, a family member hid his treasure there. There is also something strange about the well house; one of the family dogs repeatedly barks at something invisible in one corner.

One room in particular has been the scene of many strange occurrences. Not so long ago, the late Sir Cuthbert de Hoghton was writing letters in this room when he heard the rustling of skirts and heard laughter behind him as if someone was looking over his shoulder. He re-read what he had just written and, indeed, it was quite amusing…

There is also a legend of devilry attached to Hoghton Tower, involving a visitor called Edgar Astley and "The Demon of the Oak."

Edgar was in mourning for his lost love—she had married someone else and died not long afterwards. He kept to himself for much of the time, without being rude to his hosts, spending hours poring over black books beneath the ancient oak tree in the grounds. His hosts, knowing his heartbreak, were sympathetic. The servants, however, were more suspicious of his behaviour, particularly as they had seen strange lights in his apartments long after he should have retired to bed.

Finally, one of the servants was delegated to spy on Edgar and find out what he was up to. At midnight, the servant crept to Edgar's door and peeped through a knothole. There he saw Edgar with a mysterious book before him, dropping a mysterious substance into a brass cup and setting it alight, releasing the most awful smell. And then, to the servant's horror, he heard a conversation, for Edgar was not alone! It became clear that Edgar's visitor was the devil himself and, as the conversation went on, the servant heard Edgar strike a bargain with the devil—a soul in exchange for the return of his lost love.

The servant was so terrified that he fainted and when he came to his senses again he saw Edgar standing before him. Edgar made the servant swear to stay silent about what he had seen. He also made him accompany him the following night, at midnight, when the devil had told him to perform one last spell and then he would see his lost love again.

And so, the next night, despite a raging storm, the two of them crept from the house and made their way to the ancient oak tree, where Edgar laid out the ingredients for his spell and performed the ritual. As soon as this was completed, there appeared in front of the two men a beautiful girl in white—Edgar's lost love. Edgar stretched out his arms to take hold of the girl but, all too soon, she vanished.

The servant, terrified, threw himself on the ground and to his horror felt something grasp his wrist and pull him towards the oak tree. It became clear that the soul Edgar had promised to the devil was that of the servant, not his own. But then the family rushed from the house, awoken by the dreadful storm and seeing the two men in the garden. The Lord of Hoghton Tower, realising what was going on, came towards them and said loudly and clearly, "In nomine Patris!" The servant felt his wrist released, the storm ceased and all was quiet again.

Edgar had quite lost his mind and remained so until he died. As for the poor servant, he was forever marked with the imprint of the unearthly hand that had been clamped around his wrist. The marks were red and angry and he bore that devil's mark for the rest of his life.

Incidentally...there is a legend that when James I visited Hoghton Tower, in August 1617, he was so pleased by the entertainment that was laid on for him that he knighted a piece of beef—the cut was known ever afterwards as "Sir Loin." This may be partly true, but Pimp Hall in Essex also claims to be the place where the beef was knighted.

It is also said that during James' visit, as part of a pageant in his honour, several traditional dances and ceremonies were performed. A contemporary report describes a rush-bearing ceremony, "in which a man was enclosed in a dendrological foliage of fronds, and was the admiration of the company." This is surely a representation of the Green Man in human form.

Local Legend

The old and well-used rabbit warrens in this area are also home to many fairies. Once there were two poachers who knew this area well, but they had been caught poaching once too often and their dogs and their nets had been taken from them. Undeterred, they went rabbit hunting again, with only a ferret and a couple of sacks in which to store their booty. They knew the best place to hunt, and so it wasn't long before their ferret had rooted out the inhabitants of a warren and, with their sacks over the entrance holes, it was a simple job to catch their quarry. However, they could not see exactly what they had caught.

They were walking home, with the sacks slung over their shoulders, when one of them heard a voice from his sack calling out: "Dick, wheer artta?" At once another voice called out from the other sack: "In a sack, on a back, riding up Hoghton Brow!" Shocked, the poachers dropped their sacks and ran away.

Next day, they retraced their steps and found their abandoned sacks, neatly folded by the side of the road. And that was the end of their poaching days; the sacks were used for potatoes and the men went back to earning an honest living with their weaving looms.

(See Barley for an identical tale.)

HORNBY

Hornby Castle

The first documentary evidence of Hornby Castle is in 1226, when it was already well established. The castle we see today is a modern Gothic-inspired building, dating from 1847. But that in no way spoils the story.

Edward Stanley of Hornby Castle was born around 1460. He was knighted by Richard III in 1482, then after great valour at the Battle of Flodden Field, he was honoured by Henry VIII with the Order of The Garter. As the Stanley's family emblem was the eagle, he adopted the title Lord Monteagle. As a symbol of his gratitude for the victory at the Battle of Flodden, he built a remarkable eight-sided tower at St. Margaret's Church in the village.

However, local legend would have us believe that the octagonal tower came into being for a completely different reason. The legend paints Lord Monteagle as a rather wicked character, a materialist who did not believe in God. Neither did he believe in heaven; he said that "the soul of a man was like the winding-up of a watch; when the spring was run down, the man died, and the soul was extinct." He was believed to practice unholy rites late at night in the turret of Hornby Castle and the local people would cross themselves when they saw the light in the turret window. It was also rumoured that he had only married his wife for her money and when her brother died, it was said that Monteagle must have murdered him.

One night Lord Monteagle summoned the parson from Slaidburn, intending to have a good argument about theology. The two men argued for hours until finally the parson could stand it no longer. He stood up and told Lord Monteagle that only fear was preventing him from believing in God—fear of dying and going to Heaven and having to face his brother-in-law Harrington, whom he had murdered. Lord Monteagle was silent, because the parson was right; he was scared. And then the room became very still, and a white mist formed and moved around the place...it was Harrington's ghost!

From the moment he saw Harrington's ghost, Lord Monteagle was a changed man. And it was then that he built Hornby Chapel, as a demonstration of his new belief. He also began to build a chancel and planned to be buried there, but he died before it could be consecrated. He was buried temporarily in the priory churchyard, with a plan to bury him in his own church eventually. But then Henry VIII dissolved the monasteries, including Hornby Priory and Lord Monteagle's remains never were removed. It's believed they lie there still, in the old priory churchyard, which is now no more than a field near the River Lune.

Hornby Church

As well as its interesting octagonal tower, Hornby Church is notable for its churchyard cross, which now resides inside the church for safety and reasons of preservation. A carving shows the story of the loaves and fishes and another shows a figure with a halo. One of the most beautiful examples in Lancashire, the carving is so clean that it is difficult to believe it was executed almost a thousand years ago.

Hornby Park

A woman named Meg Brackin was out in Hornby Park one evening, looking for kindling for her fire. She came across another woman and wondered what she was doing there, as the day was ending and it would soon be dark. She spoke to the woman, who then came close to her and took hold of her hand—and that was the beginning of a dreadful experience for poor Meg.

An old poem, in local dialect, describes how the strange woman in a white dress (who was in fact a ghost) gripped Meg's hand tightly and led her on a break-neck journey through the park, ignoring pathways and plunging through brush and brambles without stopping even to drink at the stream. Indeed, Meg grew so thirsty that, as the night wore on, she was obliged to drag the hem of her dress through the dew-soaked grass and suck the moisture from it. The ghost would not let Meg rest until daylight came again—at which point she vanished. It is said that Meg had always been a well-covered lady, but after the awful experience of running about the countryside all night, she was thin.

The White Lady, known locally as the Park Mistress, is believed to be the ghost of Lady Harrington, who was, allegedly, a murderess. We are not told who was the victim of her murderous tendencies; perhaps she was in league with Lord Monteagle, who allegedly murdered her brother?

However, Meg Brackin certainly lived; the records show that she was born in 1745, and died in 1795.

HUNCOAT
Black Bull

The Black Bull pub on Lowergate was once visited by Cromwell's troops. Now, people complain of being followed by something or someone unseen, particularly when they go up or downstairs. On occasion, the service bells in the bar have sounded during the night, when no one was there to sound them.

HURST GREEN
Punch Bowl Inn

In the eighteenth century, the highwayman Ned King was often in residence at the Punch Bowl Inn, hiding away in the barn with the full knowledge of the inn's landlord.

He would watch the travellers arriving at the inn for the night, select the wealthiest, and then lie in wait next day to rob them farther along the road. His spoils would be shared with the landlord. Eventually, Ned's whereabouts became known and he was arrested and hung on Gallows Lane, close by. The landlord's collusion, however, appears to have gone unpunished. Perhaps it is this sense of injustice that keeps Ned's ghost at the Punch Bowl.

Ned's ghost caused all kinds of disturbances for over a century until, in 1942, a Stonyhurst priest was summoned to exorcise him. Things did quieten down, but it seems that the exorcism wasn't completely successful because subsequent landlords have complained that they hear the sound of fast footsteps and sometimes things go missing. The barn where Ned would hide is now the pub's dining-room, so the haunting, rather than being confined to an outbuilding, is within the Punch Bowl itself.

In 2006, a friend of the landlady took her family to the Punch Bowl for an evening meal. In the middle of the evening, the daughter of the family was given permission to go into the pub's kitchen to fetch a chocolate cake from the fridge. She turned to see the shape of a man; he seemed to be standing in a mist, but even so the child could see that he wore a black coat, black boots, and a triangular hat. At first, the girl was thrilled because she had always wanted to see a ghost, but things became scarier when some soup bowls were lifted by the ghost and thrown on the floor. Of course, the noise of smashing crockery summoned her mother to the rescue.

The child's story was given more credence later that evening, when the door between the kitchen and the bar was seen to swing open and closed a number of times, although there was no draught in the building.

Stonyhurst College

Stonyhurst College was established in 1794, a refuge for a Catholic school, which had already existed for two centuries in France, but was forced to move during the French Revolution. The college is home to many interesting religious relics, including a prayer book reputed to have been held by Mary Queen of Scots during her execution. Other relics are a chalice used by St. Edmund Arrowsmith and some of St. Edmund Campion's writings.

There was once a timber castle at Stonyhurst and a mound in the vicinity is sometimes pointed out as being the likely site. In fact, this mound is more likely to be a burial mound—a barrow. It was excavated in 1894 and found to contain the remains of several people, all young. These remains were dated at 1250 BC. There are, in fact, two more barrows on either side of the river at a place where the Rivers Ribble, Hodder, and Calder converge.

The legend about the mound is, however, more romantic than the truth. It has been said that some of Cromwell's men were buried inside—a tale that may have been mistranslated from another, older legend. In deeper legend it was said to be the site of

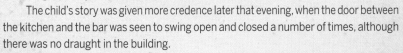

an ancient battle, won by the ancient King Eardwulf. His slain opponent was said to have been buried in the barrow seated in a grand chair, with a casket of gold by his side.

Lastly, between Stonyhurst and Ribchester there is a crossroads that was a meeting place for the devil and local witches.

HURSTWOOD
Local Legend

Hurstwood's boggart was either a black dog or a piece of white linen, depending on which version of the story is believed. It may have been this same boggart who is reported to have pulled the bedclothes off one family and was often seen in an old yew tree, dressed in white. Hoggarth's Cross is close to where the boggart was eventually "laid," after it had promised never to cause trouble again as long as the stream through Holden Clough kept flowing.

INGLEWHITE

St. Anne's Well

Built into the stonework of the bridge at Goosnargh, there is one large stone that bears the inscription "Fons Sanctae Anne." "Fons" is Latin for fountain and the name of the Roman goddess of water. St. Anne was the mother of Mary. The stone was taken from the lining of St. Anne's Well at Inglewhite—the spring still exists, but is hard to find.

Village Green

In old times, it was said that will o' the wisps would regularly come to play on the village green. It has even been said that this may have inspired the village's name, Inglewhite, as one possible origin is the Gaelic word *aingeal*, which means "fire."

KELBROOK

Dissenter's Well

Behind a farm here is a well, its site marked by a stone on which is carved a cross. The stone's name is Tom's Cross, but no one can say why. The ancient moorland spring close by Tom's Cross was enclosed into a stone trough a few centuries ago. It was much used at that time by those Christian believers who refused to "conform." The Act of Uniformity in 1662 defined Nonconformists—Dissenters—as those who belonged to a non-Anglican church or, indeed, any non-Christian religion. This included Presbyterians, Congregationalists, Baptists, and Quakers who were forced to find private places to conduct their worship. The well is simply known as the Dissenter's Well. If ever it bore a saint's name, as most holy wells do, it is long-forgotten.

Old Stone Trough

The Old Stone Trough pub dates from the 1840s and is thought to have been built on the site of an old farm, although it has itself been a pub since the day it was built.

The pub is haunted by a female ghost who has been nicknamed Scary Mary by the staff, although a visiting psychic wasn't happy with the "scary" part of that name. According to the psychic, the woman who haunts one of the pub's bedrooms was in her middle age and waiting to meet her lover. Not scary at all.

Whilst Mary is quite a friendly presence, the same cannot be said for the vision of a rifle-bearing soldier seen by a guest, or the fact that on one occasion the upper floor was stricken with a terrible smell that persisted even after the carpets had been assiduously cleaned. Several weeks later, the smell disappeared, just as suddenly as it had arrived.

KELLAMERGH

Birley Arms

Many years ago, a cottage near the Birley Arms was the scene of repeated poltergeist-like occurrences: doors would open and close on their own and there were cold draughts with no apparent source. One day, the occupants, Mr. and Mrs. Singleton, were startled by the sound of smashing crockery, but when they ran to their kitchen, all was intact. That night, they were woken from their sleep by the same terrible noises, but again, they found nothing broken or out of place.

The final straw for the Singletons came one afternoon when relatives were visiting: there was a sudden noise that sounded just like beads bouncing off crockery. One of Mrs. Singleton's relatives was so convinced by the sound that she exclaimed, "Oh, Emily, your beads!" Mrs. Singleton's necklace still hung safely around her neck. She and her husband moved out of the house soon afterwards.

KIRKHAM
Bell and Bottle

It is believed that two ghosts haunt the Bell and Bottle pub, but no one knows anything about the identity of the first, who walks along a corridor. It's thought that the corridor may once have been part of a room, but this gives no clue as to the ghost's identity. The second ghost is that of a young stable lad who died when he was accidentally kicked by one of his equine charges. The stable buildings are now the pub's restaurant area and it is here that people sometimes report seeing a sad young boy dressed in clothes from an earlier age.

Kirkham Church

A monstrous child was born here on June 20, 1643, so says a pamphlet written by the minister of Kirkham parish, Mr. Edward Fleetwood.

At that time in religious history, Kirkham's inhabitants were divided in their opinion. The Papists in the town had great hatred for the Roundheads and their sympathisers. The Roundheads were brutal in their treatment of those they discovered to be still worshipping in the old way. The fact that one local Catholic, William Haughton, was "burnt in his own entrails" serves to illustrate that brutality.

William Haughton's wife, who was with child, had fervently sworn that none of her family would ever be Roundheads. Those she was speaking with argued that her children, as they grew, might see things differently and help her to see the good in the new religion. Mistress Haughton responded that she would rather her child had no head at all than grow up to be a Roundhead.

When Mistress Haughton eventually gave birth, her child was a headless monster; it did not live and midwife Widow Greenacres had it buried at once. Widow Greenacres kept quiet about the monstrous child for a while, but at last she had to confess what she knew to the vicar, for she knew what Mistress Haughton had sworn and she saw God's will at work.

Edward Fleetwood, the vicar, had the grave opened up and the child examined and it was as the midwife had said: the child had no head. As his tract explains: "unto the place where the paps usually are, and a nose upon the chest, and a mouth a little above the navel, and two ears, upon each shoulder one."

Railway Inn

There are tunnels beneath the pub here, discovered in the 1990s by a new landlord. At the moment one of the tunnels was opened up, an apparition was seen in the bar upstairs.

KNOWLE GREEN
Written Stone Lane

Written Stone Lane is now little more than a country footpath, part of an old Roman road running from Knowle Green to Longridge. It takes its name from a large slab of stone on the wayside, on which is written "Ravffe Radcliffe Laid This Stone to Lye For Ever A.D. 1655." The words are deeply cut into this stone, which is huge—nine feet long, two feet wide, and a foot thick.

Tales speak of a horrible murder committed here, the victim's subsequent troublesome spirit being exorcised or "laid" under the stone. Several members of the Radcliffe family did pass away just before the date on the stone, so perhaps the victim was one of them.

If the laying of the stone was indeed intended as an exorcism, it does not seem to have been successful. Local people were always convinced that a boggart still haunted the stone. One doctor, passing the stone on horseback one night, was thrown from his seat when his horse reared at some invisible threat. The story says that the doctor, not to be outdone, went up to the stone and threatened the boggart, who then materialised and tried to throttle him!

Many years later, the residents of the nearby farm decided the slab of stone would be ideal for use in their new buttery. Paying no heed to the old legends, the farmer went with two of his horses to drag the stone down the hill to his farm. Despite the fact that the route was all downhill, the task took hours and the horses, when they had completed their work, were exhausted.

After the stone was installed in the buttery, it very soon became apparent that there might have been some truth in the tales after all. Nothing would stand up straight on the stone, which seemed to be able to tip off any dish, or jug, or kettle placed upon it. What's more, when the farmer was in bed at night, he could not sleep for the noise of smashing crockery. He realised that the stone would have to go back where it obviously belonged.

Next day, he set about moving the stone again. This time, even though the return journey was uphill, only one horse was needed and the job was over in no time. And no one has ever tried to move the stone again.

LANCASTER

Alexandra Hall

Footsteps have been heard running along an upstairs corridor in this building, which is now a pub but was once a notorious dance hall frequented by soldiers. It is said that a maid died here—but any further detail cannot be found.

Gallows Hill

Williamson Park and the gloriously self-indulgent Ashton Memorial overlook the city of Lancaster laid out below. From here, the castle can be clearly seen. The park comprises over fifty acres of woodland, but the focal point is the memorial, a white building capped with a green dome that is visible from almost everywhere in the city. This is a popular place for recreation and relaxation, even though locals are aware that it is also the site of the ancient Gallows Hill, where prisoners were brought from the castle to meet their deaths.

The exact spot of execution is not quite clear but it was here—with that glorious view—that the Pendle Witches were hanged on August 20, 1612. It is thought that the hanging was carried out by putting the noose around the prisoner's neck, while they stood on the cart that brought them there, and that would then be moved away, leaving them dangling.

Anne Whittle died here, as did Anne Redfern, Jane and John Bullock, Alice Nutter, Katherine Hewitt, Isobel Robey, and Elizabeth, James, and Alison Device. Elizabeth Southerns would doubtless have died here also, had she not expired in the misery of her cell at Lancaster Castle.

Their bodies would have been buried near this place, but as they were judged to be witches they were not given a Christian burial, nor were their resting places marked.

Golden Lion

The notice outside the Golden Lion proudly tells of its connection with the last journey of the Lancashire Witches, on their way from the castle to Gallows Hill where they would meet their death. The notice may not have all its facts correct, but it is true that in those days it was traditional to allow condemned prisoners to have one last drink before they went to meet their Maker.

(See also the Three Mariners pub, which has an equal claim to having been the prisoners' last drinking place.)

Grand Theatre

According to legend, the ghost at the Grand Theatre is the ghost of Sarah Siddons, who, in the eighteenth century, was described as the greatest of English tragic actresses. She was "Queen of Drury Lane" for more than twenty years. When she made her final performance as Lady Macbeth, it was so perfect that the audience insisted she repeat the scene several times before they would allow her to continue with the rest of the play. During this most successful part of her career, she appeared at Lancaster's Grand Theatre on several occasions and it's thought that something of her has remained behind.

In the late 1950s, two stage decorators spent some weeks working in the theatre late at night. On more than one occasion they heard footsteps when they were supposed to be alone in the place, followed by a banging of the doors that led into the circle area. The two of them toured the building in search of the intruder, but found nothing.

Three decades later, a female member of the Footlights Company had a similar experience. It was carnival time and the float was outside the theatre all ready to go, when it was realised that a costume item for the main character was missing. The lady concerned unlocked the theatre and, as she ran upstairs, she heard running footsteps behind her own. She called out, "Who's there?" but received no reply. Reaching the wardrobe area and still hearing the footsteps, she looked behind her in time to see one of the doors that lead to the circle swing open and then swing shut again. Yet, when she ran into the circle to catch the culprit, the place was quite empty.

Another Footlights member was once working on some props in a dressing room when she looked up and caught sight of herself in a mirror. Standing behind her was a woman in old-fashioned dress but, of course, when she turned around, there was no one there.

In September 1995, a lady in the audience for a VE Day celebration show was struck by the incongruous dress of a woman at the left-hand side of the stage; the cast wore Army and Land Girl costumes, but this woman was wearing a mob cap, long dress, and a frilled shawl. When the cast began to sing wartime songs, this woman didn't open her mouth. And when the show ended and the house-lights went on, that part of the stage was entirely empty.

This story was investigated. The musical director of the VE Day show confirmed that no one in the cast had been wearing a long dress, mob cap, and shawl, and she commented: "If she didn't open her mouth, then she definitely wasn't one of ours—none of them are allowed not to sing!"

In 2009, an elderly lady contacted the Grand to tell them of her experience when she had been working there as an usherette before the Second World War. One morning, she was cleaning the Circle when she saw a girl who was "bonny with a lovely figure, wearing a purple veil." The ghostly woman turned and smiled, then floated down the stairs.

Unfortunately, much as the Footlights Company are unanimously fond of their ghost—who causes no trouble, apart from a few surprise appearances—a little research shows that she is unlikely to be Sarah Siddons. All the recorded reports describe a woman in Victorian dress, whereas Sarah had performed in the previous century. However, during Victoria's reign, the Grand Theatre was almost destroyed by fire, so it may be that the theatre's beloved ghost has an origin more tragic than anyone ever thought.

Lancaster Castle

There has been a castle on this site since around 100 AD. For centuries, it was a working prison, but in 2011, the prisoners were transferred elsewhere and now the castle is fully open to tourists. Lancaster Castle holds the dubious honour of having put to death more people than any other place in Britain, apart from London; some of those names are mentioned in the pages of this book, including Father Ambrose and the Lancashire Witches. It would be surprising, then, if the castle did not have a reputation for being haunted.

Visitors often complain of feeling someone invisible push them. This is such a frequent complaint that tour guides are no longer surprised. Ghosts are seen rather less frequently, but those most commonly spoken about include a girl child in a blue dress with ringlets in her hair (who is also sometimes heard running), a woman of middle age, a very old woman, and a monk. Sometimes the young girl and the old woman have been seen together. In the courtroom itself, a gentleman in old-fashioned dress is sometimes seen standing at the back of the room, watching the proceedings.

The many prison officers employed here over the decades have their own stories to tell. One officer reported that he had seen a stocky, red-haired, and bearded man, wearing brown trousers and a white shirt with no collar, who had disappeared after a few moments. Other officers have reported seeing a judge in full regalia, a serving-girl, a ragged dancing woman, and a man who seemed to be dressed as a pirate.

Perhaps the strangest tale comes from one of the castle's tour guides, who had come to that point in the tour where visitors could volunteer to be briefly locked inside one of the oldest cells, in order to experience the isolation and total darkness. He is positive that four people went into the cell—but only three came out...

Penny Street

A house in Penny Street, now demolished, was haunted by a headless ghost. It appeared in the upper rooms only, but very regularly, so that the family who lived there had long since ceased to be disturbed. No other phenomena were ever experienced, so despite the scary fact that the ghost had no head, it was never considered a problem!

Priory Church

The Priory Church, as old as the castle that stands next to it on Castle Hill, has on display some wonderful Anglo-Saxon crosses, brought into the shelter of the church to preserve them from the weather. One of the crosses that used to adorn the churchyard was deemed so remarkable that it is now in the British Museum. The crosses probably date from the seventh century and their carved illustrations show various symbols of good and evil, intertwining snakes, a hound pursuing a stag, and representations of the crucifixion. There is also a Green Man in the church on one of the arm rests in the choir stalls.

The Priory Church is the setting for a tale of mystery involving two vagrants who had decided to shelter there one night. One of them, waking early in the morning, decided to steal the valuable plate and candlesticks that were openly displayed on the altar. He had no intention of including his companion in this plan, so he crept to the altar very quietly to avoid waking him. His companion's sleep, however, was soon disturbed by a horrible scream. He jumped up and immediately looked for his friend—and found him lying in the front of the altar, dead, still holding a candlestick.

Radio Station

The Bay Radio station on St. George's Quay is situated in an old building, so it is little surprise that a ghost has been seen here: a man in an old-fashioned, voluminous shirt. Doors have also been seen to open and close on their own.

Three Mariners

The Three Mariners pub on Bridge Lane is by far the oldest pub in Lancaster as it dates from 1440. It was connected to Lancaster Castle and it's said that prisoners were often brought here for a final drink before being taken up to Gallows Hill.

There is often a strange atmosphere in the place, a sudden uncanny coldness in the air. In the area of the ladies' room, a blonde woman wearing "a large dress" has been seen. A man wearing a tricorn hat and an outfit that seems to date from the Jacobite wars has also been seen, many times. He is seen in the pub itself and also wandering along what remains of the cobbled lane, outside.

The Tinker's Tale

In a curious story from the sixteenth century, it seems that the "Black Arts" included lock-picking and other tricks of thievery. Certainly there was artfulness amongst those who made their living from this crime. The tools for picking locks were highly prized and cleverly made, some of the best being specially imported from Italy.

A certain knight in Bolton-by-Bowland, known for his sympathy and courtesy to the tenants on his land, was approached by several of them over a matter of days, complaining that their locks were being picked in the dead of night and their valuables stolen. They came to ask the knight for assistance and it transpired that many of them suspected a tinker who had recently come to the town. During the day he was earning an honest living by mending pots and pans, but who knew what he was up to when darkness fell?

One day the tinker called at the knight's great house asking for work, and the cook brought out some kettles to be mended. The knight made the tinker welcome, gave him beer and food, and engaged him in friendly conversation. Thus reassured, the tinker did not suspect anything when the knight feigned interest in his toolbag and made to examine its contents. There, the knight found what he was looking for—lock-picking tools—but he quietly returned them to their place and said nothing.

When the tinker had finished his work, he told the knight he was moving on to Lancaster. That suited the knight's intentions very well. He had a friend who was the jailor at Lancaster Castle and so he told the tinker he was sure there would be work for him there. The knight said he would ask his clerk to write a letter of recommendation and the tinker took the letter gladly.

And so the tinker was tricked, for the letter told the jailor that the tinker was a thief and he should jail him at once. The jailor, on reading the letter, welcomed the tinker inside the prison gates with a smile, but once inside, the tinker was quickly shackled and put in a cell. And there the tinker stayed until the next court was held, and then he was hanged for the wrongs he had done to the knight's tenants, and none of his mysterious Black Arts were of any use to him at all.

LANESHAW BRIDGE

Barnside Hall

An entry in the Burials Register of St. Bartholomew's Church, Colne, records in detail the death of a young woman called Hannah Corbridge. No one was concerned when Hannah went walking with her boyfriend that Sunday morning in 1789—after all, she had been walking out with Christopher Hartley for some time and he was the father of her child. But when she did not return home that evening and it was discovered that Christopher had also disappeared, Hannah's father imagined the worst and organised a search for his daughter. The search went on for some days, fruitlessly, until a neighbour had a strange dream in which he saw exactly where the body lay. And so Hannah was found, in a ditch near Barnside Hall, horribly murdered. Her boyfriend was caught in Flookborough, found guilty of her murder, and executed a short time later.

Barnside Hall was haunted by Hannah's ghost for many years; she was usually seen on Sunday evenings. So frequent were the sightings that an exorcism was performed, but it seems it was only a partial success. In recent years, it is said that Hannah has been seen on Laneshaw Bridge—which was built after her death using stones from the then-demolished Barnside Hall.

Hallown Well

Emmott Hall no longer stands, but its grounds were once the home of the Emmott Cross that now graces St. Bartholomew's Churchyard in Colne. The cross stood near the so-called Hallown Well, which still exists in the grounds of the old hall. The name Hallown is interesting; it is close to a stream called Hullown Beck and it is entirely possible that both names derive from the word hallowed or even the name of a saint, to which this holy well would certainly have been dedicated. The well is also known as Saint's Well.

The well is a large pool of dressed stone, almost square, measuring eighteen feet by sixteen feet. It is ten feet deep and has fourteen steps down into the water. Its size meant that it was probably used as a baptismal pool as well as providing holy water for the faithful—although it was a sacred place long before Christianity stamped its mark here. Is this the Fairy Well that local people once spoke of? Perhaps, for the water had magical qualities and was renowned for its efficacy as a cure for rheumatism.

LARBRECK

Well

In Larbreck, there was once a well so very cold that fish were unable to survive.

LEYLAND

Charnock Old Hall

Charnock Old Hall on Balcarres Road is a Grade II listed building and dates from the fourteenth century. In the seventeenth century it was home to the Charnock family, famous for their adherence to Catholicism in a time when it was mortally dangerous to do so. One Charnock went so far as to will the house to a friend with the stipulation that it and the adjoining lands should be dedicated for the use of priests and clergy. The case went to trial and his house and lands were forfeited to the king, but a petition had this decision overturned and the estate was indeed given to successive vicars of the area. It is no surprise then that its ghostly visitors are those of numerous priests and nuns. Footsteps have been heard and electrical appliances have malfunctioned, but these occurrences are outnumbered by the sightings of ghostly monks.

Very recently, the building was up for sale and the estate agents handling the transaction were quick to assure prospective buyers that the Old Hall was, in fact, not haunted at all. They blamed the rumours on superstition. On the other hand, they were all too happy to stress that amongst the building's other charming attributes, there was a secret door leading to the attic…

Halfway House

The Halfway House dates from the eighteenth century when it was originally a coaching house. The place is believed to be haunted by at least three separate ghosts, one of which is quite troublesome. Nicknamed Sid, this ghost is blamed for creating an uncomfortable atmosphere that makes people feel unwelcome. Lights have been known to turn themselves on or off and sometimes a voice is heard, although the words it says are indistinct.

Another ghost is said to walk upstairs very noisily and make small objects rattle. The third ghost is more peaceable and has been seen sitting quietly in the bay window of the pub. However, it seems that only the staff are disturbed by these events; visitors to the Halfway House never notice anything amiss.

LG Kitchens

A ghost at this modern kitchen manufacturer's property might never have been discovered if not for burglars at another factory nearby. The managers of LG Kitchens were asked to examine their CCTV footage in case the burglars had been caught on film. They saw no burglars, but what they did see was very strange indeed. Attempting to describe what he had seen, a manager spoke of "a ring of light" that developed into a mist, within which he could see the shape of a body.

Now strange occurrences are taken more seriously. Lights are sometimes mysteriously turned on and footsteps are often heard. On one occasion one of the managers was so sure he could hear his partner walking heavily upstairs, he called his mobile phone to ask what on earth he was doing to make so much noise. His partner was mystified, because he was twenty miles away at the time.

Police Station

In 2011, an old police station on Golden Hill Lane reopened its doors as a café called Coppers Tea Rooms. However, the family who ran the café believed the building was haunted by the ghost of an inspector, who had died on the premises. The police station was built in 1882, and one of the inspectors by the name of Hewitt was apparently so well thought of that a street beside the building was named after him. It is thought to be Inspector Hewitt who haunts the building.

Adding credence to the ghost story is the fact that one of the upstairs rooms was sealed up by the police who worked there after Hewitt's demise. In addition, the staircase that led to the sealed-up room was dismantled completely. The room still exists, but remains inaccessible.

Runshaw College

Runshaw College now occupies a building once known as Runshaw House and, whilst it is now claimed to be entirely ghost-free, during the early 1970s local stories told of many sightings of a ghostly lady dressed in black, or maybe a black skirt and white blouse, drifting through the house and disappearing into walls.

St. Andrew's Church

Long ago, the people of Whittle-le-Woods set about building a church. All the townspeople helped, so that by the end of the first day the foundations were already laid. The next morning, the priest was visited by a farmer from Leyland, complaining about the church that was being built upon his land without permission. Confused, the priest followed him and found that, indeed, the foundations laid down the day before in Whittle-le-Woods were now firmly set in a field in Leyland!

The townspeople were gathered and spent the day moving the stones back to their proper place and, that night, two of them kept watch so that such a thing could not happen again. However, they were so tired by their exertions that they fell asleep and woke to find that the stones had indeed been moved again, to Leyland.

Once again the stones were moved back to Whittle-le-Woods and that night even more men stayed to keep watch, determined to catch the culprit. This time they managed to keep each other awake and at the stroke of midnight, they were frightened out of their wits by the sight of a terrifying beast like a huge cat that carried off the stones one by one in his huge claws. Unsurprisingly, they were too scared to approach the beast and the Leyland farmer, hearing their tale, was too scared to argue. So the church stayed where it was, in Leyland.

If you doubt this story, look closely at the stones of this church, for on one of them there is a carving of the great cat itself.

Towngate

A shop on Towngate is home to the ghost of an old lady who must have lived there once upon a time. At one point the building housed a Sue Ryder charity shop and the staff would sometimes report that boxes of stock were mysteriously moved from one place to another. Later, the shop reopened as a stationery shop. The two women who owned the business became quite used to seeing an elderly lady with grey hair walk across the shop and disappear. She often left behind her a vivid scent of violets.

There was at least one incident that was decidedly less peaceful. Workmen were given access to the building over one weekend and were repeatedly disturbed by the sound of banging, coming from the front of the building when they were working at the back. They checked the building each time they heard the noise, but could find no explanation. They had locked the front door behind them so were sure they were alone.

Worden Hall

The site of Worden Arts Centre used to be known as Worden Hall and, according to paranormal investigators, this explains the strange things that happen here. The remains of the hall, which was destroyed by fire in 1941, still stand and the surrounding grounds are now a public park.

Staff at the arts centre have felt themselves touched by invisible hands, they have seen lights going off and on again, crockery in the café has been moved and figures have occasionally been seen disappearing through doorways.

The investigators claim that these events are evidence of two spirits, a gentleman and a maidservant, who died when Worden Hall was damaged by fire in 1941. Research may or may not prove the truth of these claims—but the ghostly occurrences remain.

LONGRIDGE
Local Legend

One night, a man called Gabriel set off from the White Bull pub to walk home. It was late and he had a long walk ahead of him to Kemple End, but he had spent the evening in cheerful company so it was no hardship. He had covered a fair distance and was away from the town when he saw a woman walking ahead of him, dressed in cloak and bonnet, with a basket on her arm. She seemed to be walking very slowly and so he caught up with her very quickly. He was surprised that she did not turn to see who was following her, for she must surely have heard the sound of his clogs on the road. So, as he came close to her, he spoke, intending to put her at her ease. He commented that the night was fine and she replied that it was fine indeed and her voice was sweet. Gabriel would have liked to see her face, but she did not turn her head to look at him.

Gabriel became concerned for the woman, who seemed too respectable to be out on her own so late, so he enquired after her family; was one of them ill? Was that why she was out so late, perhaps going for a doctor? The woman didn't answer, perhaps too upset by the bad news that had brought her from her hearthside. So Gabriel, being a gentleman at heart, offered to carry the woman's basket for her. She handed him the basket without a word and he heard a voice say: "You're very kind, I'm sure," but the voice seemed to come not from the woman, but from somewhere else. And then, from the basket that Gabriel now held, there came laughter. Shocked, Gabriel dropped the basket on the ground, It tipped over and out rolled a head! And now the woman turned to him and he saw that the bonnet she was wearing was empty...

LOSTOCK HALL

Tardy Gate

Tardy Gate is an area of Lostock Hall named after the old tollgate that was owned by John Tardie. The Tardy Gate pub is believed to be haunted, but by whom, no one knows. Recent events have included a beer glass that shattered when no one was near it and apparitions caught on the pub's close-circuit television—which was checked after noises of midnight revelries could be heard when the pub was entirely closed and all doors locked.

LOWER BARTLE

Swillbrook House

Swillbrook House on Rosemary Lane is now a care home, but the building dates from the sixteenth century. The rather gruesome legend attached to it also dates from those ancient days.

A jealous husband, about to leave his house on business, suspected that his unfaithful wife was planning to take her lover into her bed that very night. He decided to set a trap for the two of them. He positioned two swords beneath the bed in such a way that the weight of two people would cause the swords to slice through the mattresses and kill the unfaithful pair. Sadly, he had not reckoned on his young daughter's enthusiasm for bouncing on her mother's bed. The girl—his only child—lost her life.

Now, footsteps are sometimes heard in the corridor outside the room and, from inside the room, there comes a noise resembling the rhythmic motion of a rocking-chair—or is it a bed being bounced upon by a child?

LYTHAM

Lytham Hall

An ancient priory used to stand close to the site of Lytham Hall, built by Benedictines in the late twelfth century. The monks were ousted during the Dissolution and the priory fell into disrepair. Several decades passed before the land and buildings were bought by Cuthbert Clifton, who built the original Lytham Hall on the site, incorporating some of the priory buildings. The present hall's Georgian architecture is the result of rebuilding after fire destroyed much of the house in the eighteenth century, but the building still retains some of the original architecture. The Cliftons remained at Lytham Hall for three centuries and were beneficent towards the local populace who respected them.

Considering the fact that this site has been almost continually inhabited for at least the last eight centuries, it would be odd indeed if it were not rumoured to be haunted. The Long Gallery, part of the oldest section of the hall, is frequented by a White Lady who drifts down the room and disappears—she was first reported publicly by servicemen convalescing there during the Second World War. Modern-day visitors have also reported strange things. One particular room on the top floor carries a disturbing atmosphere, although nothing has been reported to actually happen there—but in another room, known as the Duke of Norfolk's Room, the door is reputed to sometimes open on its own and footsteps and dragging chains have been heard.

Ship and Royal Hotel

A tall man dressed in dark clothing has often been seen in this hotel on Clifton Street, usually on the second floor. Staff, whilst disturbed by their experiences, have learned to accept them. He is sometimes seen by customers, who have been known to mention him to staff members, thinking he is waiting for their attention.

If anything more physical happens here, it is usually helpful. On one occasion, an order for meat was written up and left on the desk, ready to be phoned to the butcher next day, but in the morning the butcher said he had already received the order—it had been left in a message on his answerphone during the night by someone with a "gruff' voice.

It is fondly believed that the ghost is that of Squire John Talbot Clifton, who lived in nearby Clifton Hall. He fits the general description of the ghost in that he was certainly very tall—well over six feet in height. Squire John was a regular customer at the Ship and Royal until he died in 1928. He was an adventurer and any account of his death always notes that he "died at Tenerife," although the adventure he was then undertaking is not specified. After his death, his wife wrote a fond biography of him and it presents him as a kind man who, if he did remain in one his favourite places as a ghost, would certainly be respectful and helpful rather than harmful.

One other occurrence is a little more confusing: a phone on the internal system has been known to ring when there is no one in the building to make the call—when the phone is answered, no one is there.

The Ship and Royal also has other ghosts: those of a mother and son who, at the beginning of the twentieth century, drowned themselves in a suicide pact. Upstairs in the building are several unused rooms in which there is no operational plumbing, but nevertheless it is from one of these rooms that the sound of running water is heard.

St. Cuthbert's Cross

Near St. Cuthbert's church is a way marker, the inscription upon which tells that in 882 AD this was the spot where St. Cuthbert's body rested for a while. The saint's body was being carried by Lindisfarne monks, retreating from the invading Danes. The cross that originally stood here has long since disappeared, replaced by the current cross in 1912, but the base into which it is set is undoubtedly medieval. St. Cuthbert eventually came to rest at Durham and a shrine was built for him inside the Cathedral. It is said that the coffin was opened once, and his body was found to have suffered no decay.

Witchwood

Running between the Lancashire towns of St. Annes and Lytham is a long, narrow tract of woodland that in 1974 was designated a protected site by the Duke of Edinburgh. The trees of this densely wooded area are all protected by preservation orders, and the wood itself is cared for by the Lytham St. Annes Civic Society. Access is only allowed to those on foot, so the place is popular with local people and their dogs. It is such a lovely site that even people from farther afield pay regular visits there to watch the changing course of nature through the seasons.

If you visit the wood at any time, you may stumble upon the reason this place is called "Witchwood," for buried somewhere in the undergrowth is a marker stone—a gravestone barely three feet high—whose inscription may send a shiver down the spine: "The Witch—Died Jan 5th 1888."

So who was "The Witch"? And why was she buried here? It would seem to make sense that a witch should be interred in unconsecrated ground. Though witches were, in 1888, no longer burned to death or drowned, they were hardly accepted members of polite Christian society.

For many centuries this land was owned by the influential Clifton family, who lived in nearby Lytham Hall. It is thanks to them that Lytham bears the nickname "Leafy Lytham," for they were responsible for foresting the area. We must also thank the Cliftons for giving us Witchwood and a potential local legend to go with it, for it was they who buried "The Witch" and marked her place for posterity. The Witch of Witchwood was, in sober historical fact, a horse.

MARTON MOSS

Boar's Head

The Boar's Head on Preston Old Road is thought to be haunted by a mischievous child—and maybe other ghosts as well. In 2008, the landlady suffered sleepless nights because of mysterious bangs and she also complained that items of her jewellery regularly went missing. She was certain that she was not responsible for mislaying them.

A group of mediums called to investigate the events claimed to have communicated with a little boy called Sean, who had died in 1855 and who admitted playing with the landlady's jewellery. They also said the pub was often visited by George, a local farmer who had died in 1838. In the pub was a small locked room where bottles of spirits are kept and which the landlord had suggested would be worth investigating. The group placed some plastic on the floor and shook talcum powder over it, before leaving the place and locking the door. On their return, two initials, "A" and "M," could clearly be seen traced out in the talc. This was impressive, although neither initial refers to the little boy or the farmer. Does the Boar's Head have a third ghost?

Higher Hall Farm

This old farm, built around 1850, may well no longer exist because the firm that bought it in 2006 was aware that with all the defects of its long life, the company might not be able to leave the house standing much longer. For many years, the farmhouse was inhabited by two sisters who continued their deceased father's dairy work until they themselves died in the 1970s. Their nephew inherited the farm and lived there with his wife until they too passed on in the 2000s.

The last resident of the house had several ghostly tales to tell. One day, he found a very old pair of glasses in a drawer that had only just been deliberately cleared out. He also remembered one day when some tradesmen were working upstairs; the youngest of the pair suddenly screamed, ran downstairs, and refused to come inside again. He never would say what had scared him so much. If the old sisters who had spent their lives here were responsible, then it seems their cat was also still in residence, because one day a deep dent was found in a quilt on a freshly made bed, looking for all the world as if a cat had just been asleep there.

North West Gas HQ

Strange things have been said to happen here in the dead of night. Staff on the night shift often feel someone invisible beside them, and sometimes door handles turn when no human is around. It is thought that the invisible staff member was the victim of a terrible accident here in the 1950s, when a man was killed by a coal wagon.

Whitegate Farm

Marton has an old and famous story of a ghost, sometimes described as a headless boggart, but more usually the figure of a man. The figure was often seen around the old Whitegate Farm and was supposed to be the ghost of a certain Farmer Greatrix who lived early in the last century. He lived at Whinney Heys, an old mansion that had become no more than a farmhouse and that used to stand near where Victoria Hospital now stands.

The story says that Greatrix's daughter had taken up with a young man by the name of Daniel Owen of whom Greatrix disapproved so much that he refused to let the two lovers meet, let alone get married. Then one day he went to Preston Market and failed to return. He was later found murdered, and his murderer was none other than the young Daniel Owen.

Owen was not brought to justice for his crime, but justice was done all the same—and in a most strange way. Owen found himself being constantly haunted by the ghost of his victim and he became plagued with remorse at having committed the heinous crime of murder. Indeed, he felt so bad that he eventually drowned himself in the sea off Blackpool's foreshore. Greatrix's ghost, however, did not rest easy after his murderer's death, but until Victorian times continued to haunt the place where he was murdered, near the old farm.

Witches and Wizards

At Marton, there once lived a man named Caldwell, who was renowned for seeing visions of death and disaster. The scores of people who visited him swore by his accuracy, so much so that he believed it himself. Once he saw a vision of his own child's death and so, believing in his vision, he set about preparing the child's grave in the churchyard. The stories do not tell us how he felt when his child remained hale and hearty and grew to be an old man—glad that his child survived, no doubt, but cast down because he could no longer trust his visions? Perhaps he saw it as a lesson from God, showing him the error of his ways.

Also at Marton, there lived a woman by the name of Bamber, who was well-known for her ability to check bleeding, simply by uttering some magic words. People would walk twenty miles to see her.

When a charity school was opened here in 1717 by Mr. Baines, it was welcomed wholeheartedly, for surely education was the best way to stem the tide of such superstitions.

MAWDESLEY
Lane End House

Dating from 1625, Lane End House was once a fine mansion, but now is a farmhouse. It is locally known as Skull House, for in the attic there is a skull reputed to be a relic of martyred priest George Haydock. He was only twenty-six when he was arrested and killed at Tyburn. His head was brought north and first rested with his family at Cottam before the Jacobite uprising caused the family to flee to Mawdesley.

In fact, it is uncertain whether the skull belongs to George Haydock or his close relative William, who was also martyred. However, the attic of Lane End House was transformed into a secret chapel and worship was conducted there until 1832, when a church was finally built. The skull has healing properties; it is said that teeth were taken by those who were ailing, in the belief that they would thence be cured.

(See Chaigley for a similar story.)

Mawdesley Blue Stone

There is a standing stone at Mawdesley that gives its name to the lane on which it once could be found: Bluestone Lane. Quite recently, the council, not recognising the stone's importance, took it to the tip when they were repairing the road—but a certain Mr. Rigby had it returned and installed in the safety of his farmhouse garden.

A stone that was removed and then returned: normally in such stories there are disasters of one kind or another that result in the stone's reinstatement. In the future, if this story passes into legend, they will certainly be told.

Mawdesley Hall and The Black Bull

Mawdesley Hall was once said to be haunted by a bad-tempered old lady nicknamed "Madam." Her exploits became so troublesome that eventually her spirit was exorcised from the place, trapped in a bottle with a candle and thrown into a deep pit nearby.

When the pit was subsequently drained, the landlord of the Black Bull Inn produced an old bottle containing a candle and proclaimed that this was the very bottle in which Madam was imprisoned. It was a clever ploy, because people came from miles around to see and handle the bottle—and trade at the inn was brisk.

However, those who lived locally were disturbed by this. If the bottle really was the genuine article, what would happen if one of the visitors dropped and broke it, releasing Madam's spirit once again? The landlord could not argue against such superstition and so he was forced to throw the bottle away again, down the kitchen well.

The Black Bull was also known as Hell Hob...but the name probably came from the enormous hob (enclosed fire) in the place, which gave out enormous heat.

MEDLAR-with-WESHAM

Mowbreck Hall

Mowbreck Hall was destroyed by fire years ago, but its ghostly history deserves to be remembered.

It was late in the sixteenth century and the night before All Soul's Day. Resident priest Vivian Haydock was about to celebrate Midnight Mass in the chapel at Mowbreck Hall when he saw a terrible vision above the altar. The vision was of his son George Haydock—who was also a priest—and it was terrible because Vivian could see that George's head had been severed from his body.

It is said that Vivian saw the lips of the severed head mouth the Latin phrase "*Tristita Vestra Vertetur in Gaudium*" that translates as "Your sorrow will turn into joy," but this was of no comfort to Vivian, who knew this motto of old. His wife had died soon after their son George was born, and on her deathbed, in an effort to comfort Vivian, she had made him take note of that same motto, which was embroidered on the foot of their bedcover: "*Tristita Vestra Vertetur in Gaudium.*"

That motto had brought no comfort to Vivian then and its association with death brought no comfort now. Horrified by the vision of his dead son, he died soon afterwards and was interred in the chapel at Cottam Hall.

In fact, George was not yet dead, although Vivian's vision had not been wholly inaccurate; he had been arrested in London and was executed the following year.

As the story of the severed head spread, Mowbreck Hall developed a reputation for being haunted, and those living locally avoided it, especially at night. There is one tale of a nervous milliner called to deliver a hat to the lady of the house one evening—she managed to make her way up the drive to the door and pull the bell-cord, but when the door was opened, the butler found her in a dead faint on the path. She would never speak of what had frightened her so, but those hearing the story were quick to make up their own minds on the subject.

The vision of the severed head has been seen again at least once, in 1874 by Jocelyn Fazakerly Westby, whose family owned the hall. Since then, residents have often reported strange events in the building that has stood there in one form or another since the twelfth century. In recent times, it was a restaurant and the proprietors complained of ghostly footsteps, the sound of someone whistling, and things being moved by unseen hands. During renovations, one day a priest-hole was uncovered. That very night, footsteps were heard climbing the stairs and heading for the priest-hole, before fading away. A cat and a dog on the premises at the time were inconsolable, frightened out of their wits.

If the ghost of Vivian Haydock remains here, he is not alone. The ghost of Lord Derby, who once owned the premises, has sometimes been seen, as well as an old butler, who apparently took his own life here and now makes his presence felt.

MELLING

Local Legend

Many, many years ago, throngs of people flocked to Melling to inspect a certain sycamore tree, as it had been reported far and wide that the sap exuding from the bark had fashioned itself into the form of a man's face. What's more, the face was recognised as a man by the name of Palmer, who had been buried without a coffin and was using this method to make his anger known. The contemporary report ends by noting that "inns in the area reaped a rich harvest..."

Melling Hall

During the First World War, this lovely house was put to use as a military convalescent home. Lady Darlington, who allowed her ancestral home to be transformed for the purpose, loved the place so much, it seems she has never left. Melling Hall is now a hotel and Room 10 is noted for the occasional sightings of a woman standing before the mirror, wearing a dress similar in colour to the one worn by Lady Darlington as she assisted on the convalescent wards.

Todd Cottage

Todd Cottage, built in 1687, stands opposite the Norman Church, which may explain why the ghost of an old canon still haunts here. One resident, a Mr. Mulroy, saw the man several times, always wearing clerical dress and dog-collar. Eventually, he mentioned his experience to the vicar of the church, who suggested he take a look at an old photo that hung on the vestry wall. There, looking out at him was the very man he had seen so many times in Todd Cottage: Reverend Greenside.

The Reverend Greenside was vicar of Melling for almost fifty years until his death in 1913. He did not ever live in Todd Cottage, but it is known that he wanted to do so and would have bought it in a moment, had the opportunity presented itself. As one would expect, this apparition is a kindly one and causes no physical disturbances at all.

MELLOR

Mellor Moor

It has long been believed that there is a fairy city here, underground, proven by reports from people who have heard bells sounding forth. The fairies have also been seen at least once. A man was walking near the Roman camp on Mellor Moor when he saw a fairy dressed for hunting. His description was full and detailed: the little man wore a green jacket, a red cap, boots with spurs, and he carried a whip.

Others who heard the sound of subterranean bells did not believe in fairies, but said instead that the bells were ringing in a subterranean church.

MELLOR BROOK

Sykes Lumb Farm

There are two stories told about Sykes Lumb Farm. Or perhaps one is the explanation for the other—who knows. The first story concerns a boggart haunting, typical of its kind—the boggart was sometimes helpful and, at other times, very unhelpful indeed. Often the farmer would find the cows milked and fed, the horses harnessed, the carts loaded. If any disrespect was shown, however, the cows and horses would be turned loose, crockery would be smashed, and the butter would refuse to come. At night, the farmer and his wife would be awakened from their sleep to find their sheets had been torn from their beds and sometimes they would be dragged down the stairs by their legs.

Now, for the other story: Sykes Lumb Farm was so named because, in the time of the Wars of the Roses, its owners were a farmer and his wife by the name of Sykes, and it was close to a deep place in the river, the Anglo-Saxon word for such a spot being "lumb." Farmer Sykes and his wife were careful with their money and had managed to amass a considerable sum, which they were relying on to give them a comfortable old age. They hid their treasure in earthenware jars that they buried in the orchard, under an old apple tree.

In time, Farmer Sykes died, and then so did his wife—so suddenly that she had no chance to tell anyone about their treasure. Her relatives searched for it, because they suspected there was a hoard somewhere, but they did not find it.

New tenants moved into Sykes Lumb Farm, but they were not alone, for Old Sykes's wife was seen there more than once, walking along the road or standing in the orchard under an apple tree. One minute she was not there, explained one poor man, but the moment he went to pick an apple, there she stood, right in front of him. He ran away and so did anyone who saw her, for they did not want to be involved with a ghost. And so many generations passed, but Old Sykes's wife remained at her farm. She was unable to tell anyone about her treasure, for it is the way of ghosts that they cannot speak to the living unless they are first addressed.

At last, a new tenant of the farm saw her in the orchard. He had spent his evening at the inn and so, taking courage from the ale inside him, he decided to approach the ghostly woman and ask her what she wanted. This was what she had waited for and, in answer, she pointed to the roots of an old apple tree. The man understood her meaning in a moment and ran for a spade. And there he found Sykes's treasure, still in the earthenware pot.

Old Sykes's wife has never been seen again.

MORECAMBE

Clarendon Hotel

It has been said that the Clarendon Hotel is built on land that originally had been set aside for the building of a church and had already been consecrated—a fact that surely should guarantee against hauntings. However, the hotel is indeed haunted—by a Grey Lady. It is thought that she is the ghost of someone who took her own life here.

Midland Hotel

The Midland Hotel, a gem of art deco design, has recently been fully renovated and restored to its original state.

During the Second World War the building was used as a hospital for RAF officers; deceased men would temporarily be housed in the cellars and it is thought that at least one of them remained—as a ghost.

Two porters were responsible for this story. The first witnessed a shadowy figure emerge from the door leading to the cellar and make its way to the lift. The lift doors then closed and the machinery started up, taking the lift up to the second floor. There, the second porter watched, mystified, as the lift stopped and opened its doors. It was, of course, empty.

Palace Theatre

The Palace Theatre was closed in the early 1980s, but it seems the theatre ghost must have heard the rumours, for suddenly strange things started to happen. One poor electrician, working quite alone, heard someone invisible say quite clearly, several times, "The theatre will not die!"

This was not the first time something strange had been reported at the Palace. Some years previously, theatre staff were surprised when a celebrity photo fell off the foyer wall, despite being screwed in place, not balanced on a nail. In the photo was Stanley Massey, a theatre friend. The next day, the manager heard by telephone that Stanley Massey had died the previous night.

Royalty Theatre

There is now a shopping centre on the site of the old Royalty Theatre on Cheapside. When the old building was being demolished, workmen heard a ghostly theatre organ playing.

Winter Gardens Theatre

Morecambe's Winter Gardens is a Grade II listed building, erected in 1897 (it is named after the gardens that used to be here, surrounding the salt-water baths). Like many theatres, the Winter Gardens suffered from a lack of public enthusiasm at the end of the 1970s and closed its doors, remaining empty and unused until 2006 when it was bought by a charity: The Winter Gardens Preservation Trust.

The building has a wealth of reported paranormal activity including phantom footsteps, unexplained bangs and knocks, and poltergeist activity. Many people have reported being pushed by unseen hands. Investigators from TV's *Most Haunted* also heard a woman singing. The only part of the building that has a definite legend attached to it is the main staircase, where the presence of a woman is sometimes felt. It is thought that she fell—or was pushed—down the stairs during an argument with her partner.

✷✷✷✷✷✷✷

NELSON

Engineer's Arms

There was once a pub in Nelson called the Engineer's Arms. Robert Adams was once landlord here and after he died, it seems he did not want to leave, despite the fact that he had died in Aberdeen and was buried there!

An Aberdeen newspaper, in 1909, carried a report about Adams, whose ghost was behaving most disgracefully in the dead of night, singing loudly and drinking behind the bar. One man, passing the pub after closing time, was surprised to hear noise inside the building, so he looked through the window and saw Adams there quite clearly.

At the time of the newspaper report, the landlord in residence had enlisted his friends to try to get rid of the ghost, one of whom definitely identified Adams, because he had been a good friend of his in life. He claimed he had quite distinctly seen his "burly figure" in the bar. However, the team reported that Adams easily escaped their clutches, going upstairs to the bedrooms, where he caused noisy disturbances.

The newspaper report ended with the wonderfully indignant lines: "Nelson feels that something must be done. Such a ghost as this is nothing less than scandalous."

Marsden Hall

Built in the sixteenth century, Marsden Hall and its parkland now belong to Nelson Corporation, complete with all the improvements of centuries, including the Ladies Garden, mysterious tunnels, and the charming Wishing Gate. It is traditional, when passing through this gate, to pick a laurel leaf and place it in one of the crevices of the gateway, which ensures that whatever is wished for when passing under the archway will come true.

Another feature in the parkland is the faux Roman Bath—it is all but closed up entirely now but once was a favoured spot. One evening, late, a group of local people saw a white glowing figure standing in a recess close to this pool. Time will tell what legend is appended to this unidentified White Lady.

NEWCHURCH
IN PENDLE

Jinny Well

A large stone up on the hill used to roll down to this well to drink on certain nights of the year. That is, until a priest heard about it. Deciding that an evil spirit must be at work, the priest exorcised whatever spirit might be responsible and then broke the stone into pieces.

Local people knew more about the stone than did the priest, and they knew the spirit contained within it was called Jinny. After that, the stone was unable to roll, so it came to the well no more—but Jinny was not so easily held back. Now, Jinny herself wandered the path between the stone and the well, her head snapped clean off by the priest's axe.

Another priest was more successful at laying poor Jinny's ghost, but the well still bears her name.

(Jinny was probably Jenny Greenteeth, a water-spirit who, given half a chance, would drag children to their death in deep water.)

Newchurch Church

On the tower of this church is a carved stone resembling an eye, commonly believed to represent the eye of God and to protect the village from evils and witchcraft—very appropriate for the area that later became known as the home of the fabled Lancashire Witches.

In fact, closer inspection reveals that this is a tiny window that has been blocked up. Long ago, it was used by the sexton to watch for approaching wedding or funeral parties.

Rossendale Wizard

When farmers in Newchurch found their animals suffering sicknesses that could not be cured by normal means, they suspected witchcraft to be the cause. The more they shared their stories, the more they became convinced.

The farmers agreed that this run of bad luck was being caused by an old man living in Rossendale who was known to practice astrology and other arts of wizardry. So, as a last resort, they decided to undertake all the ceremonies they knew to "kill the witch." They sacrificed a chicken, then made a cake of oatmeal and cow's urine, which was marked with the wizard's name and burned. In the midst of their efforts, a knock came at the door and there was the wizard, begging to be admitted as a dreadful storm had blown up and he was far from home, soaked to the skin, and

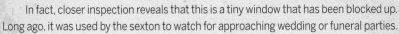

freezing with cold. The farmers refused him, knowing that if they should let him in, all their spells would be for nothing.

The wizard managed to make it to his Rossendale home, but fell ill straight away and was dead before the week was out.

Tynedale Farm

Tynedale Farm and Lower Well Head Farm lie close to each other. The latter, which dates from the sixteenth century, is rumoured to have been habitually used as a morgue at one time in the distant past. Evidence of this is the nearby footpath known as Corpse Way. Footsteps were often heard coming from the upper floor in the farmhouse, when it was known that no one was up there.

Nearby Tynedale Farm was probably built at the same time, although the current building dates from a century later. The area around Tynedale Farm is known for an apparition of a monk, who is seen either walking or kneeling beside the road. A young woman in a cloak has also been seen on more than one occasion, moving swiftly between the two farmhouses.

NEWTON IN BOWLAND

Walloper Well

On the fell above Newton-in-Bowland is Walloper Well, whose name derives from an ancient word for a freshwater spring. Its name is the focus of a story immortalised in a folk-song of the area, in which a man and his wife were climbing the fell arguing all the way, when a passing pedlar piped up: "I'll tell thee what I'd do if she were my wife. I'd wallop her, wallop her, wallop her well."

The water still flows today into a stone trough and the water is pure and clean. It is tradition to drink each time you pass the well, thus ensuring you will come back again.

OLD LANGHO

Black Bull Inn

A cavalier haunts this pub. He was not a local man, but was in the area on Cromwell's business. It is said that he was desperate with longing for a barmaid at the Black Bull, but unfortunately she already had a serious suitor. Undismayed, the cavalier set about getting what he wanted by killing the inconvenient suitor. We are not told if the barmaid then accepted the determined cavalier, but one assumes it would be unlikely.

Perhaps he was stricken with guilt over his act of murder, for he remains at the Black Bull. He is blamed for items that go missing and doors that lock themselves. He is also said to be responsible for one stunning event: a little girl fell downstairs and then was seen to land unharmed on the bottom step, as if a pair of invisible arms had caught her and stood her upright. Perhaps the cavalier was not so heartless after all.

It is suggested that the cavalier was one William Dutton, and certainly a man by this name was connected to Cromwell; he was his ward, educated by the poet Andrew Marvell, and at one time in the running to become Cromwell's son-in-law. It would be interesting indeed if evidence could be found that Dutton visited Old Langho at some time.

ORMSKIRK

The Plough

The ghost haunting the Plough pub is thought to be Nancy Balshaw, once landlady of the public house when it was called The Tavern. Nancy Balshaw's father originally ran the pub, and it seems Nancy, who never married, took over the place when he died. She was thirty-six years old. She was not without family, indeed she became responsible for four young nieces and nephews when her brother died, but the Plough was her means of support for most of her life.

Nancy died in 1863, but she had already retired from the Plough by then and was living with relatives in St. Helens. Also, the pub has been almost completely rebuilt since Nancy's days. However, as the Plough was such a big part of her life, perhaps it is indeed Nancy who is responsible for strange things happening there.

The trouble began when a car crashed into the Plough and caused great damage to the structure of the building. It is commonly thought that such damage to (or renovation of) an old building can somehow stimulate paranormal activity. The first intimation that all was not well at the Plough was when a bottle of gin fell from a shelf in full view of a bar full of customers. After that, bottles were seen to move on several occasions, and once the landlady felt someone's hand resting on her back.

Nancy is a source of interest for the customers, who regularly enquire if she has been around lately. However, during the day all is quiet—only at night does the spirit make herself felt. The landlady reporting these events simply said she hoped Nancy would eventually find what she was looking for.

Rufford Old Hall

William Shakespeare himself is said to haunt this place—a young man in hose and a high-collared jacket. Certainly a William Shakeshaft did once perform here, in 1585, as one of a travelling company of players. This tallies with what we know about Shakespeare's life at that time, for we know very little except that he was part of such a troupe, and at that time, he was away from his family.

The Old Hall also claims Elizabeth I as a ghost—an Elizabethan lady so regal in bearing, it could not have been anyone else.

However, the Grey Lady is the best-known ghost, and her story is tragic. She was Elizabeth Hesketh, whose husband was summoned to a war in Scotland on their very wedding day, leaving so suddenly that he was forced to abandon their wedding feast. Some days later, a soldier called with a message from him, saying that he would be home very soon. Heartened by this news, Elizabeth donned her wedding dress once more, arranged a new wedding feast and summoned all the original wedding guests for a great celebration.

Hours passed, days passed, and still Elizabeth's new husband did not return. Elizabeth swore that she would wear her wedding gown until he did arrive, convinced he would return the next day...or the next.... Gradually, Elizabeth grew weaker from her sorrow and she continued to refuse to eat until her husband came to take food with her. Finally, she reached the point of death. With her dying breath, she vowed that she would wait at the hall for her husband forever, even as a ghost.

The Grey Lady haunts the hall, its grounds, and has also been seen on the drive that leads to the church—still waiting for her husband to return.

Historical note: an Elizabeth Hesketh was betrothed, in 1580, to a young man who then went to fight in the Netherlands and died at Zutphen. The legendary details may be marginally incorrect, but the tragedy does not alter.

St. Anne's Church

A Green Man can be seen on one of the window frames on the front of this church.

St. Peter and St. Paul's Church

This church is unusual in that it has both a tower and a spire. The prosaic explanation is that the spire was part of the original church building and the tower was a later addition, built especially to hold the eight bells that came here after Burscough Priory was broken up.

A more attractive tale is the one that explains that two wealthy spinsters by the name of Orm, who had provided much of the money for the building of the church, were unable to agree on whether it should have a spire or a tower—and so they each paid for one.

A Green Man graces the organ here, high up, on the right-hand corner of the mounting.

OSBALDESTON

Osbaldeston Hall

Osbaldeston Hall is now a private home, but its history goes back to the thirteenth century and quite possibly beyond. The oldest parts of the building are largely Elizabethan, but the Osbaldeston family are known to have lived here for over 700 years.

Sometime around the beginning of the seventeenth century, Thomas Osbaldeston argued with his sister Elizabeth's husband, Edward Walsh. The reason for the argument is almost irrelevant because the disagreement escalated until the only way to settle it was for the two men to fight it out to the death. Swords were drawn and Edward Walsh lost the fight, dying where he fell, his blood pouring out onto the floorboards. It is said that the stain of his blood remains, and nothing can remove it.

The blame for this death would seem to rest entirely on Osbaldeston's shoulders, for it is said that Walsh actually put up little resistance. Consequently, Osbaldeston was tried and convicted for his brother-in-law's murder at Lancaster Assizes. There is no record that he was imprisoned, but he was certainly divested of much of his land as a punishment.

The Osbaldestons left the hall over 200 years ago, but the ghost story lives on. It is still said that sometimes the Hall is disturbed with the sound of swordplay—and this is taken as a warning that the ghost of Edward Walsh may soon be seen, moaning and staggering to his death.

OSWALDTWISTLE

Duckworth Hall Inn

Landlords here have heard the sound of moving chains and footsteps. A shadowy figure wearing a long cloak has also been seen outside the inn. It is said that he is perhaps a Catholic priest, perhaps connected to Whalley Abbey, held here on his way to martyrdom.

Stanhill Lane Post Office

This cottage was once the home of James Hargreaves, who, in 1764, invented the Spinning Jenny, one of the machines that triggered the Industrial Revolution. He remains one of Lancashire's best-known sons. His cottage also remains, although until relatively recently it was better known as the village's Post Office.

The cottage is known to be haunted by a White Lady. Perhaps she was one of James Hargreaves' descendants, because the cottage remained in the possession of his family until at least the turn of the twentieth century. The White Lady was often seen by both residents and guests, who would wake to find the lights switched on.

PADIHAM

Gawthorpe Hall

A superb Jacobean building, Gawthorpe Hall is now a National Trust property. Like so many Lancastrian great halls, it was originally a simple pele tower, a defence against marauding Scots. The mansion attached to the pele tower was added nearly two centuries later. The initials "KS" that appear in the masonry are relatively modern, dating from 1842 and commemorating the marriage of James Philips Kay to Janet Shuttleworth—they took as their surname Kay-Shuttleworth.

The hall is one of many places connected to the Lancashire Witches' story, because both Old Chattox and Anne Redfern lived on Shuttleworth land. In addition, a servant of the Shuttleworth family was one of the witch's accusers.

It is said that there may have been a murder at the hall; some visitors have complained of feeling a sudden pain in the chest. This is only one of the strange occurrences reported, for it is believed that several entities haunt the place, including the ghost of Rachel Shuttleworth, who was the last Shuttleworth to actually live there. Rachel is well-remembered at the hall, for she was a skilled lace maker and her collection of lace books still remains in the hall's library.

Pendle Street Footbridge

In January 1952, the *Burnley Express* carried an article about William Grimes, who was retiring from his employment as a "knocker-up" after half a century. His job was to wake mill-workers by knocking on their bedroom windows with a long pole, so he was often out-of-doors in the very early morning. The journalist interviewing him commented that he must have seen some strange things in those early hours. William certainly had; the most unusual thing he had seen was a ghost! He had clearly seen a nurse in uniform climb the steps of the railway footbridge on Pendle Street, and when she reached the top, she disappeared.

Red Rock

The ghost at the Red Rock pub, christened Mary, has been blamed for all kinds of odd things happening. Glasses have fallen to the floor and smashed; full glasses of beer have been seen moving in front of customers' eyes. Once, a glass bowl full of mints broke and fell apart, scattering the sweets on the floor. Things have disappeared and then reappeared. Staff have seen doors opening on their own and felt the sensation of a person brushing past them.

But perhaps there is more than one ghost at the Red Rock. On occasion, people have heard the tune "Greensleeves" being played, when no juke-box is operating. Many years ago, a local policeman called Peter would habitually play that song on the jukebox—until his death.

A different ghostly character was discovered quite recently when a team of ghost hunters spent some time in the pub. The medium with the team picked up the presence of a man connected to the current landlord, someone who had suffered a stroke. When the landlord was asked about this, he produced a newspaper article about a friend of his, a well-known Padiham character called Ernie—who had indeed recently had a stroke and died.

Royal British Legion Club

A shadowy form has been reported upstairs in this building moving across the landing and into a large room, then leaving the door swinging. Sometimes objects go missing and reappear somewhere else. However, no one seems to find these occurrences worrying; regulars have become quite used to them.

PARLICK PIKE
Old Nick's Watering Pot

A well of spring water here is known as Old Nick's Watering Pot. The fabled "Old Dun Cow" was reputed to frequent this place and give freely of her milk to anyone who asked, without ever running dry—until she was bewitched.

(See the story of Dun Cow Rib Farm, at Whittingham, for the complete tale.)

PENDLE
Ashenden Clough

At Ashenden Clough on Pendle Hill, on nights when the wind is in the right direction, it is said that the faint sound of bells can sometimes be heard, calling monks to midnight prayer at Whalley Abbey. This is strange...because the five bells that had once hung in the church were redistributed to other churches centuries ago.

Devil's Apronful

Apronful Hill is named after this cairn, now rather smaller than it once was, which had the name of the Devil's Apronful. The original size of this monument can be judged by the remnants of stones surrounding the small pile.

This is where the devil stood when he flung rocks at Clitheroe Castle, making a new window in its side. The cairn was his stockpile of ammunition.

(See also Clitheroe Castle.)

Fox's Well

In 1652, one George Fox climbed to the top of Pendle Hill in response to a feeling that God wished him to do so. Once there, he had a mystical experience he described in his autobiography: "The Lord let me see in what places he had a great people to be gathered." Fox went on to found the Quakers and one of their American centres is named after Pendle. Near the summit of Pendle is Fox's Well; in George Fox's journal, he notes that he had fasted for several days, so when he discovered the spring, it must have been very welcome.

Local Legend

There are tales around Pendle Hill of one Mother Cuthbert, who lived there with her two daughters—witches all. The tales are presented in an early seventeenth-century tract called *The Famous History of the Lancashire Witches*. The work is described by the author as a story about "witches in general" and he offers it up as a piece that is "conducive to mirth and recreation." However, the stories it contains are probably suggested by the folktales of the Pendle area, not entirely from the author's own imagination. Therefore, they are worth including here.

Mother Cuthbert was not always a witch. In the beginning, she and her daughters earned a meagre living by carding wool, gathered by Mother Cuthbert when sheep caught their fleeces on hedgerows. One day, while engaged in this occupation, Mother Cuthbert saw a rabbit that changed into a dog and then into a man. Mother Cuthbert was frightened by this, but greed soon overcame her fright when the man offered her a small bag of coins, as long as she would meet him at that same place next day. Mother Cuthbert agreed and took the money.

Mother Cuthbert's daughters were overjoyed to see the money and never questioned why the man would give it so readily; they heartily encouraged her to meet him again, next day. And so she did. This time she was surprised to see a tree growing up right in front of her, which soon turned into an entire wood. Buried in the wood was a great house with beautiful decorations and tables full of beautiful food and many ladies, dancing to beautiful music. This was, of course, a house of witches.

The leader of this coven introduced herself as Mother Crady, the Witch of Penmaenmawr in Wales. Mother Cuthbert was well fed and well entertained and when at last she was invited to join the coven herself, she found it impossible to refuse. She was anointed with a magical ointment and given more to take home and use as she pleased. She was also given a small creature, like a mole, to be her familiar. She soon found that this imp could talk and did not always appear as a mole because he could turn himself into anything he wished. Now Mother Cuthbert had the tools she needed to repay all those who had mistreated her in the past...

Mother Cuthbert's first victim was the mayor of Lancaster, who had once caught her stealing pieces of his fence to burn on her fire, in a winter so cold she and her daughters might otherwise have frozen to death. He had punished her with a strong whipping and she had never forgotten this injustice. So she sought him out and put into his hands a letter, which had been touched with the magic ointment given to her by Mother Crady. The mayor read the letter and, to the surprise of his companions, he immediately stripped off all his clothes and ran out into the street, whipping himself until the blood ran. His friends ran after him in horror, whilst the townspeople laughed till they cried. When the mayor recovered his senses, he told his friends that he had imagined himself in a horse-race and had never felt the lashes of his own whip, imagining that he was instead whipping his horse to go faster.

Realising the strength of her new power, Mother Cuthbert initiated her two daughters, Margery and Cicely, into the magical arts. Margery was the first to use her magic, when she was jilted by Roger Clodpate in favour of a dairymaid called Dorothy. One day, Margery followed the pair as they went courting and because she was jealous, she cast a spell to summon a heavy rainstorm. It rained so heavily that Roger and Dorothy could walk no farther because the streams and ditches overflowed all around them. At that moment, Margery changed herself into a black mare and cantered up to them, as if to offer them a ride. But as soon as they were both astride her, Margery reared, threw them into the stream and galloped away, leaving them to walk home all wet through.

Later, Margery Cuthbert came across Roger and Dorothy while walking and they threw insults at her, calling her Leaden-Heels. She walked on as if she had not heard, but a little farther along the road Roger and Dorothy had cause to climb a stile and then could not climb down because of the deep pools of water that suddenly surrounded them! The spell was broken when some passersby pointed out that there was no water there at all. Later that day, Margery found the pair in a barn, discussing this strange event and, making herself invisible, Margery sprinkled magic dust on Roger, so that when Dorothy looked at him she saw a donkey instead!

A story about Margery's sister Cicely tells of her love for a gentleman—love that was, of course, unrequited. When the gentleman went hunting, Cicely often turned herself into a hare, so that he would hunt her and she would at least be able to be close to him. This was a dangerous pastime. One day, as Cicely raced back towards her house, one of the gentleman's fastest hounds caught up to her and managed to nip her buttocks just as she disappeared inside. The young man, puzzled that he always lost sight of the hare just as it reached this particular house, followed it inside. But although he saw Cicely rubbing her buttocks to ease the pain, he did not guess her secret.

After that, Cicely went a-hunting no more, but her love for the gentleman did not waver. When she heard that he was about to be married, she was distraught and went looking for his bride-to-be. She enticed the girl into a deep wood and worked a spell to make her sleep for a day and a night. Then she cast a spell on her beloved gentleman so that he would think Cicely was his love and marry her instead! Fortunately, Cicely realised she had done something terribly wrong by using her magic this way. She worked another spell to put her new husband to sleep, brought the young lady from the deep wood and laid them down together. When they woke, neither had any memory of Cicely's trickery, which was just as well.

Likewise, Mother Cuthbert's magical powers were not always used in spite. On one occasion, she came across a poor man being taken to Lancaster Gaol for a debt that, though small, he had no hope of paying. She argued with the men arresting him, but they would not take any notice of her. So, she took from her pocket a magical pipe that the Witch of Penmaenmawr had given to her and started to play a tune. The men, thus bewitched, immediately began to dance and jig about and could not stop, much as they tried. Mother Cuthbert led them a merry dance through fields and hedgerows whilst the poor debtor made good his escape. She only abandoned the men after she had made them dance into a stagnant pond.

On another occasion, Mother Cuthbert heard some thieves boasting of their latest venture and how rich they now would be. Her first thought was that she needed riches as much as they did, so she cast a spell over them and the horses on which they rode. Suddenly the thieves heard a tremendous noise and thought themselves pursued by angry hordes of people, but much as they tried, they could not make their horses move from that spot. And so they dismounted and ran away, leaving Mother Cuthbert to gather up their spoils and take them home with her. However, not long afterwards, she learned that the people who had been robbed were known to her, and they were not rich, but quite poor. And so, as she was not an evil-minded woman, she returned the stolen belongings to their rightful owners.

These tales, written down at a time when many so-called witches were being persecuted and killed, are interesting. Where is the evil in these tales of witchcraft? Mischief and the righting of wrongs are all they describe.

(See Woodplumpton and the tales of Marjorie Hilton, for another example of a witch turning herself into a hare and being nipped by hounds as she reaches her house.)

Pendle Witches

Six of the Pendle Witches came from two families: the Southerns and the Whittles. Elizabeth Southerns was otherwise known as Demdike and was in her eighties at the time of her arrest. Anne Whittle, also in her eighties, was known as Chattox because of her habit of constantly muttering to herself. Both these old women were locally regarded as witches for their abilities with medicinal herbs, but their powers also led people to believe that they were capable of doing ill as well as good.

Also accused were Southerns's daughter Elizabeth Device and her grandchildren James and Alizon Device, as well as Whittle's daughter Anne Redfern. Non-family members dragged into the accusations were Jane Bulcock and her son John, Alice Nutter, Katherine Hewitt, Alice Gray, and Jennet Preston.

Roger Nowell of Read Hall was the JP (Justice of the Peace) for Pendle and was actively pursuing the Royal decree that he should list all recusants in his jurisdiction, those who refused to give up the old church and take on the new religion. So when one John Law, a pedlar, complained to him that young Alizon Device had put a curse on him, he was ready to listen. Alizon had asked the pedlar for some valuable pins, but he had refused and so she had cursed him—a few minutes later his horse had stumbled and fallen and so he believed it was her doing.

We do not have records of how the witches' confessions were extracted but in all likelihood torture was used. Alizon confessed that she had sold her soul to the devil and her brother James said that she had confessed to bewitching a child. When Alizon's mother was called, she said only that her own mother, Demdike, had a mark on her body that could be a witchmark, where the Devil had sucked her blood.

Alizon was also questioned about Old Chattox and her reputation as a witch, and she readily named her as such because, it is believed, the two families were not friends.

On April 2, 1612, Demdike, Chattox, Anne Redfern, and Alizon Device were committed for trial. On Good Friday, Elizabeth Device called a meeting at the family home, Malkin Tower, and several friends attended. It was said that they were making plans to blow up Lancaster Castle, amongst other things, and when Nowell heard about this, he had the whole group arrested. Seven more people were sent to Lancaster for trial on charges of witchcraft; one, Jennet Preston, was sent to York as she lived over the border.

A few days after the trial began, three more women were added to the list: the Samlesbury Witches Jane Southworth, Jennet Brierley, and Ellen Brierley. Their charges included murder by witchcraft. Also brought to the trial were Margaret Pearson from Padiham, accused of killing a horse through witchcraft, and Isobel Robey from Windle, who was accused of causing sickness.

The main prosecution witness was Jennet Device—a nine-year-old girl. Nine of those accused were found guilty. Elizabeth Southerns had already died, waiting to come to trial. Alizon Device, Elizabeth Device, James Device, Anne Whittle, Anne Redfern, Alice Nutter, Katherine Hewitt, John Bulcock, and Jane Bulcock were all found guilty and hanged at Gallows Hill on August 20, 1612. Jennet Preston, in York, was also found guilty and hanged.

Lancashire has a plethora of charming folktales about witches, but the case of the Lancashire Witches reminds us just how lethal that particular superstitious belief could be...

PILLING

Carr House

Carr House Farm was home to boggarts in the form of horses, who would be heard—but never seen—galloping along the road away from the farmhouse. Mrs. Sherdley, who lived there as a girl, remembers hearing them many years ago, when she and her fiancé were standing at the yard gate saying good night after a lovely day out in Blackpool. In those days, there was no street lighting, but it was a lovely moonlit night—and then, all at once, the two of them heard a sound like horses galloping across the cobbled yard. The youngsters ran over to the stable, but found that the farm's own four horses were all present and correct, all quite safe and calm.

Many years later, well into married life, Mr. Sherdley spent an evening with the church Fellowship group. After the meeting, some of the men stayed behind to chat and the conversation turned to ghosts. For the first time, Mr. Sherdley told of his experience and was startled when another chap exclaimed, "Oh, it's t'Carr House Boggart you've heard!" He had worked at Carr House Farm before the Sherdleys had lived there and there had always been much talk about the boggart—who was said to sound just like galloping horses.

For many years. Mr. and Mrs. Sherdley said nothing to their family about their strange experience—until one evening when Mrs. Sherdley found herself telling her brother all about it. "Aha!" he said, "that accounts for it!" And he went on to describe a night when he too had heard horses in the yard. Although he had been comfortably warm in bed, the sound was so convincing that he had been obliged to get up and check the stables and, just like Mrs. Sherdley, he had found nothing but a full complement of horses, all neatly stabled. And, of course, it was another moonlit night.

Fluke Hall

Fluke Hall dates from the eighteenth century and was built by Richard Cardwell Gardner, who was a JP and also mayor of Liverpool for a time. The word "fluke" is a local name for flatfish, and five of these fish are carved in stone above the entrance to the hall. It is believed that the wood panelling in the entrance hall came from the smoke room of the liner *Mauretania*, whose fixtures and fittings were used to grace several establishments around the country when she was broken up in 1935. For several years in the twentieth century, the building was a restaurant and then it became a retirement home.

Staff at the retirement home have grown used to strange happenings, particularly overnight. A chandelier in the lounge is sometimes seen to be moving and has a habit of shedding its light bulbs. Staff going into the kitchen sometimes find the door locked behind them, although no one was around to turn the key. In 1995, one chef was reported to have had many strange experiences in his kitchen, but he preferred not to discuss them...

One night, in the 1990s, the deputy matron was staying overnight in the large room above the main lounge. She awoke early for her morning shift and was startled to see a figure appear before the window and drift across the room, disappearing when it reached the fireplace. From its size and stature, the deputy matron judged the black silhouette to be male and it appeared to be wearing a black cloak. She had been sceptical of the tales until then.

Olde Ship

The Olde Ship is a listed building and it's clear that some of the timbers used to build it may truly have come from old ships. The place was originally built and paid for in the eighteenth century by George Dickinson, but stories differ as to the source of Dickinson's money. He was a captain, and some say he retired to his native village of Pilling after years sailing the South Seas and East Indies, trading in spices and silks. Others, however, say he built the Olde Ship on the less moral proceeds of his involvement with the slave trade.

A succession of landlords and landladies have had strange experiences in the Olde Ship, but none have ever been frightened by the presence, which seems entirely benign. Indeed, one landlady came to feel that the success of her business was actually helped by her invisible guest. Initially a sceptic about such things, living in the Olde Ship had caused her to rethink, but she refused to use the word "ghost," preferring to describe it as "a feeling that something is living with us that we can't actually see."

On one occasion, when her husband was alone in the building, the kitchen radio suddenly went quiet. On examination, he found that the radio had been switched off—and unplugged. Another time, when her husband was alone overnight, he was awakened by voices outside his bedroom door. He got out of bed, opened the door, and heard the voices fade away. He checked the house, but he was still alone in the building. His mother had her own experience when she came to stay: she saw a ghostly woman with a "pale and troubled face," dressed in clothes from the Georgian period.

Later owners of the Olde Ship also reported inexplicable things. One morning after the lounge bar had been thoroughly cleaned, a flower was found lying on the hearth. It was just an ordinary garden flower—but not of a type that grew in the Ship's own garden. The strangest occurrence happened one day when the owners' daughter returned from school, went upstairs, and came straight down again to ask, "Why have you moved my bed?" The bed hadn't simply been shifted along the wall; it had been turned 'round through a ninety degree angle and was now facing in a different direction. Yet the family weren't scared. There was never a forbidding atmosphere in the Ship, and a variety of pets that also lived there never exhibited any fear.

As for the reason for the haunting: there is one old tale, that may or may not be true, about a murder. At the time, Pilling was an important potato-growing area and Irish labourers would come for the picking season, receiving their wages when picking was over. One evening, an Irish worker came to the pub, full of high spirits, flashing his wages and buying drinks for everyone. At the end of the evening, he left the place rolling drunk and was never seen again. Perhaps he was followed and murdered for his money, because many years later, when the land behind the pub was developed into a council estate, it's said that they found a skeleton. Maybe that's the answer. But there's no explanation for the sighting of the Georgian lady with the "pale and troubled face."

Pilling Moss

There is a small bridge over a stream called Broadfleet in the fields surrounding the village of Pilling that has a connection to the tale of the Devil at Cockerham. The devil decided to make his home at Cockerham and was so troublesome that the local schoolmaster was engaged to strike a bargain with him. He set three tasks for the devil, on the understanding that if he couldn't complete them, he must leave. The devil was defeated and was so angry at this result that he flew into the air and landed on this bridge. His footprint can still be seen today.

(See Cockerham for the full devil story.)

PLEASINGTON
Playing Fields

In 1965, a local constable watched a girl wearing a long, black dress and white head-scarf walk down the road towards him. She stopped before a bench across the road as if to sit down. He did think it marginally odd that he heard no footsteps, but as he picked up his bike and made his way over to have a friendly "policemanly" chat with the young lady, he was shocked to realise that she had disappeared. Later, he learned that others had also seen her from time to time. She was believed to be a young seventeenth-century nun who had been expelled from the nearby priory because of an episode of bad behaviour.

Pleasington Old Hall

Pleasington Old Hall was built in 1587, and was home to Dorothy Winckley. Dorothy married a Southworth of Samlesbury Hall, then a de Hoghton. It could be this Dorothy who is named in the legend of Samlesbury Hall's White Lady, as that family actually has no Dorothy in its genealogy.

(See Samlesbury Old Hall at Samlesbury for the full story.)

POULTON-ʟᴇ-FYLDE
Local Legend

Many families have a tradition of some kind of supernatural entity that only makes its appearance when death approaches. Such is the boggart claimed by a family named Walmsley, of Poulton-le-Fylde. The boggart's activities took the form of alarming noises for which no natural explanation could ever be found and that always preceded the passing of another poor Walmsley. There is no record of how often this occurred, but there's no doubt that it must have been a dreadful thing to live with—a sure harbinger of death with no way of avoiding the sad outcome.

Poulton Church

P Early in the seventeenth century, Robert Hey of Poulton-le-Fylde had become known as the Wise Man of the Fylde because of his accuracy in telling fortunes. In 1611, his reputation came to the attention of the vicar of Poulton Church, who was so concerned that he brought him before the bishop of Chester to be castigated for his irreligious practices. However, it was noted that Robert was a good Christian who took communion regularly and actually took no pleasure in his fame as a fortune-teller. His penance was painless—he was simply required to attend the church the next Sunday, promise to read no more fortunes and publicly renounce his title of Wise Man of the Fylde. Given that this was the era of witch-hunts, Robert was fortunate indeed to be so lightly punished.

PREESALL

Hackensall Hall

There may have been a hall here as long ago as the ninth century, as it is believed the name of the place comes from Haakon, a Viking settler who chose to make the place his home. The hall, now standing near Knott End Golf Course, was built in 1656, and there was previously a moated house on the site. Initials carved in stone over the doorway of the hall indicate that it was built by Richard and Anne Fleetwood of Rossall. The towns of Rossall and Fleetwood are not far away, across the waters of the River Wyre.

Hackensall Hall is best known for its boggart, which took the form of an industrious horse who would work on the farm overnight, so long as a fire was left burning in the kitchen hearth for it to sleep by when its work was done. If the fire went out, the household would be rudely disturbed by the noises of an angry horse stampeding in the kitchen!

Lesser known is the fact that Hackensall Hall was also thought to be haunted by two human ghosts, whose rest was disturbed when their skeletons were found during restoration work on the hall in 1873. It was rumoured that these two unfortunates, both women, appeared to have been deliberately walled up and left to die. The ensuing reports of haunting were so disturbing that a priest was summoned to perform an exorcism.

Town Foot

Preesall had a boggart cat who was often seen at Town Foot, dressed in a smart red military uniform.

PRESTON

Avenham Park

In the southeast corner of Avenham Park is a charming little grotto housing a Victorian drinking fountain, which late in 2010 was subject to a proposal to restore it to full working order. The fountain is of great interest because it stands on the site of an ancient well that was reputed never to run dry and whose water was a certain cure for eye diseases. Sadly, the fountain will not use that ancient source of curative water—which was some time ago judged to contain "impurities."

Christ Church

Christ Church was built in 1836. Three years later the Reverend Clark planted an ivy by the wall and there it grew for twenty-five years, covering a large part of the church wall, as ivy does. He left the church in 1864, whereupon his ivy promptly fell off the church. Knowing how ivy embeds itself so securely, it's no surprise that this occurrence was seen as meaningful! The church was largely demolished in 1971, but the facade was preserved, and now forms the front entrance of an office block.

Friargate

In December 1877, the *Manchester Evening News* was just one of the papers reporting a disturbance on Friargate, Preston, outside the house of Edward Foster, a druggist (chemist). He was a controversial character for two reasons: he was opposed to vaccination and he was a spiritualist. About six o'clock one Sunday evening, someone thought they saw a ghost at the window of an upstairs room and convinced many passersby that it must be the result of a séance they imagined to be taking place in that room. Word spread, crowds gathered, the road was blocked, and after two hours of mayhem, the police had to be called. By that time, the newspaper stated, hundreds of people were saying they had also seen the ghost...

The George Hotel

The buildings now housing Ted Carter's tackle shop include one that was once a pub, The George, which hit the headlines in the early 1990s as landlord Tom Harrison had been terrified by a ghost.

Tom Harrison and his wife were new landlords of The George when the trouble erupted. The cobblestoned cellar floor had been replaced for safety reasons, but workmen had also removed a larger slab of stone that turned out to be a gravestone. There was nothing intrinsically wrong with this—in earlier times it had been legal to bury family members on private property—so it was deemed unnecessary to excavate either this grave or a second one, that was discovered a few feet away.

Before the new concrete floor was laid, however, Tom examined the ground and found a gold ring that was enamelled in white and inscribed. A historian at Preston Museum deciphered the writing: "Robert Clay OB 28 Mar 1786 aged 40" and explained that it was a woman's bereavement ring—but this was a lover's ring, not a wife's. Black enamel was the norm for a bereaved wife's ring, but if the wearer was not married to the one she mourned, white enamel was used.

Early one morning, Tom was awoken by loud thumps from the room above where his son slept, followed by heavy footsteps descending the stairs. Annoyed, Tom went to his bedroom door and found himself facing not his son, but a stranger—a tall man with long, thin features, intense eyes, and a shortcut beard. He wore a hat, a long black coat, and a shirt with a square-cut white collar. The man was there—and then he was not. Tom was so shocked that he could not move—until he heard the outer door downstairs bang shut. He ran downstairs and found that the door was still locked. It could not have been opened and then noisily closed again.

More disturbances quickly followed over the next few days: in the pub, a man told Tom he'd better check the Gents' toilets, because someone was kicking down one of the cubicle doors. The room was empty. Another evening, a woman was heard crying out and Tom found her pinned against the wall by an invisible force, with her feet a couple of inches above the floor. He ran to assist and the woman dropped to the ground. Business started to suffer…

Tom had always been a down-to-earth man, but when an elderly customer suggested a séance might be in order and recommended a medium, he decided there was nothing to lose. The story told during that séance claimed that Robert Clay had abused and murdered two young girls and buried their bodies in the cellar. He had suffered enormous guilt over his actions, and his trouble-making now was simply his way of getting his story out, so that he might find forgiveness and peace at last.

As for the bereavement ring, the medium told Tom he should always wear it, saying that it would protect him. He did wear it but never believed it could protect him, until he went on a deep-sea fishing trip. Several miles out to sea, Tom got a bite from an enormous fish, lost his balance, and was dragged into the water. He sank like a stone—but then, suddenly, he felt someone's strong arm around him and he was on his way back to the surface. He broke the surface with a smile on his face.

Despite the proof of Robert Clay's existence in the form of the dated ring, a hunt for him in the records was inconclusive. However, there was only one Clay family in Preston at the time. Whilst Robert was not amongst the names, there was one family member whose age suggested that he could have been Robert Clay's father. He just happened to be in charge of the House of Correction—situated directly opposite The George Hotel.

If Robert Clay really was a murderer, it makes sense that his name cannot be found in any official records. In those days, if someone committed a heinous crime, their family could arrange to have his or her name excised from the records completely.

(See Stone Cottage Inn for another, less troublesome, pub cellar gravestone.)

Ladywell Street

Bannister Doll was the name given to the ghost of the Mayor's daughter, Dorothy Bannister, who lived on Snow Lane. When Dorothy confessed to her father that she was with child, Mayor Bannister was so angered that he dragged poor Dorothy from the house, tied her to a post, and whipped her so mercilessly that she died. The post where Dorothy met her death was situated where Ladywell Street meets Heatley Street. It was made of cast iron and more usually used to tether horses. It was only removed when British Rail built Ladywell House there, many years later.

Bannister Doll was said to haunt the area and many a misbehaving child would be taken to the whipping-post and told the terrible story, to scare them into changing their ways. She was also said to haunt the churchyard at Holy Trinity Church, where it is believed she was buried. However, recent research has found no record of her burial there.

Whatever the truth of this story, it is an enduring one in Preston. For many years, people would tell of seeing a White Lady in the area of Ladywell Street, or in the churchyard. Eventually, a special service was held for her in Holy Trinity Church, to help her poor soul rest. Bannister Doll was never seen again.

Local Legend

Preston's own boggart takes the form of a black dog and is said to appear before some calamity befalls the town. Some reports claim it has no head—and yet it howls...

Moor Park

It was said that along a path from Moor Park to Cadley Mill there was a bottomless pool.

New Hall Lane

In 1934, an electrician working in an empty shop here saw a black-haired woman in a shimmering white gown rise up out of the floor, staring at him all the while. He left the building fast. Coverage by the local newspaper brought to light the story that thirty years previously, the tenant of the shop had learned that his drunkard wife had been unfaithful to him—and he had murdered her there.

Our Lady's Well

Close to the site of the old Franciscan Friary, now disappeared, there was once a holy well called Our Lady's Well—which in all probability was destroyed when the Lancaster Canal was constructed. It is from this that Ladywell Street takes its name. The exact site is somewhere under Ladywell House. The piece of canal responsible for the demise of Our Lady's Well was later supplanted by the railway. Progress?

Playhouse Theatre

The first building on this site on Market Street was a Quaker Meeting House, built in the early eighteenth century. In 1847, the building was replaced by the Playhouse Theatre that stands there still. The costume store in this old building is said to be the most haunted part and costumes hung here have been seen to move on their own. In the cellar, people have seen ghosts who appear only from the waist up.

Railway Station

Staff at Preston Railway Station are convinced that several ghosts haunt the platforms and the office buildings. It is thought that the offices may once have been a ballroom and ghostly forms have been seen there several times. The clock tower also has a reputation for being haunted. Even the platforms are sometimes visited by ghostly travellers, particularly platform two, where a young man has been seen at different times of the day and night. Staff who work on night-shifts are never keen on venturing out of their offices!

In 1886, at the old Deepdale Bridge Station, Margaret Banks reached for a passenger's hand, became caught on the moving carriage and was dragged under the wheels of the train. She died instantly. She was just fifteen. It is said that she haunts nearby Miley Tunnel.

Spindlemaker's Arms

The ghost here is well-known to regular customers, although no one can say who it once was. The ghost's presence is felt when the air turns cold or when items disappear and reappear. Staff are reluctant to be alone in the building, because of the sounds of coughing, tapping, footsteps, and moving furniture.

Stone Cottage Inn

In the cellar of Stone Cottage Inn on Egan Street a tombstone was discovered. It could not be mistaken for some other kind of stone slab, because it bore the inscription "In memory of Jane, the wife of Corporal Vernon, of the 85th Regiment, died Feb 11th 1851 aged 31 years." Research has proved that a woman of that name did indeed die on that date, but there is no explanation for why the memorial resides in such a place. Perhaps the pub was a private home at that time? It was certainly not illegal to bury one's loved ones on one's own property. The presence here is assumed, of course, to be Jane Vernon, but she is not troublesome, causing little more than an odd atmosphere and an occasional beer-pump malfunction.

(See The George Hotel, Preston, for another pub cellar gravestone.)

Town Hall

Preston's Town Hall is haunted by a "Dickensian" man. The reports first came from cleaners, working when the building was deserted and quiet; there were strange noises, doors would unexpectedly open or close, and it sometimes felt very cold for no reason. They also saw a man whose clothes led to their description of him as Dickensian. The man was once seen by the head porter early in the morning of (appropriately) Remembrance Sunday.

Additionally, there was a persistent problem with the building's lighting system; lights would flicker as if the bulb was about to blow or as if there was something badly wrong with the whole wiring system. One night, the police became involved when someone reported that lights were on in the Town Hall. They searched the building but found nothing untoward—apart from their police dog's reaction when they tried to take him into the basement. He simply would not go. The wiring system was checked by electricians who could find nothing wrong, so the conclusion was that all these strange events are being caused by the Dickensian man.

Wellington Inn

In 1839, two regulars at the Wellington Inn in Glovers Court had a disagreement that escalated during the evening and ended in a knife-fight outside their homes in the Avenham area of town. The root of the argument was a single penny piece, but it cost one of them his life and the other spent the rest of his life in prison for the murder.

Now, the Wellington Inn is plagued with strange noises and the feeling that someone invisible is wandering around the place. Glasses fall off shelves when no one is close, and once a corkscrew flew across the room. The perpetrator of these strange events is thought to be the ghost of the murdered man, still looking for the penny he was owed. In recent years, a photograph taken here seems to show the ghost itself, as a cloudy white shape.

White Bull

Customers in the White Bull pub have sometimes seen the top half of a ghostly man floating past them. Young experimenters once spent the night in the cellar—but left in a hurry after asking questions of the ghost and hearing definite raps in response.

RAWTENSTALL
Railway Inn

The Railway Inn's ghost has been christened Jane by those who know her. She is tall, slim, and dressed in grey. She has been seen in various bedrooms and once she walked through a wall—that, of course, was not there when she was alive.

REEDLEY
Oakes Hotel

This hotel was built as a private home in 1883, and was originally called Oakleigh. Later it became the local council's headquarters and then, in 1984, it was converted into a hotel. No mention had been made of a ghost before then, but when renovations began, several people witnessed a ghostly girl in a white dress wandering around the building. It has been suggested that she was a servant here, employed by the Altham family who built Oakleigh.

RIBCHESTER
Hothersall Hall

Hothersall Hall was plagued by a boggart that was so troublesome that it was eventually laid by a priest under a laurel bush near the house. It is said that as long as the laurel survives, the boggart will be at rest. It is also advised that the bush should be regularly fed, with milk, to keep the spell alive. Neither the hall nor the laurel bush survives, but the story does. Another version of the tale says that it is the devil himself who was laid under the laurel bush. He is trapped there until he works out a way of spinning a rope from the sand of the River Ribble.

(See Cockerham for another mention of spinning a rope of sand.)

RIVINGTON

Ornamental Gardens

Lord Leverhulme was the founder of the soap manufacturing company that became Unilever and he was a great philanthropist, building the entire town of Port Sunlight to provide houses for his workers. He lived in a bungalow at Rivington that was surrounded by ornamental gardens that he designed and arranged himself. He loved his gardens and was often seen wandering amongst the shrubs and flowers, enjoying his creation. Leverhulme died in 1925, but his spirit lives on here; several visitors have seen his unmistakable figure, wearing a distinctive suit of maroon checked with gold. He is seen to walk down a particular flight of steps, and then disappear.

Rivington Castle

Rivington Castle has long been believed to be haunted by a mysterious white figure. She wanders in a variety of areas from the highest point to the foundation stones. Five men working near the castle very early one morning saw the figure travelling the route from the base of the castle walls up to the top—and repeating the route several times. A local resident also reports that when he takes his little dog for their regular walks up to the grounds of the castle, the dog always pauses by one small bench, wagging her tail enthusiastically and barking. Perhaps the White Lady, taking a rest from her wanderings?

Rivington Pike

A ghostly horseman haunts the moors here and is sometimes identified as Lord Willoughby, a brave Parliamentary captain who refused to submit in battle or, indeed, in death. Others claim that the horseman is the devil himself and a detailed story is offered as proof.

One day, late in the afternoon, some men out hunting took shelter from a storm in a ruined tower. As they waited for the storm to pass, a horseman galloped past and one of the men, Mr. Norton, thought he recognised the rider as a missing uncle, so he quickly mounted his own horse and set off in pursuit. The rest would have followed, if not for the intervention of one of their servants, who held them back and insisted that this was not Norton's uncle, but the spectral horseman long feared in the area.

The servant then explained that his father had been out poaching one night when a similar man on a huge black horse had asked to be taken to the stones known as the Two Lads. When they arrived there, the stranger asked that one of the stones should be lifted and, beneath it, the servant's father had seen a large pit, wherein lived the devil and the smell of the pit was so terrible it had caused him to faint. When he woke, the stranger was gone and the stone was as it had been before.

Once the storm abated, the rest of the hunting party returned to their accommodation for the night and were disturbed to find that Norton had not yet arrived there. They went at once to the Two Lads, and found him unconscious on the ground, looking as if he had been in a terrible fight.

When Norton eventually regained consciousness, he explained that the horseman had indeed been his uncle, at least in part. He had been claimed by the devil and allowed to return to earth only on condition that someone else could be found for the devil's spirit to possess. As Norton had refused to submit, even to save his uncle, the devil would have to hunt for another victim.

ROSSENDALE
Local Legend

Somewhere in the Rossendale Valley lived Old Gamul the woodman. He is the hero of a story that is very strange indeed. Gamul had only one enemy: the wood-keeper. Once, the keeper dug a huge pit, covered it with branches to hide it, and waited for Gamul to fall in. He went back next day, but he had covered his pit so carefully that he forgot where it was and fell into it himself. After a long time, he heard someone coming and cried out for help. To his shame, the passerby who rescued him was none other than Gamul. Gamul let down a rope into the pit but was surprised to rescue a lion, then a serpent, and then an ape, before finally his enemy appeared.

The keeper was very angry that his plan had failed, but he forced a smile and invited Gamul to his house—whereupon he hit him with a club and, believing him dead, threw him out of the house. But Gamul was not dead and when he recovered, he went home and next day resumed his work in the wood. To his surprise, he saw again the ape he had rescued, who helped him in his work. Next, he saw the serpent, who gave him a magic stone. Finally, he saw the lion he had rescued, and the lion led him to a cave that was full of riches.

The keeper was so infuriated at Gamul's sudden riches that he hung himself, and the woodman became Sir Gamul, always ready to help those less fortunate than himself.

SABDEN
Coffin Stone

The Coffin Stone sits upright beside an important prehistoric route across the Pennines and so probably has a much older significance than its later use, which gave it its name. A hundred yards or so up the hill is Our Lady's Well, known for its curative water. Centuries ago, before the church of St. Mary was built at Goldshaw Booth in 1544, mourners would have to carry the coffins of their deceased loved ones to Whalley, along this route. The mourners would rest the coffins at the Coffin Stone and refresh themselves at the well.

SALWICK
Hand and Dagger

This pub on Clifton Road dates from the seventeenth century. It has long been thought to be haunted by a ghost named Fred, although no one knows anything more about him. In the restaurant, upstairs, male voices are sometimes heard when the room is empty and occasionally chairs and tables are rearranged. Beer mats and menu cards have also been known to move. Fred causes only mild disturbances—nothing too scary—but the proprietors of this lovely canal-side pub would love to know more about him.

SAMLESBURY
New Hall Tavern

In the seventeenth century, this pub on Cuerdale Lane was a cobbler's establishment, with a piggery in the buildings behind it. A young boy has often been seen in the bar area, wearing a cobbler's leather apron. Sometimes he has appeared alongside a man wearing a tall black hat. The third ghost in the New Hall Tavern is, unusually, a pig!

Samlesbury Hall

During the Lancashire cotton riots in 1878, a young sub-altern was garrisoned with his company at Samlesbury Hall, near Blackburn. In the early morning, he was awakened by the sound of a woman crying bitterly in the corridor outside his room. He got out of bed to investigate, but could find no one; the next morning he mentioned this to his host and hostess and saw the look that passed between them. He had witnessed the White Lady of Samlesbury Hall.

In 1926, when he was an elderly colonel, he wrote to the *London Morning Post* and told them the whole story. In view of the years that had passed, the colonel may have misremembered the details when he wrote his letter, but he certainly experienced something that morning that he was never able to satisfactorily explain.

In 1960, the papers again carried reports of strange happenings at Samlesbury Hall and on the road close by. Several motorists had reported seeing a woman dressed in white at the roadside—some stopped to offer her assistance or a lift, others saw her walk into the road and were sure they had hit her, only to be shocked when they realised that she wasn't really there. A couple walking their dog saw a woman in a light-coloured coat walking towards them—she passed them without lifting her feet, in effect walking straight through the dog's lead. A bus driver stopped at the bus-stop outside Samlesbury Old Hall to pick up a lady in a white coat, who had promptly disappeared. The driver had then had an argument with the conductor, who swore no one had been waiting at all.

It is assumed that all these incidents were sightings of Lady Dorothy, the White Lady of Samlesbury Old Hall, although the staff at Samlesbury Hall claim never to have seen the White Lady and are sceptical of her existence.

In the sixteenth century, Samlesbury Hall was the seat of the Southworth family, who were Catholics. Like many Lancashire families, they risked their lives by giving sanctuary to priests hiding from the authorities. Sir John Southworth supported Mary Queen of Scots and wished to see her reinstated on the throne. His nephew John was ordained as a priest and later canonised as the last Catholic to die for his faith in England. His son Christopher was an equally devout defender of their faith and it is he who is the villain of this piece, for unfortunately his love of his religion caused him to turn against two of his own family members: Jane and Dorothy. He conspired for Jane to be tried as a witch and he also murdered Dorothy's Protestant lover.

Jane came to be tried as a witch in 1612, because she began to show signs of taking up the Protestant faith. In all, nine Samlesbury people were accused of witchcraft, three of whom, Jane Southworth and Janet and Ellen Bierley, were taken to Lancaster to be tried. The case was regarded as so important that it was tried in the same assize session as the infamous Pendle witch trial.

The main witness was a simple girl of fourteen, Grace Sowerbutts of Samlesbury, the granddaughter of Janet Bierley and the niece of Ellen. Grace accused all three women of bewitching her so that she began to waste away, and she said that her grandmother Janet had turned herself into a black dog that had walked on its hind legs and tried to talk Grace into drowning herself. All three women were accused of taking Grace to a twice-weekly Sabbats (witches' gatherings) on the banks of the River Ribble where they were joined in their demonic parties by "four black things, going upright, and yet not like men in the face…" Fortunately, the judge found Grace's statements hard to believe and cross-examined her. Under pressure, she admitted that she had been persuaded to denounce the women by Christopher Southworth. Jane and the others were acquitted and Christopher's plot against his own sister-in-law was foiled.

Christopher's treatment of his sister Dorothy was to prove even more tragic. Dorothy fell in love with a young man of the de Hoghton family, from nearby Hoghton Towers; he would have been suitable enough had he not renounced his faith in favour of the Church of England. Dorothy's father strictly forbade the union, but true love never will be denied and Dorothy and her lover continued to meet and planned an elopement. Unfortunately, Christopher became aware of this plan, ambushed de Hoghton and his attendant and murdered them outside Dorothy's bedroom window. Dorothy witnessed the awful deed, threw herself from the window and was killed. Another version of the story claims that Dorothy was sent away to a convent on the continent and there went mad with grief and died.

Credence was lent to this story in 1826 when road construction work near the hall uncovered two human skeletons. Unfortunately, the Southworth pedigree shows that Sir John had no daughter named Dorothy. Perhaps she may have married into the family, in which case she would not have been recorded in the pedigree. Not far away is Old Pleasington Hall, and a daughter of the family there was called Dorothy. This Dorothy married a Southworth, then a de Hoghton, then Thomas Ainsworth, who was likewise a Protestant. On the other hand, as mentioned earlier, it was not unusual for families to arrange for any member who had transgressed beyond forgiveness to be totally excised from the records. But despite the difficulty of proving exactly who the White Lady is, if you should be driving down the A677 past the beautiful black and white building that is Samlesbury Hall, be aware that if you see a lady dressed in white standing by the roadside, she isn't really there—particularly if the month is August, for this is the anniversary of her death.

Another ghost haunts the interior of the hall: a male ghost who, apparently, prefers blondes—they feel a gentle tug on their hair. The ghost is thought to be Joseph Harrison who bought the hall in the 1860s. Just after Christmas in 1878, learning by letter that his bank holding all his monies had collapsed, he killed himself with one shot to the head.

When another Lord of Samlesbury died, a man-servant was appointed to stay with the body in the Old Hall before the lord's burial in the churchyard. During the night, the servant awoke to the sound of piano music in the room below, a mournful dirge accompanied by screams of sorrow. The music repeated at intervals and did not finally stop until daylight came. Needless to say, the servant refused to spend another night in the Old Hall.

The bells at Samlesbury Old Hall also have a habit of sounding all by themselves. One employee half a century ago was often disturbed by the courtyard door bell ringing, when no one was waiting outside. On one occasion, he was upstairs by a window and so was sure that no one had come up the drive to the hall, but he still went to open the door when the bell rang—only to find no one there.

The hall was bought in the 1920s by a preservation committee, who soon noticed that the line of old room-bells had a habit of ringing on their own. A member of the committee was walking past the row of bells one day when one of them rang, but on investigation he found that only two other people were in the building and neither was responsible. On another occasion, the caretaker was showing some visitors around the place and, as they approached the oriel window, one of the room-bells rang. One of the visitors investigated, sure he would prove a natural cause, but he could not. Then, as they descended the stairs, another of the party saw a woman wearing an old-fashioned dress and her hair loose, with an odd faintness to her appearance. Assured that no one of that description was actually in the building, the party left convinced they had seen the famous White Lady.

Finally, inside Samlesbury Hall there is a fourteenth-century Green Man, carved into one of the stair panels on the outside of the staircase.

St. Leonard the Less Churchyard

Samlesbury's church was originally intended to be built elsewhere, but the foundations were repeatedly moved by goblins or fairies to the church's current site. Moving them back made no difference; the next night they were shifted once again. In the end, like so many churches in Lancashire and around the country, the builders gave up and the church was erected where it now stands.

There's also a tale about a very old and cracked grave slab in the churchyard, horizontally placed, that is fastened down with puzzling iron bars. The cracks may well be the result of vandalism or simply repeated exposure to inclement weather, but the bars are less easy to explain. Some refer to it as "the witch's grave" and say the iron bars were put in place to keep the witch firmly in her place. Others say that this is the grave of Nan Alker, who had spent her life tormenting her husband Tom with her endless nagging.

Nan Alker had threatened on her deathbed that she would haunt her husband if he dared to take another woman when she was gone. After she had died, Tom buried her decently in the churchyard, under the slab that no doubt at one time bore her name. There were no iron bars at first—they came later. Patient Tom spent many months in peace and quiet after burying Nan but, as time passed, loneliness got the better of him and he began to spend time with a farmer's widow, Ellen Hayes. And then the dreams started, dreams in which his dead wife returned to him, shouting and nagging just as she had threatened. Then, one day, Tom was told that the slab had been moved from his wife's grave—not an easy task! He found help to replace it, but the stone was mysteriously moved several times in the following months and several times it had to be replaced. And the dreams (or nightmares) continued.

Finally, Tom had some iron spikes made, drilled holes in the grave-slab and hammered the spikes deep into the earth. Nan never bothered him again and he and Ellen lived happily ever after.

SAWLEY

Spread Eagle

The tale of Nicholas Gosford describes him as an honest tailor who was a little too fond of his ale. Most of his earnings were spent at the Spread Eagle instead of on his family and he never had enough money for all his needs. One night, a drunken stranger in the Spread Eagle described how a man he knew had come into sudden wealth by selling his soul to the devil. So Nicholas decided to give it a try.

We are not told what method Nicholas used to raise the devil, but it worked. The devil agreed to make a deal with Nicholas; he would claim his soul twenty years hence in return for three wishes right now, made either by Nicholas himself or his wife.

The first wish was used up quickly when Nicholas went home expecting a meal and there was only oatcake and butter to be had. His wife said, "I wish I had a backstone for the fire, so that I could bake." At once, a backstone appeared on the fire and Nicholas was so angered by this waste of a wish that he shouted, "I wish that backstone was smashed to pieces!" And so it was. The third wish was similarly thrown away next morning, when Nicholas wished he had some hot water for his shave.

Twenty years later, the devil came to claim Nicholas's soul. Nicholas complained that it was not a fair exchange, as the wishes had never done him any good and he surely deserved one more. The devil thought about it, then he agreed. But Nicholas had thought about it for longer than the devil. With no hesitation, he pointed at a horse in a nearby field and said he wished the devil were riding into Hell on that horse, never to come back!

The devil—and the horse—disappeared in a flash. As for Nicholas, he had learnt his lesson all those years ago and had saved his money instead of spending it on drink, so he gave up tailoring and bought himself a pub instead. Business was very good, for people came from far and near to meet the man who had tricked the devil.

(See Chatburn for a similar story—but with different wishes.)

SCOTFORTH

Bowling Green Hotel

Many years ago, a family was walking near the Bowling Green Hotel at Scotforth when the mother fell down, claiming she had fallen over a black dog that had got in her way. The rest of the family were quite sure there had been no such dog...

SILVERDALE
Hawes Tarn

An enormous serpent used to live in Hawes Tarn, near Yealand Conyers and Silverdale. When it was hungry, it would leave the Tarn and slither to a large rock known as the Buck Stone, conveniently situated in a field that was often full of sheep. It concealed itself by coiling around the stone and lying still, until a sheep came too close, when it would strike and swallow the sheep whole. When the serpent was eventually killed, the proof of its diet was a wad of wool, lodged inside a hollow tooth.

The Buck Stone, also known as the Rocking Stone, is ten feet high and thirty-three feet around, so the serpent must have been terrifying indeed...

Where did the serpent come from, you may ask? A clue might be found in the name Yealand Conyers, for the area was the dowry of a daughter of William de Lancaster, who married Roger, known as Roger de Conyers. Roger was known and revered in several Durham towns as a dragon-slayer or worm-slayer. This is a strange coincidence. Perhaps a serpent pursued him to the area with the intention of clearing up some unfinished business?

St. John's Church

Many years ago, some monks praying for the recovery of one of their sick brethren noticed a scent in this church—a strong smell of roses. The sick monk recovered. This has happened quite often since; those praying for the recovery of a sick loved one will also smell the distinctive scent of roses, and they will find that their loved one has recovered. By way of explanation, it is claimed that the scent indicates the intercession of St. Teresa of the Roses.

SIMONSTONE
Huntroyd Hall

In 1594, no less than seven members of a Huntroyd family were possessed by evil spirits. Nicholas Starkie and his wife lived in the large house with their two children John and Anne. The children were the first to be afflicted by spirits and an exorcist by the name of Edmund Hartlay was summoned. Hartlay rapidly dealt with the spirits by the use of magical spells, but it seems he was unwilling to leave. He told the

Starkies that only his continued presence in the house would prevent a recurrence of the trouble. He even went so far as to demand forty shillings a year, on top of his free accommodation.

Three years later, Nicholas Starkie was growing increasingly tired of his house guest and told Hartlay he must leave. There was a heated argument and then it became apparent that the two children were once again possessed—as were two of the servants, Starkie's three female wards, and an innocent visitor to the house. All eight began shouting and shrieking, and Hartlay was blamed; it was said that he had breathed the devil into whoever he had kissed in greeting. The "possessions" lasted for days; the afflicted suffered terrifying delusions, such as imagining beasts were inside their own bodies, seeing huge angry dogs before them, and hearing voices. They ran about madly and one even tried to hurl herself from a window. They spoke in strange tongues at great speed, they howled, and shook with fear.

Dr. John Dee, Queen Elizabeth's own astrologer and alchemist, was called to assist in exorcising the afflicted, but he refused to be involved with such meddling, which he saw as conjuring on the part of Hartlay. He suggested that religious men be summoned instead. The two ministers who attended were George More and John Darrell, and it is the latter we have to thank for writing down all that transpired at Cleworth and for giving the poor afflicted people the name "demoniacs." More and Darrell gathered all the demoniacs together and laid them on couches. They brought thirty people to pray with them for an entire day. By the next day, all eight were delivered from their torment, although some of them were reported to bleed from the mouth and nose as the deliverance occurred.

As Edmund Hartlay was clearly responsible for the so-called "demonic possessions," he was tried for witchcraft at Lancaster Castle. At first, the judge could find no basis on which to convict him, despite the trouble he had caused. Then Starkie came forward and swore that he had seen Hartlay draw a magic circle into which he had invited Starkie to step. This kind of witchcraft was a felony so, much as Hartlay denied doing anything of the kind, he was sentenced to death.

Darrell wrote about the case in a book, accusing the family of Starkie's wife (who had been married before, to Thomas Barton of Smithells Hall) of bringing about the whole affair by their prayers. They were Catholics and were said to have prayed for the death of all her male children from both her marriages, so that Cleworth would not be inherited by them. Whatever the reason, Starkie's two children John and Anne suffered no lasting damage from their demonic experiences; Anne grew up and married happily, and John became sheriff of Lancashire.

SINGLETON
Mains Hall

At ancient Mains Hall, now a small hotel and restaurant, a lady is sometimes seen on the first floor, standing at the head of the staircase with a sad expression on her face. She has been called Lily and it is thought she was deserted by her lover. She is often observed to be looking at a particular section of wall where recent excavations uncovered the remains of an original window.

Cavaliers are often seen in the hotel, in the area that was once the main bar. One evening when they were seated at dinner, a cavalier was seen by all twelve hotel guests. Other presences here include a man in riding gear, a lady looking out of a window towards the river, a children's nanny, and many children.

Mains Hall has a religious history; it was once referred to as Monks Hall. It was a regular hiding place for Cardinal Allen, escaping the king's men. The hall contains more than one priest-hide. It is said also that a dozen monks who were lay preachers and farmers here died of plague and were each buried under a separate tree in the grounds. There are many tales of ghostly monks making appearances, both in the hall and outside.

Physical effects of this crowd of spirits are many; objects are moved, whispering voices are heard, doors open and close, and sometimes even lock themselves, and electrical equipment malfunctions despite a new wiring system.

Shard Riverside Inn

The road here crosses the River Wyre smoothly, but once there was a toll bridge, owned by the family who lived in the house beside it. Before the toll bridge was built, crossing the river was only possible by fording it at low tide, or paying a ferryman.

In 1905, Norman Renshaw drowned here, trying to save his beloved dog, Jack. Jack survived and lived for another ten years. Norman and his dog knew the Shard Inn well and indeed the inn is haunted, but not by drowned Norman. It is Jack, his little dog, who still wanders in the bar.

SLAIDBURN
St. Andrew's Church

There are no less than eight Green Men on the seventeenth-century screen inside this church, four on either side.

SLYNE

St. Patrick's Well, Slyne

St. Patrick's Well is close to the house called Belmont. It is known that St. Patrick came to England by ship from Ireland and the many occurrences of his name in this area lend credence to the idea that his ship was wrecked on St. Patrick's Skeer, a treacherous bank off the coast at Heysham. Landing at Heysham, he gave his name to the church and chapel there. Then, progressing north, he needed water and could find none, so he struck the ground with his walking staff and a spring began to flow. The spring was revered for its effects on diseases of the eye.

ST. ANNES

Anthony House

Anthony House is now a prosaic job centre, but its lift is home to a ghostly resident— a workman.

Kilgrimol

Kilgrimol was a small village in an area that is now underwater off the coast of St. Annes. Kilgrimol certainly had a church as early as the twelfth century, for it appears on maps. Earlier still, a story tells of Oswald the Gentle, a Culdee monk at Kilgrimol's Benedictine cell. His name was appropriate for someone who chose a life of service, living apart and taking in the sick and poor, even lepers, when no one else would help them. The Culdees, active in the eighth century, were an Irish order who spent their lives in service to God rather than building up stores of wealth.

The massive storm that devastated the Spanish Armada also devastated this coast and Kilgrimol was deluged, submerged forever. The name alone remains, its memorial a street name in St. Annes. However, legend has it that sometimes the bell from the old church at Kilgrimol can still be heard, over the waves. It is a worrying sound, for it foretells storm and disaster...

Old Links Golf Club

The remains of Kilgrimol's burial ground now lies under the tenth fairway of St. Annes Old Links golf course. Strange occurrences were reported from the Old Links Golf Club in the 1950s. In addition to footsteps and moving furniture, one young waitress staying overnight in the clubhouse was pulled from her bed by unseen hands.

Sand Dunes

Kathleen Breaks's body was found in the dunes on Christmas Eve 1919. Her boyfriend had shot her three times. He was soon caught and charged, however, because he had carelessly left his gun and bloodstained gloves at the scene of the crime. Kitty's ghost has often been seen wandering the dunes.

Wood Street

I once lived in an old house in Wood Street that had been a large, three-storied family home; now we inhabited the top two stories and the ground floor was rented as a shop. My husband worked late into the evenings and my children were always in bed early, so I spent many hours alone. One evening, when I was sewing quietly in the room between the lounge and the kitchen, I felt someone—a woman—standing behind me. Of course, there was no one there. A few weeks later it happened again and then once more, but I told no one, because there was little to say.

This invisible presence was later confirmed by a medium who described me alone in a room, turning my head to see someone who wasn't there. The woman had lived in the house long ago, I was told.

Some time later, I took the proprietor of the shop to see the same medium, who talked about a ghost in her shop. I hadn't told the medium about our connection. Neither had I told my friend about the ghost. To my surprise, my friend agreed that she had indeed felt someone. We were told the ghost's name was "Alice."

A few months later, my small son saw Alice walk through a wall. Too young to explain what he had seen, he ran to a blank wall and banged his fists on it, first on one side of the wall, then on the other. Unwillingly, I asked if he had seen a lady walk through the wall. He nodded and leapt into my arms for a cuddle. Despite my misgivings, I found myself telling him that the lady's name was Alice and she meant no harm.

When we moved from that house, the new owner called me one night, having sought out my number from my friend in the shop. He had turned my sewing-room into an office and was often there late at night. On more than one occasion, he had felt that a woman was in the room with him...

I later visited my old flat. In the blank wall where my son had seen the lady disappear, there was now a door. The new owner had obtained the original plans for the house and put the door back where it had always been.

And some time after that, a different medium visited my new home. She told me a lady was there, but she didn't know why, because the lady wasn't a relative and had nothing to do with my new house—although she approved of the place very much. She told me her name was Alice...

Coincidence?

ST. MICHAEL'S ON WYRE

Old Hall

Near the present St. Michael's Hall, which is really a farm, there used to stand a much grander hall. It was built in 1590 and stood for almost 300 years. One of its most notable residents was Major Ralph Longworth, whose lifelong and distinguished military career included fighting with the Royalist armies against Cromwell's Roundheads at Preston. After his death, at the end of the seventeenth century, Old St. Michael's Hall was repeatedly haunted by his presence, who frightened those living there by banging doors and furniture and, oddly, rattling cutlery. He was also regularly seen outside, parading in the lane by the hall's gates.

Major Longworth's haunting became so persistent and troubling that both the Protestant vicar and Catholic priest were summoned to exorcise his spirit. They laid his ghost under the bridge near the hall, commanding him to lay quiet "so long as the water flows down the hills and the ivy remains green." The hollow in the ground that was Major Longworth's spirit's ultimate resting place can still be seen.

STAINING

Local Legend

An old farmer was ploughing at the break of day when no one else was awake, when suddenly he heard a little cry, soft as a choirboy's voice. "I've broken mi speet!" the little voice cried. The farmer turned to see who owned that lovely voice and saw a tiny girl, as pretty as could be. She was certainly a fairy. In one hand she held a tiny broken spade and in the other some tiny nails and a tiny hammer. She smiled at the farmer and held out the spade and hammer; and the farmer, not quite believing what he was seeing, gently took them from her. Then he sat down and, as was clearly required of him, he took the little hammer and the little nails and he mended the tiny spade. When he had finished, the fairy gave him a smile so sweet it shone like the sun, before taking her spade and giving him a handful of silver. That was the only time the old farmer ever saw a fairy, but he never tired of telling the story…

Staining Hall

Staining Hall is an ancient place. At one time it had a moat and according to tradition was once honoured by a visit from King John, when he was staying at Lancaster Castle. It also has a boggart.

The story of Staining Hall's boggart seems to stem from the time of the Jacobite Rebellions, when many hundreds of brave men lost their lives fighting for their beliefs. The story says that a Scotsman was cruelly killed near Staining Hall and buried near a tree, in the vicinity of the old moat.

The ghost of the old Scotsman was seen many times over several centuries, a sad and forlorn figure wandering around the area; but, as time passed, his ghost grew less distinct and appeared less often, until finally it disappeared entirely. However, his memory was kept alive by the tree that marked the site of his burial, because it perfumed the soil around it with the unmistakable smell of thyme. In those days, thyme was believed to ease the passing of the dying and so was used to fragrance coffins. It was also carried by warriors as it was thought to magically impart courage—but the legend gives another reason for the scent at the Scotsman's grave. It is said that his wife was travelling from Scotland to be by his side and he desperately tried to stay alive until she arrived. With his dying breath, he called out, "Time! Give me time!"

(See Freckleton, the Road Ghost, for another mention of this phrase.)

STALMINE
Local Legend

A boggart at Stalmine was known as the "Hall Knocker" and he made himself useful at many of the farms in the area. He must eventually have started to misbehave, however, as most boggarts do, for he is said to have been laid under the threshold stone of Stalmine Church.

STYDD

Stydd Almshouses

Near the Church of St. Peter and St. Paul are Stydd's almshouses. They were built in 1728, using money left in the will of John Sherburne of Stoneyhurst, for the purpose of providing housing for local, poor Catholic women. Residents were also provided with fuel and money. To this day, the almshouses still provide shelter for Catholic ladies. The old well still survives in the grounds. The houses were described by the architectural historian Pevsner as "very curious and very engaging" and it is thought that the pillars in the front of the almshouse building were once part of an old Roman fort.

One night, a resident heard a knock on her door and opened it to see a tall man, his face hidden in the cowled hood of a cloak—who vanished almost as soon as he was seen. Perhaps it was John Sherburne himself?

THORNTON

Ashley Conservative Club

There have been reports here of footsteps in the upstairs games room, when it is known to be empty. Snooker balls have sometimes been seen to move on their own. The ghost causing these effects has not been seen, but has been christened Harold.

Local Lane

One evening, in 1939, two women were cycling along a country lane in Thornton when they saw a light approaching and, assuming it to be a delivery van, they stopped and pulled their bikes to the side of the narrow lane. The light came towards them and passed them, but there was no sound—and no van. They told their parents when they returned home and to their surprise they were told that the light had been seen before. It was rumoured to be seen when war was approaching...

(See also Bispham, Robin's Lane—the lane skirts Thornton and may be the location of this story.)

Local Legend

One day, a milkmaid in Thornton was peacefully milking her master's cow. She was very surprised when an invisible hand suddenly placed a jug and a sixpenny piece carefully at her side. It was clear that the sixpence was supposed to be in payment for a full jug of milk, so the milkmaid filled the jug and tucked the sixpence in her pocket. She told no one about her experience, however, for her father had always warned her that if she ever had dealings with a fairy, she must not tell a soul. Also, she was afraid of being thought mad.

Later that day, she saw that the jug had vanished and thought that was the end of it, but a few days later, the invisible hand once again placed a jug and a sixpence at her side. Once again, she filled the jug and kept the sixpence, but said nothing to anyone about how she came by it. Over the next few weeks, more jugs and sixpences were brought to her and, as it became a regular occurrence, the young milkmaid found it harder and harder to keep it to herself.

Her downfall came when her boyfriend asked her to marry him. She was thrilled and could not help but tell him about the fine nest-egg she had built up from the fairy sixpences. And that was her mistake—for once she had spoken about the friendly fairy and its generous gifts, the fairy never came to buy milk from her again.

Pennystone Rock

Once, the coastline of the Fylde was at least a mile and a half farther out to sea. The land was known as Thornton Marsh and beyond it a village thrived: Singleton Thorpe. There were several large standing stones here that were said to have once been a "Druidical Circle." All the stones bore names: Old Mother's Head, Bear and Staff, Carlin and the Colts, Higher Jingle, and Lower Jingle.

The largest stone was known as the Penny Stone. It stood beside the village's pub, whose owner was the first in the Fylde to offer the newfangled "beer." The drink differed from ale because of the addition of hops, and people came from far and wide to try it. The pub owner fixed a large, iron ring to the Penny Stone, to give riders somewhere to tether their horses. His beer was so strong and so tasty, he could sell it at a penny a pint—instead of the usual twopence a gallon—and legend has it that this is how the stone acquired its name of Pennystone Rock.

The entire village of Singleton Thorpe was destroyed in July of 1588 by the same storm that destroyed the invading Spanish Armada. Other stones of the "Druidical Circle" may have been washed away, such was the force of the storm and the vicious tidal surge, but some remained, including the Penny Stone Rock. It is too far away from the shore to be explored, except by the most foolhardy.

The spit of red clay on which the village of Singleton Thorpe stood was also washed away and deposited elsewhere. It became known from the colour of its earth as the Red Bank. This led to a local saying, "Penny stood, Carlin fled, Red Bank ran away," and in memory, the village of Bispham's main thoroughfare is called Red Bank Road.

The inhabitants of the village set up a new home safely inland (at Singleton) and the Singleton family moved to Whittingham and built Chingle Hall. But Sir Richard Singleton never recovered from the shock and dismay of losing his beloved home and some believe he died of his grief. It is said that he haunts the area around Pennystone Rock to this day.

Police Station

The old police station in Thornton, which is now privately owned and thus inaccessible, has long been rumoured to have a ghost. Heavy footsteps were often heard in an upstairs room. Nothing is known of the ghost's true identity, but he was nicknamed Fred.

THURNHAM

Ashton Hall

Ashton Hall on Ashton Road is currently the club-house for Lancaster Golf Course, but its history stretches back at least to the fourteenth century. The oldest part still standing is the red sandstone tower house, originally built by Roger of Poitou, then inhabited by the Lawrence family, who lived here for over two centuries. It has unusual smaller towers at each corner, set at angles. At some point in the 1500s the tower gained battlements and the present windows also date from that time—the outlines of the original windows are still visible. The tower house was grand enough to host royalty; King James I and Charles II both stayed there in their time. Another building was added in the seventeenth century but was demolished in 1856, to make way for the limestone mansion-style building through which one enters the club-house.

It is the ancient tower house that is of interest here; the tower and particularly the battlements are haunted by a White Lady. She was the wife of a Jacobite sympathiser, whose husband was so jealous and mistrustful of her that when he went to war he gave orders that she was to be locked in the highest room in the house and kept there until his return. Or perhaps he simply feared for her safety and her imprisonment was his way of protecting the woman he loved. Whatever the reason, the result was that the unfortunate woman died in her cell, waiting vainly for her lord and master to return and release her.

Fate took revenge on the family for the White Lady's unfortunate demise. Ever since then, the estate passed down the female line of the family; never was it inherited by a man.

TOCKHOLES

Churchyard

In the churchyard is a large stone that supports what is left of an ancient preaching cross. The cross is precisely dated at 684 AD. It is known as the Toches Stone and it is from this that the town takes its name. The stone is visited by those who need to have their wishes granted, and touching the stone while wishing guarantees a good result.

(See St. Bartholomew's Church in Colne for another Touch Cross.)

Hollinshead Hall

Near the ruins of eighteenth century Hollinshead Hall is a holy well that is of great interest. It is covered by a seventeenth-century well-house that is believed to have been a restoration

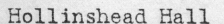

of an earlier, medieval construction. The restoration may well have been carried out by the Radcliffe family as their coat of arms can still be seen on one of the walls. Sadly, the well-house is often found to be locked, but two windows allow a good view of the interior. Under a lovely vaulted ceiling are two large stone baths holding water and a decorative lion's head from which water would have gushed. (Now it does little more than drip.) Many ledges and niches set into the walls would, in medieval times, have held bread for the hungry or offerings from those praying for a cure from the healing waters.

There is a strong tradition that this was an ancient holy well, used since medieval times by pilgrims who believed in the water's healing properties. Like many such wells, its water was believed to be especially good for ailments of the eyes. It may well have been used as a baptistery in the turbulent sixteenth century and would certainly have been dedicated to a saint, but it now carries no name apart from "the holy well."

Whilst there is a belief that pilgrims have visited this site since medieval times, it is likely that they actually came to a second pool just above the well-house, whose ancient stone lining betrays its age. Water from this pool feeds the baths in the well-house and, as access is unrestricted, a visit is recommended.

Lastly, the well-house is believed to be haunted, but by whom or by what, there is no clue.

Red Lee Farmhouse

An inscribed stone over the lintel of the main door proclaims that this farmhouse was built in 1674 by a couple named Aspden. The house is reported to be haunted by boggarts and one of the flags in the stone floor is avoided because no butter would ever come if the churn was placed there.

Royal Arms

There's a friendly smoke-piping ghost in this pub on Tockholes Road and he is generally seen sitting quietly in the corner. The building only became a pub in the 1930s, when it was converted from two adjoining cottages.

TORRISHOLME
Torrisholme Hall

Notes and Queries is a respected scholarly journal that has published collections of short articles since 1849. The fact that it publishes only factual stories lends great weight to the following, found in an early edition. The narrator had not heard any hint of a story or legend about Torrisholme Hall prior to her experience there. As was the habit in days gone by, the name of the hall concerned was changed to Bair Hall, but as discussion of this case continued in later editions of the journal, the true location was shown quite clearly to be Torrisholme Hall.

Two ladies stayed overnight at Torrisholme Hall, in an old-fashioned bedroom complete with an old press wardrobe. The narrator woke very early and saw an old gentleman in an armchair. Convinced that this was a delusion, she closed her eyes and, when she reopened them, the old man, complete with armchair, had changed position and was now seated against the bedroom door. She woke her friend, who could see nothing—indeed, the apparition had vanished.

The ladies were so distressed by this experience that they went quickly to their hostess's bedroom, where they told her what had happened. She was unsurprised and asked if they had opened the wardrobe at all; yes, in fact they had. Their hostess then explained that her uncle, now deceased, did not like anyone to interfere with his wardrobe, which still contained his clothes. Another effect of his presence was that it seemed pointless to lock doors at night, as they were often found open again by morning. His presence disturbed other family members, she said, but she herself did not mind him.

TRAWDEN

Lad o' Crow Hill

Above Trawden, on Crow Hill, there is a curious stone bearing the inscription "Lad Orscarr On Crow Hill." This is probably a boundary stone, but the inscription is less easy to explain. It is said that a young boy lost his way and died on this spot and, as his identity was unknown, it fell to the parish to bury him. But which parish? For the boy lay at the boundaries of three parishes: Haworth, Stanbury and Trawden. Trawden eventually relented and buried the boy, thus claiming a little more land for their own.

(See Wiswell Moor and Jeppe Knave's Grave for another burial at a spot where three parishes meet.)

Local Legend

One long-ago Christmastime, a farmer here was sure witchcraft was at work because his cattle, usually so calm in their stalls, were unsettled to the point of injuring themselves with their repeated turnings and stampings. Suspicion fell on an old woman who lived nearby, although the farmer could see no reason why she might have cursed him or his cattle.

Then, one day, some boys playing football were pestered by a bad-tempered cat and they chased it, but when one of them kicked at the hissing creature, it disappeared in a flash of flame and smoke! The cat was never seen again, but soon they heard that the old woman suspected of being a witch had mysteriously broken a leg...

TUNSTALL

St. John the Baptist Church

There is a Green Man here, in one of the fifteenth century stained glass windows.

TURTON

Bull's Head

In 1997, this pub on Bradshaw Road featured in the local newspapers because it seemed to be very haunted. The ghost was thought to be female, although it was difficult to be certain, as those who had reported seeing it were only able to describe it as having long grey hair and wearing a long grey smock. Witnesses included the landlord, his son, and five of their regular customers. All of them saw the apparition in one of the pub's front rooms, where it would drift across the room and disappear through the wall close to the fireplace. Many other people had reported feeling a chill in this room, despite the central heating. Other more physical occurrences included kitchen equipment and crockery being removed from their shelves, and music coming from the empty rooms upstairs.

Intriguingly, the landlord had also found an old photograph in the pub, dating from 1921 and showing the exterior of the pub itself. In the photograph, a misty white form could be seen standing at one of the first-floor windows.

Hanging Stone

A large stone here is known as the Hanging Stone, but others know it as the Giant's Stone, as legend says it was thrown by a giant from Winter Hill across the valley. They say that the marks of the giant's hand can still be seen upon it: depressions made by the strength of his fingers as he grasped the huge boulder. It measures fourteen feet by almost six and a crude cross is carved into the surface.

Turton Tower

Turton Tower now houses Blackburn Museum. The original Tower dated from the fourteenth century, but it was entirely renovated in 1835, and few traces of the original construction can be seen today. The many ghosts, however, remain.

Upstairs, near the Chetham Room, people have felt the sweep of a woman's long skirts brushing past them and the rustling of stiff silk can also be heard. At night, there are heavy atmospheres and strange noises, especially in the Ashworth Room. An antique rocking cradle brought here from Bradshaw Hall is sometimes heard rocking all by itself.

Outside, a ghostly horse-drawn coach races across the moorland where once there was a Roman road. It drives up to the old Tower entrance, before vanishing. A lady and her dog have been seen walking outside—so solid is the apparition that one elderly man raised his hat to the lady, who promptly disappeared. A man has also been seen, apparently waiting for a bus. One bus driver who stopped for him was mystified when he did not board the bus and could no longer be seen anywhere in the vicinity.

An old lintel stone lies in the garden, brought here when Timberbottom Farm was demolished. Timberbottom was also known as Skull House, for it was home to two skulls found by the farmer, who chose to keep them in the house resting on the family Bible. One of the skulls was very old and fragile, but still in one piece, whilst the other bore obvious signs of having been severely damaged by a sharp instrument. They were rumoured to be the remnants of a tragic event when a husband killed his wife and then himself. When alarming things began to happen in the farmhouse, the farmer tried to get rid of them, but without success. The skulls were several times buried in Bradshaw Chapel's graveyard, they were also thrown into the river, but they always had to be brought back because the Farm's occupants had no peace without them.

ULNES WALTON

Gradwells

Croston Farm and its grounds are now home to the Royal Umpire Caravan Park. It was once better known as Gradwells, after the Catholic family whose home it was centuries ago. It was a very Catholic house; many members of the Gradwell family became priests, and other priests knew that it was a safe house. One priest in particular, Father Winckley, had a close connection to the family and a priest-hole was constructed for him under the hearth of the main hall. His memory is preserved by a stone cross standing in the grounds.

Croston Farm also has a Grey Lady, commonly called the Sarscowe Lady, who is the ghost of a young girl who lived at nearby Sarscowe Farm. She was Father Winckley's lover, but of course that was a secret. Naturally, their secret love was destined not to last and the end, when it came, was a double tragedy. First the priest sickened with a fever and lost his life. Then the bereft girl died after developing a fever herself and wandering in her sickened state, falling into a well on the grounds. As the well was forty feet deep, the fall was certainly enough to have killed her.

Local people avoided Gradwell's on their journeys home, for fear they would witness the ghost of the girl on her way to the well where she met her death. The Sarscowe Lady was also often seen inside the house, her long skirts rustling as she made her way down the staircase, but the last sighting of her was in 1958. Coincidentally, this was the day that Father Winckley's memorial cross was moved from its place in the orchard to a new situation nearer the house. On that day, a bus driver stopped at a bus stop at the end of the drive, in order to pick up a woman standing there—a woman who then could not be found. The driver was mystified, especially when his conductor said he had never seen her in the first place. The coincidence was noted and the stone cross returned to its original site.

In the years since then, heavy breathing has been heard in the barn next to the farm and, once, stones fell out of the air from no apparent source.

Praying Crosses

Praying Crosses were so called because they were used as places to rest coffins during their journey to churches. In Ulnes Walton, there are two stones that were the bases of such crosses, although the crosses themselves have long since ceased to exist. One can be seen behind Lostock Bridge.

The second cross-base, still known as the Roecroft Cross, has an amusing story attached to it. Work was being done to widen the road, and in order to preserve the stone, it was moved to the opposite side of the road where it would be safer. Overnight, it moved back again. This happened several times—until some local boys dressed themselves as ghosts and moved it themselves. This time, perhaps recognising that it was actually being treated with respect, the stone stayed where it was!

UPHOLLAND

A Cottage

A young governess living here in 1807 kept a diary that survives to this day. In the diary, Miss Ellen Weeton recorded that when her mother had died and she was living in their cottage alone, she often heard the sound of breathing coming from her late mother's room. She fought her fear and went into the room to satisfy herself that no living presence was there. As the days passed and the sound happened again and again, she became quite used to it and even found it a comfort.

Church Street

Over a century ago, a house next to the White Lion Inn became known locally as "the Ghost House." Night after night the house was full of flashes of light, strange noises, and many times stones were thrown. It all began when Mrs. Winstanley, the resident there, was about to cook a meal for her family of seven children. She was having trouble with the fire, whose flames were a rainbow of colours, and she blamed the children, thinking they must have put paraffin or something of the kind on the fire. Much as they pleaded their innocence, she chased them out of the house.

That night, two of the boys went to bed as usual, but were repeatedly disturbed because the curtains, which hung on a simple bamboo rod, kept falling onto their bed. Then knocks were heard in the room, a brick fell from the fireplace, and lights flashed, although the house had no power source beyond candle and lamplight.

This was the beginning of nightly disturbances. The performances became so regular that local people would gather outside, from where they could easily hear heavy stones being thrown and see the mysterious lights. The story was widely reported in newspapers across the country, including the *Derby Daily Telegraph* on Tuesday 16 August 1904. The headline read: "The Lancashire Ghost. A Whole Village For Audience." The report said that although many of the people standing outside came to laugh, they soon stopped laughing when they were invited into the house to see the mayhem the "ghost" had caused. A bricksetter had been called in to investigate the walls, but had found no explanation for the mysterious noises.

A week later, an article in the *Manchester Courier* said that a local resident, aged eighty, had pointed out that the knockings and stone throwing were not new; they had been happening at intervals for years. A local councillor who had made a study of such things had investigated this most recent outbreak, observing the phenomena closely and performing some experiments. He confidently stated that the occurrences had not been caused by any of the family. In one of his experiments he had placed a tiny piece of paper on top of a stone that was on a shelf, making sure the boys who slept in the room did not see what he had done. When the light was extinguished, noises were heard and the stone was found to have been thrown onto the bed—but the tiny piece of paper still lay on top of it.

The same article also quoted the eldest son of the family, who asserted that the phenomena had stopped a few days previously. There had been no knockings or stones for a few nights. He did not know what had caused them, neither did he know why they had stopped.

At one point, it was suggested that the cause may have been the ghost of George Lyon, a notorious highwayman who is buried in the graveyard opposite the house. We will never know for sure because the house no longer exists. It is interesting, though not necessarily relevant to the haunting, that when the house was demolished in 1927, it became apparent that it was of very ancient construction. Its roof was made of whole tree branches laced together.

WALTON-le-DALE
St. Leonard's Churchyard

In 1560, three men met in this churchyard with the intention of bringing a corpse back to life. The corpse rose up, revealed the site of hidden treasure, and made a variety of predictions. The men were the famous occultist Dr. John Dee of Manchester, his close associate Edward Kelly, and the seer Paul Wareing. A very famous, very old engraving shows this event.

There is another story about this church—or rather, about a clergyman who lived here once upon a time. This clergyman was very studious, but his studies were of dubious quality, and whilst he did give his time freely to those parishioners who needed his advice and ministrations, he was suspected of being involved in rather blacker arts than a man of God should have been.

One day a package of peculiar bottles arrived at the clergyman's house and news of it travelled quickly, passed from mouth to mouth and changing along the way, until the story eventually described how the clergyman had, with the aid of the contents of those bottles, successfully raised the devil.

The parishioners began to avoid the clergyman, crossing the road if they saw him approaching, and children ran away. Then it was noticed that the clergyman had begun to spend a great deal of time with Old Abraham, a man who had old knowledge of herbal remedies and traditional spells. Abraham was respected by the villagers, who trusted his knowledge of herbal lore, but his intense friendship with the clergyman worried them—for if he knew how to heal with herbs, surely he would also know how to harm?

During one of their talks, the clergyman mentioned an old tradition he had heard, that anyone waiting out the night in a church porch on Christmas Eve would be guaranteed to see visions of those destined to pass away during the coming year. The pair agreed to meet in the church porch and see if such an experiment would work.

They met close to midnight in the porch and after performing various rituals and uttering certain prayers, they settled down to wait. Very soon, they realised that their experiment had worked, for they saw a procession of ghosts walking through the churchyard, ghosts whose faces were all recognisable as parishioners. Then, suddenly, the clergyman fell to the ground in a dead faint. The last ghost, Old Abraham now saw, had the face of the clergyman himself.

The clergyman left Walton-le-Dale soon afterwards and Old Abraham received news that he had died, after a terrible fever. The parishioners heard the story of the Christmas Eve vigil and were constantly begging Abraham to tell them who else he had seen, but he would not. He had to live out the whole year unable to share his knowledge, watching those around him die before the year was out, just as he had seen.

The following Christmas Eve, several parishioners came to him and offered to accompany him for another Christmas Eve vigil in the church porch...but Abraham, wisely, refused.

WARTON
(NEAR BLACKPOOL)

Wrea Brook Court

Wrea Brook Court is home to HM Land Registry. During the construction of the building in 1994, lights were often switched on by some unknown hand. This happened so often that an explanation was sought and a ghost, Black Bob, was blamed. He was, apparently, a US airman who had been murdered at that place.

WARTON
(NEAR CARNFORTH)

Fairy Hole

The Fairy Hole is on the east face of Warton Crag. It was anciently occupied and human remains were found here many years ago. The cave extends far into the rock and it is said it may even go as far as Leighton Hall. Tales of fairies seen here include details of piles of precious metals, silver or gold, and sightings of the fairies washing their linen.

WATERFOOT
Railway Inn

The ghost of a Woman in Grey haunts this pub on Bacup Road, appearing in bedrooms and sometimes removing bedclothes from sleeping guests. Sometimes her footsteps are also heard. She is known to the hotel staff as Jane.

WEETON

Eagle and Child

One of the oldest pubs in the Fylde, the Eagle and Child at Weeton on Singleton Road was built in 1585, and there are many relics from older times on the premises, such as an ancient sword that was uncovered during renovation work. There is also a resident ghost known as Murph, who has frightened many customers with his moaning! He is thought to be a highwayman from London who somehow found his way to Weeton and stayed here, hiding from his crimes and his pursuers.

Local Field

Weeton is graced by a "Hairy Boggart" that was unintentionally released from an ancient cairn by a farmer ploughing his field. His horses were so frightened by the experience that the farmer never dared to investigate the spot further. Many years passed before the stones comprising the cairn were appropriated for re-use in building—many urns and pieces of pottery were then unearthed.

WEIR

Local Legend

In this area of Bacup, there was once a young woman who was married to an old man and dissatisfied with her lot. When night came, she would steal away from her husband's bed and go wandering, but where she went was a mystery.

A neighbouring farmer was suffering nightly visitations from someone—or something—that would overturn milk cans and steal the cream. One night, he stayed awake with his son, determined to catch the thief. In the early hours of the morning, a black cat crept in through a window and the farmer and his son attacked it energetically with pots and pans. At last, the cat, battered and bruised, managed to escape.

Next morning, the old man made no comment as he watched his young wife bathing her cuts and bruises. He had a feeling she would never be wandering abroad at night again.

WEST BRADFORD

Barn

In the 1820s, workmen dismantling an old barn at West Bradford came across a piece of paper, folded and secreted in the rafters. The strange symbols upon it were deciphered by a scholar from the British Museum and found to be a "magic square," made up of six rows of six squares each, all of them containing numbers. The numbers in each row added up to 111, so the total was 666, the ultimate magical number. Elsewhere on the paper were many astrological and magical symbols and also words.

The whole piece was a charm and it ended with the following words in a mixture of Greek and Latin, which only add to its mysterious nature: "As it is said in the seventeenth chapter of St. Matthew, at the twentieth verse, By faith ye may remove mountains: be it according to faith, if there is, or ever shall be, witchcraft or evil spirit, that haunts or troubles this person, or this place, or these cattle, I adjure thee to depart, without disturbance, molestation, or trouble in the least, in the name of the Father, and of the Son, and of the Holy Ghost. Amen."

It is not known which of the local "wise men" was called upon to prepare this charm, or what events caused it to be necessary...

WHALLEY

St. Mary's Well

This well was visited by the faithful every May Day—the old religion mingling with the new.

Surey Demoniac

The Surey was a building resembling a barn that was used as a kind of village hall, a place for communal activities. The demoniac was one Richard Dugdale.

In 1689, this young man was just nineteen, still living with his parents in Whalley and employed as a gardener. He had always been known as a good actor, with some talent as a ventriloquist, but amongst his peers, this seems to have gone largely unnoticed when he began to act as though demons were possessing him. Richard was stricken with fits that terrified those who witnessed them because he raged against God as if he were indeed inhabited by a demon. Yet when sane he prayed to God most sincerely and begged that fast-days be undertaken on his behalf, to save his soul.

Several ministers were called to attend the possessed boy and one of the first things they did was interview his parents, who told them an astonishing story. Several months before, they said, at the traditional rush-bearing celebrations, Richard had taken a lot of drink and appealed to the devil to make him the best dancer in Lancashire. When he went home, he had many visions of evil spirits and demons who offered him all kinds of treasures if he would seal his pact with the devil—which he duly did.

During his fits, his body would shake uncontrollably, he would speak in languages unknown to him and his voice varied between high-pitched and very deep. It is said that he would vomit stones, sometimes. When it came to the dancing, for which he had sold his soul in the first place, he could leap so high and so often that those who saw him were in no doubt that this was the devil's work.

Richard often enacted his fits of "possession" in the Surey in front of a willing audience numbering, on occasion, several hundred people. In one report, the element of acting or performing is clear to see. Richard would take a blanket and wrap it around himself, arranging one of the corners over his head so that with one flick of the head it would fall over his face. He would dance about the Surey, coming close to the most gullible of his audience, and flick the blanket over his face quite suddenly, making them jump. Then he would flick the blanket back again, stare at the ceiling and quickly turn away. He had his audience entranced.

His family, especially his sisters, were suspected of being accomplices in his act; when considering his regurgitation of stones and other small articles, it was noticed that there were several nooks and crannies in the Surey where such articles could be hidden by his sisters, so that he could dance over to them and retrieve them as necessary, under cover of his blanket. Another contemporary of Richard claimed he had heard Richard say he had been taught these tricks by a witch, Sadler's wife.

At last, Richard announced that he could stand his torments no longer and he demanded that if he were not cured by March 25, he should be killed, to end his misery. In fact, his last fit occurred the day before that date. It was claimed that a medicine administered by one Dr. Chew was in part responsible for this cure. The clergy, however, claimed the cure as evidence for the power of prayer.

Swan Hotel

Soon after the Swan Hotel was built, a young girl named Mary was employed as scullery maid. Mary was very simple-minded but still an attractive girl. Sadly, this combination led to her being seduced by a hotel guest and later finding that she was with child.

The landlord of the Swan, a man named Cunningham, felt sorry for poor Mary and tried to help, but the solution he suggested was not an easy one. He told Mary that she was too simple-minded ever to care properly for a baby and so he would find someone to adopt it. Mary must have been grateful for his help—and for not being turned out into the cold—but neither had considered the emotional pain Mary would go through when she had to give her child away.

When the child was born, only to be taken from her, Mary sank into a grief so deep that she simply could not escape it. Eventually, she took her own life in the Swan Hotel. Cunningham, who had only tried to help, sank into his own pit of grief and guilt for being the cause of Mary's death and, in the end, he moved away from Whalley and never returned. The ghost of Mary, a sad and simple girl, remained at the Swan Hotel.

Whalley Abbey

This Cistercian Abbey was first established in the thirteenth century, next to the medieval church that still survives. The Abbey was dissolved in 1537, and its last abbott, John Paslew, was executed at Lancaster Castle. His crime was his involvement in the Pilgrimage of Grace, which was regarded as treason, but few local people thought it a just punishment, especially as he was around seventy years of age and already in failing health. No doubt his execution was deemed to be an example to others who might also be considering resistance to the Dissolution.

There is in existence an ancient manuscript that tells a remarkable ghost story concerning John Paslew. A monk named Edward Howarth died on May 9, 1520, and after his death he appeared to Abbot Paslew, telling him exactly how long he himself had left to live. He told him he would not live longer than sixteen years. In March of 1537, Paslew was hanged at Whalley.

Abbott John Paslew's own ghost has often been seen around the abbey, particularly in the cloisters of the abbots' lodgings. He has also been seen by travellers on nearby roads and it is even thought that he once appeared in a photograph. A dark shadow on a photo taken over forty years ago by a professional photographer (employed by the *Clitheroe Advertiser*) has never been adequately explained.

The abbot is not the only ghost to be seen here; a whole group of monks has been witnessed walking from the south transept towards the abbey's choirstalls and plainchant has been heard, when there is clearly no source for the singing.

After the Abbey was dissolved, the Abbots House passed into the hands of Ralph Assheton, whose remodelling made it more of an Elizabethan manor house. It remained privately owned until 1923, when it was bought by the Church of England. It is now home to a retreat and a conference centre. In this ancient building, doors are known to close by themselves, footsteps are heard on the stone floors, and many overnight visitors have reported seeing a disturbing bluish cloud of light that lasts for some time before fading.

There are also two female ghosts here. The first is seen in the abbey grounds, but she has also visited the resident of a house very close by. He described her as very beautiful and wearing clothes that were clearly of the medieval period. She is said to have been a nun, kept at the abbey and abused by some of the monks, finally murdered when she tried to escape.

The second female ghost is thought to be the wife of Ralph Assheton, who once owned the abbey. She appears at one of the Abbey windows and is sometimes seen standing before the main hall's fireplace.

Whalley Church has not just one, but three ancient crosses. There are two explanations for their origins. The first, from an ancient monk, says that St. Augustine himself came here and so a church was built and three crosses carved by local stonemasons. Historically, it is more likely that the missionary Paulinus was responsible for the religious settlement, not Augustine—but the crosses would seem to have been erected a century later. The carved designs on these crosses have been said to show influences from Irish Norwegians who settled in Lancashire in the tenth century.

There was once another cross at Whalley, but it was pulled down in 1642 by two men for reasons unknown, but which perhaps were not entirely respectful, because one of them was crushed by it as it fell.

Inside the church there is also a Green Man, carved on the fifteenth century misericord.

WHITEWELL

Fair Oak Circle

Near Fair Oak Farm, this is the largest of a number of possible ancient settlement sites in the area. At nearby Whitewell and Dinkling Green are fairies so the name of this farm and the circle site are full of suggestion…

Fairy Holes Cave

Set in a wooded landscape, a large cave and two smaller ones here are known as the Fairy Holes. Stone tools and some bones were found here, indicating that the caves were used for shelter in very early times. The items have been dated as Bronze Age. The ambience of the place is doubtless what led to their picturesque name.

Hodder Gorge
(A CAVE)

One day a midwife was brought here from Clitheroe to attend a woman in her labour. The woman's husband said that secrecy was paramount but that she would be rewarded handsomely, so she agreed to wear a blindfold so that she would not see her destination. She was taken into a tidy little cottage at Hodder Gorge where her blindfold was removed and she assisted at the birth of a fine baby.

When the baby was born, an old woman gave the midwife a box of ointment and asked her to anoint the baby all over—but to be careful not to get any of it in her eyes. The midwife wondered at this, but did as she was told, until her eye started to itch and she could not avoid rubbing it and a little of the ointment thus made its way into her eye. Then she saw the place differently; the tidy cottage was actually a bare and uncomfortable cave and the mother of the baby was clearly a fairy, as were the husband and the old woman. The midwife managed to stay calm and did not give away her secret. She was paid in fairy gold, blindfolded once again and taken home.

Some time later, the midwife was at market one day when she realised that someone was trying to steal apples from her basket. It was none other than the fairy husband! When the midwife shouted at him, accusing him of stealing, the fairy husband looked at her hard. "Which eye do you see me with?" he asked—and when she told him, the fairy touched it and from that time on, the midwife never saw the fairies again.

(See Staining, Local Legend, for a similar story.)

Saddle Bridge

This bridge over Bashall Brook is also known locally as the Fairy Bridge. The story says that a woodcutter was running to escape a pack of witches and, as there was no bridge across the Brook, it seemed he would soon be caught. The fairies of this place, seeing his plight, made a bridge instantly, by magic, and it is that very same bridge that stands there today.

WINTER HILL

Two Lads Cairns

Once there were two cairns here that were locally known as the "Two Lads," but a hundred years ago, the stones were rearranged to make the platform that stands there now. One legend says that the two lads were members of the Pilkington family who lost their way and died here. Another legend records the same fate befalling two much more ancient princes. Roby's *Traditions of Lancashire* tells of a ghostly horseman who roams here.

Close by is Scotsman's Stump, an iron post bearing an inscribed plate. It is a memorial to George Henderson, a twenty-one-year-old pedlar, who was murdered here in 1838. Henderson was Scottish by birth but was working as a salesman for a Blackburn draper. James Whittle, twenty-two, was charged with his murder in April 1839.

WISWELL MOOR

Jeppe Knave's Grave

This place is said to be the resting place of Jeppe Curteys (Geoffrey Curtis), a criminal who was beheaded for his crime in 1327. Once he was captured and killed, no town or village would take responsibility for his burial and so he was taken up to Wiswell Moor to be buried in a spot where three parishes meet.

In fact, the boundary between the aforesaid "three parishes" is some distance away and the pile of stones, marked as "Jeppe's Grave" by a small cross, may actually be a prehistoric monument—a Neolithic chambered tomb. If the latter is true, its size indicates a burial of someone very important indeed.

In Jeppe Curteys time, 1327, death by beheading was a sentence handed down only to nobility. Perhaps Jeppe Curteys was no common "knave" and was buried in this ancient tomb to mark his place in society?

(See Trawden and the Lad o' Crow Hill for another burial at a spot where three parishes meet.)

WITHNELL

Broadwood

In April 1921, newspapers all over the country featured a story about a ghost haunting a cottage here, one of three at the end of a lane past the parish church. The ghost was supposed to be a local woman who had been murdered twenty years previously, before the cottages had been built and when the area was just a field.

The apparition wore a dark dress and had long, dark hair, heavy black eyebrows, and was generally seen in the early hours. Mr. Forshaw, owner of the afflicted cottage, reported that the ghost had been seen three or four times a week, first just by himself, but later by other members of his family. One of the scariest occurrences was experienced by his daughter, who saw the ghost in her bedroom. The ghost said: "Follow me," and so the girl did, finding herself a few moments later downstairs and quite alone. The neighbours also agreed that the house was haunted; they had several times seen the poor ghostly woman leave the house and walk into the nearby fields.

A slightly different version of this story was related in the *Hull Daily Mail* in the April of 1933, making the point that the ghost, which traditionally was seen during Lent each year, had not been seen for some seven years. The story referred to the ghost as "Wigan Liz" and explained that she was the ghost of a woman who had been found dead in the early 1890s. She had not been murdered, but had died of exposure—there had been snow on the ground, although it was spring.

WOODPLUMPTON
St. Anne's Churchyard

St. Anne's church dates from the fourteenth century. The interior of this ancient church is fascinating and draws many tourists, but just as many come to stare at a nondescript glacial boulder that lies beside a footpath in the churchyard. The boulder marks the grave of the legendary Fylde Witch, Marjorie Hilton.

Tales about Marjorie Hilton come from all over the Fylde. One story tells how she was accused of stealing corn from a Singleton miller, although he had never managed to catch her in the act. Night after night he would see her sneaking into the mill, but when he went to look for her there was never a trace. Yet, in the morning, he would check his stores and find corn missing, again. Eventually, one evening, the miller saw Marjorie sneaking into the barn and quickly went in after her—but she was nowhere to be seen. Convinced that he had been robbed again, the miller counted his store and to his surprise found that there was one sack too many! He took a pitchfork and stabbed a sack, then another, until at last one of them let out a scream and there was Marjorie standing before him. But the miller still didn't manage to catch her, because she picked up a broomstick, jumped astride it and flew away.

Another folktale tells how Marjorie took a liking to a cottage in Catforth, owned by one Mr. Haydock. Haydock was well-known for his love of hunting and his pack of hounds, particularly one black dog that was much faster than the rest. Marjorie made a wager with Haydock: she would race against his hounds and, if she reached her home unscathed, the cottage in Catforth would be hers. Her only stipulation was that the black hound should not be released. Haydock accepted her bet, but let loose the black dog anyway. In an attempt to outrun the hound, Marjorie turned herself into a hare and managed to reach the door of her cottage just ahead of the dog, which just managed to nip the hare's heel before it disappeared inside. Marjorie had won her bet and the cottage at Catforth, but for many days afterwards it was noticed that she was walking with a slight limp...

Another story tells of a man who came across Marjorie returning from market with a fat, white goose waddling ahead of her. The lane was narrow and the bad-tempered bird wouldn't let the man pass, so he kicked it out of the way—and the next minute Marjorie was shouting at him for breaking her pitcher of milk all over the ground. He looked down and sure enough, on the ground at his feet were the pieces of a broken milk-crock, in a puddle of wasted milk. The goose was nowhere to be seen. Marjorie had found the pitcher too heavy to carry and had turned it into a goose so it could walk home on its own!

Apparently, this was a trick she used more than once. Another story tells how a farmer saw her flying over a hedge into his cow-pasture with a jug in her hand and immediately assumed the old hag was set to steal some milk from his cows. He went to see her off, but she argued that she had no jug; she had only come to graze her white goose. The farmer saw through her trick when he spotted milk dribbling from the goose's beak—he kicked at it, the spell was broken and the milk-jug lay shattered on the ground as Marjorie flew away over the hedge.

A crueller story tells of a farmer who was sure Marjorie had bewitched his cow so that it would no longer give milk. He took a traditional course of action. He invited her to warm herself at his fire, encouraging her to take the cosiest seat, in the inglenook. Before she arrived he had placed two forks, crossed, on her seat and left them there all day, and thus a spell was put on the old woman so that once seated, she could not stand up again. Having trapped her, the farmer berated her for bewitching his cow and insisted she remove the spell straight away. When she proclaimed her innocence, the farmer built up the fire until she became uncomfortably hot, but still she wouldn't confess—not until the flames were so high that they seared the old woman's skin did she at last relent and agree to remove her spell.

Today, it's easy to regard folktales like these as naive stories with no basis in fact, but a woman called Marjorie Hilton really lived and died in Woodplumpton and, according to the Parish Register, she was buried in St. Anne's churchyard on the second of May 1705. It's likely that she was simply a poor old woman, doing her best to survive by stealing small amounts of corn and an occasional jug of milk. Today, she would have been accepted as a harmless eccentric who preferred solitude to company, but at the end of the seventeenth century, with rumours of witchcraft prevalent, attitudes were very different.

Even the story of her death is shrouded in mystery. She had not been seen for several days, and when the villagers went to investigate, they found her dead. If her death was an accident, it was a strange one indeed, because poor Marjorie was found crushed between a barrel and a wall. The stories fail to record whether any human agency was suspected of killing her. The verdict of the locals was probably that it was the devil's work, that he had come to claim his own, and no further investigation was necessary.

One obvious question is why should a witch be buried in a churchyard? The answer is that whilst some villagers objected, others knew that Marjorie had been baptized a Christian and pleaded that she could not be denied a last resting-place near the house of the Lord. However, as a compromise she was buried away from other decent Christian souls, near a pathway some yards from the church and her burial took place at night, by candlelight. But in true witch fashion, she refused to stay buried.

During her lifetime, poor Marjorie had been blamed for every small mishap in the district, and in the months after her death, the villagers continued to suffer from cows going dry, hens refusing to lay, horses going lame. When someone reported having seen

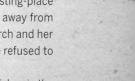

Marjorie on the outskirts of the village, it was decided that action must be taken. They dug up her body and reburied her, head downwards, with a large boulder on top of the site to make sure she couldn't dig her way out again.

Marjorie Hilton may have been dead and buried for over 300 years, but her legend lives on. One local woman remembers how she and other children used to dance round the witch-stone and spit on it. Children today, inspecting the stone, are still likely to be warned by a local not to get too close, just in case Marjorie reaches up and grabs them by the ankle!

Wheatsheaf

One evening, many years ago, a motorist stopped hurriedly outside this pub, certain she had just hit an old woman. She summoned help from those in the pub, but they could find no trace of the woman at all. It may or may not be relevant that the pub stands opposite the graveyard where Marjorie Hilton, the Fylde Witch, is buried.

This same pub is famous for a photograph, taken inside the pub by the landlord, that shows the image of a girl in a purple dress, apparently engaging in polishing the brass around the fireplace. There was no such girl in the building at the time the photo was taken.

WORSTHORNE

Bay Horse

Old Thrutch, the ghost of the Bay Horse pub in Church Square, was a local miller's wife who worked at the mill with her husband all day and then, in her spare time, worked at the Bay Horse. She managed to hide some of her earnings from her husband by secreting it at the pub, building up a nice little nest egg. Returning home to the mill one night, Old Thrutch came to the stepping stones across the stream and, because the stream was swollen from heavy rains and the stepping stones slippery, she lost her balance and drowned in the fast-flowing water. The secret of her hoard of money drowned with her.

It wasn't long before strange things started happening at the Bay Horse, focusing on one room that had always been unused. When strange noises began to emanate from this room, the assumption was that Old Thrutch was back, looking for her hidden treasure, and as the disturbances became more worrisome, the doorway to the room was bricked up.

The ghostly noises stopped, but the haunting was not entirely forgotten. Many years later, a new landlord arrived at the Bay Horse and opened up the haunted room,

despite warnings from the local people, and very soon Old Thrutch was walking abroad once more. This time, it was said that she would appear in a red silk dress and her footsteps would be heard on the stairs. The pivotal moment came when a local man was trying to come into the pub to join his friends but the door was mysteriously stuck fast. He pulled and pulled and, suddenly, he heard a voice from the other side of the door shouting "Push!" The man called back, "Push the devil! You push, I'll pull!" And at once the door opened! There was no one was on the other side of the door—but a rustling noise was heard that stopped when it reached the newly opened haunted room. The landlord saw sense then, and bricked up the doorway again.

High Halstead Farm

There was once a farm near the Roggerham Gate Inn called High Halstead, and this is the scene of the legend of the "Halstead Changeling." One day, the farmer's wife left her child asleep in its cot whilst she went to fetch some water and came back to find, instead, an ugly creature, looking like a wrinkled little man. Not knowing what to do, she went to speak with a local wise man, who announced that the thing she had found in the cot was probably a fairy and that she could find out by performing some unusual household tasks.

Back at home, she set an eggshell filled with cold water on the fire and when the water came to the boil, the little creature was so intrigued that it called out, "What are you going to do with that?" She replied, "I'm going to make a brew!" And the creature commented, "Well, I'm three score and ten and I've never seen that done before!" That statement, that he was three score and ten, was the proof the woman needed; she picked up the creature and took him down to the stream, intending to leave him there. Nearing the stream, she heard the sound of her own child crying and found him in the arms of a very old woman—the mother of the creature she had found in the cot. The children were exchanged, but no words were spoken, as both mothers were so pleased to have their own children back again.

Local Legends

Fairies were often seen here, early in the morning, little men wearing green jackets looking after their women as they stole milk from cows. They were also known to frequent the Old Jam Well, where they churned their butter. Also, in 1883, many people swore they had seen a boggart in the shape of a black dog. Then they recalled a character known as Johnny o' Pasture, a man of bad character, who had died some time before. It was said of him that he had once sold his soul to the devil, who had appeared as a huge black dog...

WRIGHTINGTON

Finch House

A prominent catholic priest, Edward Dicconson, once lived here. The son of Hugh Dicconson of Wrightington Hall, he was born in 1670 and studied philosophy at Douai in France, eventually taking his religious oath there in 1698. He remained at Douai until 1720, after rising through the priesthood to be procurator of the college and a professor of syntax. He then returned to England to minister in Staffordshire and, in 1840, was eventually elected vicar apostolic, essentially bishop, of the north of England by Pope Benedict XIV. Dicconson came to live at Finch House—or Finch Mill, as it was then known—in 1740, and conducted his religious affairs from there. He died there in 1752.

The Dicconson family are reputed to have kept a preserved skull, whose legend stems from Finch House. The owner of the skull is variously said to be either a civil war cavalier or a priest, who was peacefully dining one evening when an intruder burst in and beheaded him with his sword. Sadly for legend, the tale cannot truly be linked with Edward Dicconson, priest, as the Civil War ended a century before his death.

WYCOLLER

Wycoller Bridge and Clapper Bridge

These bridges cross Wycoller Beck. It's thought that the stones that were used to build Wycoller Bridge—a charming and very old landmark—may once have been part of a prehistoric monument. Four of them have the "cup-mark" carvings common to such stones. Archaeologists say that at least three of the carvings are probably prehistoric whilst the fourth, more pronounced and deeper than the others, is more likely to have been a medieval attempt at copying the mark, possibly dating from the time the bridge was originally built.

Clapper Bridge, close by, has the local nickname of the Druid's Bridge and is much older than Wycoller Bridge. A little distance away is a field known as Dripping Stone Field, so called because legend says it was the site of druidical sacrifice.

There is also a spring, close to the stream bank, that used to fill the stone trough that can still be seen. It was once known as Lowlands Well and the water had healing power. Whether this was derived from some saint's name (perhaps St. Lawrence?) is unclear.

Wycoller Hall

There is very little left of Wycoller Hall, for it has long been deserted. Indeed, when Charlotte Bronte used it as the model for Ferndean in the novel *Jane Eyre*, it was empty even then. The last Cunliffe had died in 1819, but it is one of his ancestors who concerns us now.

In the days when the Stuarts were on the throne, Simon Cunliffe lived here with his wife. It is said that he murdered her, or at least caused her death, because the story varies according to the source. Perhaps, as some versions say, Cunliffe discovered that his wife had been unfaithful and murdered her. Or perhaps, as other versions insist, Cunliffe's wife haunts the place because she is eternally waiting for her husband, who was lost at sea. There is, however, a much more picturesque story—perhaps this one is the truth?

Early one morning, when Squire Cunliffe was hunting with his hounds, he came across a wily fox that outran him and his hounds for several miles, until at last it came to Wycoller Hall. The door to the hall was open and the fox ran inside, looking for a hiding place. Up the stairs it ran, pursued by the hounds and Squire Cunliffe himself, still on his horse, determined to make the kill. The fox ran through another door into the bedroom where Cunliffe's wife still lay in bed. She awoke to see her husband on his wild-eyed hunter and the dogs tearing the fox to pieces. She died soon afterwards, of the shock.

Tradition says that once every year a spectral horseman rides up to the doors of the hall. The visitation is noticeable because of the sound of a horse's hooves at full gallop and the scream of a terrified woman. No one in recent years has reported the experience, but on occasion the ghost of a woman dressed in black has been seen.

Wycoller Village

In the village of Wycoller, the building known as Wycoller House is haunted by a lady dressed in blue. Visitors there have experienced her passing them on the stairs and she is known for leaving doors open or closing them unexpectedly. A Grey Lady has been seen passing through the wall in Pierson House next door. Perhaps this house and neighbouring Wycoller House were once more closely connected?

TWO LAST LANCASHIRE TALES...

There's a tale told in the south of Lancashire that seems to have no place of origin, but that is worthy of inclusion here all the same. One evening a man was sitting quietly by his fire when he was surprised to see a cat coming down the chimney. He was even more surprised when the cat said, "Tell Dildrum, Doldrum's dead!" A few minutes later, his wife came into the room with their own cat, and hearing this story, the cat said, "Is Doldrum dead?" and disappeared up the chimney! There was no explanation but that Doldrum was King of the Cats and Dildrum—their own cat—was his heir.

Our last tale is also told in other counties but claimed for this book as some sources claim it as Lancastrian. It tells of an old cobbler who had a mysterious dream.

The cobbler dreamed of a man who told him that he must go to London Bridge, where he would learn something to his advantage. He dreamed the same dream for three nights, until at last he decided he must follow its instructions. When he reached London Bridge, he expected that the dream's prophecy would be fulfilled at once, but that did not happen. So he stayed there for three days. At the end of the third day, just as he was about to give up and go home, a stranger approached him and asked why he was there.

On hearing about the cobbler's dream, the stranger said dismissively that he had dreamed that if he went to a certain Lancashire place where there was a well-filled orchard, he would find, under one particular apple tree, a pot filled with gold. But the stranger paid no heed to such superstition and had not bothered to make the journey. He advised the cobbler to go home and forget his dream.

The cobbler, however, recognised the orchard and the apple-tree as his own, so he went home with all haste, dug under the tree, and found the treasure. The gold was in a pot that had on it an inscription the cobbler could not read, for it was in Latin. However, that hardly mattered, because he was grateful for the money, which was sufficient to pay for a good education for his son.

During his education, the boy learned Latin and so, one day, was able to read the strange inscription on the pot that had held the gold. The inscription read, "Look under, and you will find better." So they dug deeper in that same place, found much more treasure and lived a comfortable life thereafter.

CONCLUSION

Fairies, witches, ghostly ladies (in white, grey, or black), haunted houses, halls, pubs, and theatres, tales of the devil—and not forgetting boggarts—Lancashire certainly has them all. It is not unique amongst English counties; each one has a plethora of ghosts and folklore to offer the interested visitor. However, some stories told about Lancashire are unique to that county and not heard anywhere else. For those who would like to compare all tales of a particular type—for example, all those describing meetings with the devil—this book includes a Topical Index for the purpose. A second Index lists basic Postcodes and general Ordnance Survey references, for those who plan to explore Lancashire and visit some of the listed places for themselves. It is the reader's responsibility to avoid trespass; I could have omitted those places which are privately-owned or otherwise inaccessible, but that would have meant leaving out some very good stories...

BIBLIOGRAPHY

Bowker, James FRGSI. *Goblin Tales of Lancashire*. London: W. Swan Sonnenschein, 1883.

Cox, Antony D. H. *Haunted Britain*. London: Hutchinson, 1973.

Dyer, T. F. Thiselton. *The Ghost World*. London: Ward & Downey, 1893. Dyer, T. F. Thiselton. *Strange Pages From Family Papers.* London: Sampson Low, Marston, 1895.

Fishwick, Lt.-Colonel FSA and Rev. P. H. Ditchfield. *Memorials of Old Lancashire.* London: Bemrose & Sons, 1909.

Gomme, George L. *Folklore as an Historical Science.* London: Methuen, 1908.

Green, Andrew. *Our Haunted Kingdom.* Glasgow: Fontana, 1974.

Grice, Francis. *Folk Tales of Lancashire.* London: Thomas Nelson & Sons, 1953.

Grinsell, Leslie V. *Folklore of Prehistoric Sites in Britain.* London: David & Charles, 1976.

Hardwick, Charles. *Traditions, Superstitions And Folk-Lore.* Manchester, Lancashire: A. Ireland, 1872.

Harland, William and T. T. Wilkinson. *Lancashire Folk-Lore.* London: John Heywood, 1882.

Harland, William and T. T. Wilkinson. *Lancashire Legends.* London: John Heywood, 1873.

Harper, Charles G. *Haunted Houses.* London: Studio Editions, 1993.

Henderson, William. *Folk Lore of the Northern Counties.* London: Longman's Green, 1866.

Herbert, W. B. *Railway Ghosts & Phantoms.* Newton Abbot, Devon: David & Charles, 1989.

Hope, Robert C. *Legendary Lore of the Holy Wells of England.* London: Elliot Stock, 1893.

Ingram, John H. *Haunted Homes & Family Traditions of Great Britain.* London: Reeves & Turner, 1905.

Lofthouse, Jessica. *North-Country Folklore.* London: Hale, 1976.

McEwan, Graham J. *Haunted Churches of England* London: Hale 1989.

O'Donnell, Elliot. *Dangerous Ghosts.* London: Rider, 1954.

O'Donnell, Elliot. *Haunted Britain.* London: Rider, 1948.

O'Donnell, Elliot. *Phantoms of the Night.* London: Rider, 1956.

Peel, Edgar & Pat Southern. *The Trials of the Lancashire Witches.* Nelson, Lancashire: Hendon, 1985.

Roby, John. *Roby's Traditions of Lancashire.* Manchester, Lancashire: George Routledge & Sons, 1882.

Thornber, William. *The History of Blackpool and its Neighbourhood.* Blackpool & Fylde Historical Society, 1985.

Underwood, Peter. *Ghosts of North-West England.* Glasgow: Fontana 1978.

Underwood, Peter. *Nights in Haunted Houses.* London: Headline, 1994.

Underwood, Peter. *This Haunted Isle.* Poole, Dorset, Javelin: 1986.

Warren, Melanie and T. Wells. *Ghosts of the North.* Bristol: Avon, Broadcast Books, 1996.

Whitaker, Terence. *Lancashire's Ghosts and Legends.* London: Granada, 1982.

Wilcock, John. *Guide to Occult Britain.* London: Sidgwick & Jackson, 1976.

Winterbottom, Vera. *The Devil in Lancashire.* Stockport, Cheshire: Cloister Press, 1962.

TOPICAL INDEX

ANCIENT MONUMENTS AND THEIR STORIES

Bacup, Hell Clough, 22
Burnley, Local Legend, 50
Carnforth, Moothaw & Shrew Tree, 55
Chorley, Astley Hall, 60
Downham, The Great Stone, 77
Halton, St. Wilfrid's Church, 99
Heysham, The Barrows, 102
Hurst Green, Stonyhurst College, 111
Pendle, Devil's Apronful, 147
Thornton, Pennystone Rock, 178
Winter Hill, Two Lads Cairns, 194
Wiswell Moor, Jeppe Knave Grave, 195
Wycoller, Wycoller Bridge, Clapper
    Bridge, 200

ARTHURIAN STORIES

Appley Bridge, Skull House, 19
Bashall Eaves, Local Area, 25
Burscough, Martin Mere, 54

BOGGARTS IN HALLS

Bickerstaffe, Mossock Hall, 26
Burnley, Barcroft Hall, 47
Chipping, Wolf House, 59
Clitheroe, Old Hall, 66
Clitheroe, Waddow Hall, 67
Clitheroe, Well Hall, 68
Cockerham, Thurnham Hall, 72
Preesall, Hackensall Hall, 155
Ribchester, Hothersall Hall, 161

BOGGARTS IN HOUSES

Blackburn, Union Buildings, 32
Bolton By Bowland, Bolton Peel
    Farm, 40
Burnley, Coal Clough House, 49
Chipping, Leagram Mill, 58
Foulridge, Hobstones Farm, 87
Knowle Green, Written Stone
    Lane, 116
Mellor Brook, Sykes Lumb Farm, 135
Stalmine, Local Legend, 175
Tockholes, Red Lee, 180
Wycoller, Wycoller Village, 201

BOGGARTS OUTDOORS

Brunshaw, Turf Moor, 46
Burnley, Hollin Hey Clough, 50
Burnley, Rowley Hall, 51
Burnley, Towneley Hall, 53
Clayton-le-Moors, Dunkenhalgh
    Hotel, 62
Darwen, Ashleigh Barrow, 76
Galgate, Hampson Green, 92
Greenhalgh, Greenhalgh Castle, 97
Hurstwood, Local Legend, 112
Marton Moss, Whitegate Lane, 131
Pilling, Carr House, 151
Preesall, Town Foot, 155
Preston, Local Legend, 158
Weeton, Local Field, 189
Worsthorne, Local Legend, 199

BOTTOMLESS POOL

Preston, Moor Park, 158

BRIDGES IN STORIES

Burnley, Hollin Hey Clough, 50
Burnley, Rowley Hall, 51
Clayton le Moors, Dunkenhalgh
    Hotel, 62

Clitheroe, Bridge, 64

Clitheroe, Waddow Hall, 67

Cockerham, Local Legends, 71

Coppull, Darkland Bridge, 74

Greenhalgh, Greenhalgh Castle, 97

Inglewhite, St. Anne's Well, 113

Laneshaw Bridge, Barnside Hall, 121

Pilling, Pilling Moss, 153

St. Michaels on Wyre, Old Hall, 174

Whitewell, Saddle Bridge, 194

Wycoller, Wycoller Bridge and Clapper
    Bridge, 200

BURIED TREASURES

Accrington, Peel Park, 16

Accrington, Tasker Street, 17

Bickerstaffe, Mossock Hall, 26

Hurst Green, Stonyhurst College, 111

Mellor Brook, Sykes Lumb Farm, 135

Worsthorne, Bay Horse, 198

CASTLES AND THEIR STORIES

Ashton, near Preston, Preston Castle, 21

Bolton By Bowland, Bolton Peel Farm, 40

Broughton, Broughton Tower, 46

Burnley, Towneley Hall, 53

Clitheroe, Clitheroe Castle, 65

Croston, St. Michael and All Angels
    Church, 75

Greenhalgh, Greenhalgh Castle, 97

Hoghton, Hoghton Tower, 106

Hornby, Hornby Castle, 108

Hurst Green, Stonyhurst College, 111

Lancaster, Lancaster Castle, 119

Lancaster, The Tinker's Tale, 120

CHURCHES MOVED BY UNEARTHLY FORCES

Burnley, St. Peter's Church, 52

Great Mitton, All Hallows Church, 97

Leyland, St. Andrew's Church, 124

Samlesbury, St. Leonard the Less
    Churchyard, 167

CROSSES

Anderton, Headless Cross, 18
Burnley, Towneley Hall, 53
Colne, St. Bartholomew's Church, 73
Foulridge, Maiden's Cross, 88
Great Mitton, All Hallows Church, 97
Halton, St. Wilfrid's Church, 99
Hornby, Hornby Church, 109
Inglewhite, Village Green, 113
Lancaster, Priory Church, 120
Laneshaw Bridge, Hallown Well, 122
Lytham, St. Cuthbert's Cross, 128
Tockholes, Churchyard, 179
Ulnes Walton, Gradwells, 184
Ulnes Walton, Praying Crosses, 184
Whalley, Whalley Abbey, 192

CURSES AND DEATH OMENS

Burnley, Barcroft Hall, 47
Burnley, St. Peter's Church, 52
Clitheroe, Browsholme Hall, 64
Cliviger, Cliviger Gorge, 69
Poulton-le-Fylde, Local Legend, 154
Walton-le-Dale, St. Leonard's
    Churchyard, 187

THE DEVIL IN FOLKLORE

Bacup, Hell Clough, 22
Blackburn, Raising the Devil, 31
Brindle, St. James' Church, 45
Burnley, Burnley Grammar School, 49
Chatburn, Dule Upon Dun, 57
Chipping, Three Lane Ends, 59
Clitheroe, Clitheroe Castle, 65
Clitheroe, Grammar SchooL, 65
Cliviger, Cliviger Gorge, 69
Cockerham, Local Legends, 71
Crawshawbooth, Village Green, 74
Extwistle, Lee Green, 80
Fair Snape Fell, Local Legend, 81
Fulwood, Withy Trees, 91
Garstang, Local Legend, 93

Great Mitton, All Hallows Church, 97
Haslingden, Haslingden Grains, 100
Hoghton, Hoghton Tower, 106
Hornby, Hornby Castle, 108
Hurst Green, Stonyhurst College, 111
Pendle, Devil's Apronful, 147
Pilling, Pilling Moss, 153
Ribchester, Hothersall Hall, 161
Rivington, Rivington Pike, 162
Sawley, Spread Eagle, 168
Walton-le-Dale, St. Leonard's
    Churchyard, 187

DRAGON

Silverdale, Hawes Tarn, 169

DREAMS OF PROPHECY

Broughton, Broughton Tower, 46
Darwen, Lower Darwen, 76
Laneshaw Bridge, Barnside Hall, 121

FAIRIES IN FOLKLORE

Barley, Barley Brow, 23
Bolton by Bowland, Rainsber Scar, 41
Briercliffe, Calf Hey Well , 43
Burnley, Rowley Hall, 51
Croston, St. Michael and All Angels
    Church, 75
Goosnargh, Local Legend, 96
Great Mitton, All Hallows Church, 97
Grindleton, Cat Steps, 98
Grindleton, Dinkling Green, 98
Hardhorn, Local Legend, 99
Hoghton, Local Legend, 108
Mellor, Mellor Moor, 135
Staining, Local Legend, 174
Thornton, Local Legend, 177
Warton near Carnforth, Fairy Hole, 188
Whitewell, Fair Oak Circle, 192
Whitewell, Fairy Holes Cave, 193
Whitewell, Hodder Gorge; a cave, 193
Whitewell, Saddle Bridge, 194
Worsthorne, High Halstead Farm, 199
Worsthorne, Local Legend, 199

FAIRY FUNERALS

Extwistle, Extwistle Hal, 79
Higher Penwortham, Church Avenue, 105

FOOTPRINTS

Brindle, St. James' Church, 45
Pilling, Pilling Moss, 153

GHOSTS OF ANIMALS

Burnley, St. Peter's Church, 52
Coppull, Darkland Bridge, 74
Fleetwood, Bourne Hall, 82
Fleetwood, Fish Market, 83
Hurstwood, Local Legend, 112
Leyland, St. Andrew's Church, 124
Preesall, Town Foot, 155
Preston, Local Legend, 158
Preston, Wellington Inn, 160
Scotforth, Bowling Green Hotel, 168
Singleton, Shard Riverside Inn, 171
Whalley, Whalley Abbey, 192
Woodplumpton, Wheatsheaf, 198
Worsthorne, Local Legend, 199

GHOSTS IN BUSINESS AND OFFICE PREMISES

Bamber Bridge, Baxi Heating, 23
Barnoldswick, Northern Costume Hire, 25
Blackburn, Byrom Street Fire Station, 27
Blackburn, Telephone Exchange, 31
Blackpool, Illuminations Building, 36
Burnley, Burnley Express Offices, 48
Burnley, Central Library, 49
Burscough, Burscough Airfield, 54
Eccleston, Grove Mill, 78
Fulwood, Fulwood Barracks, 90
Fulwood, Preston Workhouse Hospital, 91
Heysham, Heysham Library, 103
Leyland, LG Kitchens, 123
Marton Moss, North West Gas HQ, 131
Oswaldtwistle, Stanhill Lane Post Office, 144
Preston, New Hall Lane, 158
Warton, near Blackpool, Wrea Brook Court, 188

GHOSTS IN CASTLES

Clitheroe, Clitheroe Castle, 65
Hoghton, Hoghton Tower, 106
Hornby, Hornby Castle, 108
Lancaster, Lancaster Castle, 119
Rivington, Rivington Castle, 162
Turton, Turton Tower, 183

GHOSTS IN CHURCHES

Burnley, St. Peter's Church, 52
Burscough, Burscough Priory, 54
Clitheroe, Methodist Chapel, 66
Croston, St. Michael and All Angels
    Church, 75
Fulwood, Fulwood Barracks, 90
Silverdale, St. John's Church, 169
Whalley, Whalley Abbey, 192

GHOSTS IN HALLS

Bickerstaffe, Mossock Hall, 26
Borwick, Borwick Hall, 42
Bretherton, Bank Hall, 42
Burnley, Rowley Hall, 51
Burnley, Towneley Hall, 53
Charnock Richard, Park Hall, 57
Chipping, Leagram Hall, 58
Chorley, Astley Hall, 60
Chorley, Bagganley Hall, 60
Chorley, Hall o'the Hill – Chorley Golf
    Club, 61
Clayton-le-Moors, Dunkenhalgh Hotel, 62
Cliviger, Holme Hall, 70
Cockerham, Thurnham Hall, 72
Colne, Colne Hall, 73
Fleetwood, Rossall Hall, 85
Goosnargh, Chingle Hall, 94
Heskin Green, Heskin Hall, 101
Leyland, Charnock Old Hall, 122
Leyland, Worden Hall, 125
Lytham, Lytham Hall, 127
Mawdesley, Mawdesley Hall & The Black
    Bull, 132
Medlar-with-Wesham, Mowbreck
    Hall, 133

Melling, Melling Hall, 134
Nelson, Marsden Hall, 138
Ormskirk, Rufford Old Hall, 142
Osbaldeston, Osbaldeston Hall, 143
Padiham, Gawthorpe Hall, 145
Pilling, Fluke Hall, 151
Samlesbury, Samlesbury Hall, 164
Singleton, Mains Hall, 171
St. Michaels on Wyre, Old Hall, 174
Staining, Staining Hall, 175
Thurnham, Ashton Hall, 179
Tockholes, Hollinshead Hall, 179
Torrisholme, Torrisholme Hall, 180
Ulnes Walton, Gradwells, 184
Wycoller, Wycoller Hall, 201

GHOSTS IN HOSPITALS

Blackpool, South Shore Hospital, 39
Blackpool, Victoria Hospital, 40
Burnley, Victoria Hospital, 54
Chorley, Chorley Hospital, 61
Fleetwood, Fleetwood Hospital, 83
Goosnargh, Whittingham Hospital, 96

GHOSTS IN HOTELS

Blackpool, Old Coach House Hotel, 36
Blackpool, Raikes Hotel, 37
Clayton-le-Moors, Dunkenhalgh Hotel, 62
Darwen, Millstone Hotel, 77
Fleetwood, North Euston Hotel, 84
Melling, Melling Hall, 134
Morecambe, Clarendon Hotel, 136
Morecambe, Midland Hotel, 136
Reedley, Oakes Hotel, 161

GHOSTS IN HOUSES

Accrington, Hynd Brook House, 16
Accrington, Springhill House, 17
Adlington, Chaffer's House, 18
Bretherton, Carr House, 43
Burnley, Allen Street, 46
Burnley, Coal Clough House, 49
Cockerham, Invisible Harpist, 71
Fulwood, Black Bull Lane, 90

Goosnargh, The Hill Presbytery, 96

Great Eccleston, Cross House, 97

Heyhouses, Fancy Lodge, 101

Heysham, Converted Barn, 102

Lancaster, Penny Street, 119

Leyland, Police Station, 124

Lower Bartle, Swillbrook House, 126

Marton Moss, Higher Fall Farm, 130

Melling, Todd Cottage, 134

Newchurch In Pendle, Tynedale
    Farm, 140

Preston, Friargate, 156

St. Annes, Wood Street, 173

Stydd, Stydd Almshouses, 176

Thornton, Police Station, 178

Upholland, A Cottage, 185

Upholland, Church Street, 185

Withnell, Broadwood, 195

Wycoller, Wycoller Village, 201

GHOSTS OUTDOORS

Accrington, Black Abbey, 14

Accrington, Peel Park, 16

Accrington, Tasker Street, 17

Anderton, Headless Cross, 18

Bamber Bridge, St. Saviour's
    Church, 23

Bashall Eaves, Local Farmhouse, 25

Bispham, Robins Lane, 26

Blackburn, Grimshaw Park, 29

Blackburn, Holy Trinity Church, 29

Clowbridge, Clowbridge Reservoir, 70

Coppull, Darkland Bridge, 74

Galgate, Green Lane, 92

Greenhalgh, Greenhalgh Castle, 97

Heyhouses, Fancy Lodge, 101

Higher Penwortham, St. Mary's
    Well, 106

Hornby, Hornby Park, 110

Laneshaw Bridge, Barnside Hall, 121

Longridge, Local Legend, 125

Mellor Brook, Sykes Lumb Farm, 135

Newchurch In Pendle, Jinny Well, 139

Padiham, Pendle Street
    Footbridge, 145

Pleasington, Playing Fields, 153
Preston, Ladywell Street, 157
Rivington, Ornamental Gardens, 162
Rivington, Rivington Pike, 162
Samlesbury, St. Leonard the Less
    Churchyard, 167
St. Annes, Sand Dunes, 173
Thornton, Pennystone Rock, 178
Winter Hill, Two Lads Cairns, 194
Withnell, Broadwood, 195

GHOSTS IN PUBS

Accrington, Miner's Arms, 16
Adlington, Bridge Inn, 17
Adlington, Ridgway Arms, 18
Arkholme, Redwell Inn, 20
Blackburn, Duck & Puddle, 29
Blackburn, Postal Order, 31
Blacko, Cross Gaits Inn, 34
Blackpool, Riley's Snooker Hall, 38
Blackpool, Saddle Inn, 39
Burnley, Keirby Inn, 50
Burnley, Swan Inn, 53
Chipping, Sun Inn, 59
Clayton-le-Woods, Halfway House, 64
Clayton-le-Woods, Ley Inn, 64
Clitheroe, Swan and Royal, 66
Cliviger, Gordon Lennox, 70
Colne, Hole In The Wall Inn, 73
Darwen, Crown and Thistle, 76
Euxton, Euxton Mills Hotel, 79
Fleetwood, Victoria, 87
Foulridge, New Inn, 88
Freckleton, Ship Inn, 89
Hapton, Bridge House Inn, 99
Haslingden, Griffin Hotel, 100
Heysham, Old Hall Hotel, 104
Heysham, Royal Oak, 104
Huncoat, Black Bull, 110
Hurst Green, Punch Bowl Inn, 110
Kelbrook, Old Stone Trough, 114
Kellamergh, Birley Arms, 114
Kirkham, Bell and Bottle, 115
Kirkham, Railway Inn, 116
Lancaster, Alexandra Hall, 117

Lancaster, Golden Lion, 117
Lancaster, Three Mariners, 120
Leyland, Halfway House, 123
Lostock Hall, Tardy Gate, 126
Lytham, Ship and Royal Hotel, 127
Marton Moss, Boar's Head, 130
Mawdesley, Mawdesley Hall and
    The Black Bull, 132
Nelson, Engineer's Arms, 138
Old Langho, Black Bull Inn, 141
Ormskirk, The Plough, 141
Oswaldtwistle, Duckworth Hall Inn, 144
Padiham, Red Rock, 145
Pilling, Olde Ship, 152
Preston, George Hotel, 156
Preston, Spindlemaker's Arms, 159
Preston, Stone Cottage Inn, 159
Preston, Wellington Inn, 160
Preston, White Bull, 160
Rawtenstall, Railway Inn, 161
Salwick, Hand and Dagger, 164
Samlesbury, New Hall Tavern, 164
Singleton, Shard Bridge, 171
Thornton, Ashley Conservative Club, 177
Tockholes, Royal Arms, 180
Turton, Bull's Head, 182
Waterfoot, Railway Inn, 188
Weeton, Eagle and Child , 189
Whalley, Swan Hotel, 191
Woodplumpton, Wheatshea, 198
Worsthorne, Bay Horse, 198

GHOSTS IN PUBLIC BUILDINGS

Accrington, Arndale Shopping Centre, 14
Bickerstaffe, Mossock Hall, 26
Blackburn, CVS Resource Centre, 28
Blackburn, King George's Hall, 30
Blackburn, Utopia Nightclub, 33
Blackpool, Blackpool Football Club, 34
Blackpool, Blackpool Zoo, 35
Blackpool, Frenchman's Cove, 35
Blackpool, Pleasure Beach, 37
Blackpool, Ripley's 'Believe It Or Not!', 38

Blackpool, Superbowl, 40
Blackpool Tower, 35
Burnley, Smackwater Jack's, 52
Chorley, Botany Bay, 61
Chorley, Hall o'the Hill – Chorley Golf
    Club, 61
Fleetwood, Marine Hall, 84
Heskin Green, Heskin Hall, 101
Leyland, Towngate, 125
Padiham, Royal British Legion Club, 148
Preston, Town Hall, 160
St. Annes, Anthony House, 172
St. Annes, Old Links Golf Club, 173

GHOSTS IN RADIO STATIONS

Blackburn, BBC Radio Lancashire
    studios, 27
Lancaster, Radio Station, 120

GHOSTS IN RAILWAY STATIONS

Chorley, Railway Station, 62
Entwistle, Entwistle Halt, 78
Preston, Railway Station, 159

GHOSTS ON ROADS

Carleton, Crematorium, 55
Caton, The Druid's Oak, 56
Freckleton, Road Ghost, 89
Fulwood, Fulwood Barracks, 90
Samlesbury, Samlesbury Hall, 164

GHOSTS IN SCHOOLS

Blackpool, Arnold School, 34
Blackpool, St. Mary's High School, 40
Leyland, Runshaw College, 124

GHOSTS IN THEATRES

Bacup, Royal Court Theatre, 22
Blackburn, Palace Theatre, 30

Blackpool, Grand Theatre, 36
Lancaster, Grand Theatre, 118
Morecambe, Palace Theatre, 137
Morecambe, Royalty Theatre, 137
Morecambe, Winter Gardens
    Theatre, 137
Preston, Playhouse Theatre, 159

GREEN MAN CARVINGS

Great Mitton, All Hallows Church, 97
Heysham, St. Peter's Church, 105
Hoghton, Hoghton Tower, 106
Lancaster, Priory Church, 120
Ormskirk, St. Anne's Church, 142
Ormskirk, St. Peter and St. Paul's
    Church, 143
Samlesbury, Samlesbury Hall, 164
Slaidburn, St. Andrew's Church, 171
Tunstall, St. John the Baptist
    Church, 182
Whalley, Whalley Abbey, 192

LIGHTS

Bispham, Robins Lane, 26
Blackburn, Holy Trinity Church, 29
Inglewhite, Village Green, 113
Thornton, Local Lane, 177
Whalley, Whalley Abbey, 192

LOST BELLS

Ashton, near Preston, Preston Castle, 21
Clayton le Moors, Dunkenhalgh
    Hotel, 62
Pendle, Ashenden Clough, 146
Samlesbury, Samlesbury Hall, 164
St. Annes, Kilgrimol, 172

LOST VILLAGES

Clowbridge, Clowbridge Reservoir, 70
St. Annes, Kilgrimol, 172
Thornton, Pennystone Rock, 178

MARTYRS

Anderton, Headless Cross, 18

Appley Bridge, Skull House, 19

Brindle, Gregson Lane – the Holy
Hand, 44

Broughton, Broughton Tower, 46

Chaigley, Chapel House Farm, 56

Heskin Green, Heskin Hall, 101

Mawdesley, Lane End House, 132

Medlar-with-Wesham, Mowbreck
Hall, 133

MISTLETOE BRIDE

Heskin Green, Heskin Hall Heskin
Green, Heskin Hall, 101

MONSTERS, MERMAIDS, GIANTS

Burscough, Martin Mere, 54

Darwen, Darwen Moors, 76

Kirkham, Kirkham Church, 115

Silverdale, Hawes Tarn, 169

POSSESSION TALES

Simonstone, Huntroyd Hall, 169

Whalley, Surey Demoniac, 190

SECRET PASSAGEWAYS

Adlington, Chaffer's House, 18

Anderton, Headless Cross, 18

Kirkham, Railway Inn, 116

Warton, near Blackpool, Wrea Brook
Court, 188

SEVEN YEAR SACRIFICES

Burnley, Towneley Hall, 53

Clitheroe, Waddow Hall, 67

SKULLS

Appley Bridge, Skull House, 19
Blackpool, Ripley's 'Believe It Or Not!', 38
Chaigley, Chapel House Farm, 56
Clitheroe, Browsholme Hall, 64
Freckleton, Ship Inn, 89
Mawdesley, Lane End House, 132
Turton, Turton Tower, 183
Wrightington, Finch House, 200

STONES AND THEIR STORIES

Bacup, Hell Clough, 22
Bickerstaffe, Mossock Hall, 26
Downham, The Great Stone, 77
Foulridge, Standing Stone Lane, 89
Garstang, Garstang Church, 92
Heysham, The Barrows, 102
Knowle Green, Written Stone Lane, 116
Mawdesley, Mawdesley Blue Stone, 132
Newchurch In Pendle, Jinny Well, 139
Sabden, Coffin Stone, 164
Silverdale, Hawes Tarn, 169
Thornton, Pennystone Rock, 178
Trawden, Lad O' Crow Hill, 181
Turton, Hanging Stone, 182
Turton, Turton Tower, 183
Wycoller, Wycoller Bridge and Clapper
    Bridge, 200

STRANGE EVENTS

Accrington, East Crescent, 15
Chorley, Chorley Hall, 61
Eccleston, Bank House, 78
Preston, Christ Church, 156
Ulnes Walton, Gradwells, 184

SUNKEN CHURCHES

Ashton, near Preston, Preston Castle, 21
Mellor, Mellor Moor, 135

TREES IN FOLKLORE

Carnforth, Moothaw & Shrew Tree, 55
Caton, The Druid's Oak, 56
Melling, Local Legend, 134

WATER IN FOLKLORE

Blackpool, Sea-Bathing, 39
Burnley, Hollin Hey Clough, 50
Burnley, Rowley Hall, 51
Burscough, Martin Mere, 54
Charnock Richard, Park Hall, 57
Chipping, Wolf House, 59
Clayton-le-Moors, Dunkenhalgh
    Hotel, 62
Clitheroe, Waddow Hall, 67
Clowbridge, Clowbridge Reservoir, 70
Hurstwood, Local Legend, 112
Newchurch In Pendle, Jinny Well, 139
St Michaels on Wyre, Old Hall, 174

WELLS

Ashton, near Preston, Spa Well, 21
Barnoldswick, Lister Well, 24
Blackburn, Well (near the Wellington
    Inn), 33
Bolton by Bowland, Fooden Spa, 41
Briercliffe, Calf Hey Well, 43
Brindle, St. Ellen's Well, 45
Burnley, Shorey Well, 51
Chipping, Churchyard, 58
Clitheroe, Waddow Hall, 67
Colne, Craven Laithe Farm, 73
Colne, St. Helen's Well, 74
Fernyhalgh, Ladyewell, 82
Hardhorn, Local Legend, 99
Heysham, Crime Well, 103
Heysham, Sainty Well, 105
Higher Penwortham, St. Mary's Well, 106
Inglewhite, St. Anne's Well, 113
Kelbrook, Dissenters Well, 114

Laneshaw Bridge, Hallown Well, 122
Larbreck, Well, 122
Newchurch In Pendle, Jinny Well, 139
Newton In Bowland, Walloper Well, 140
Parlick Pike, Old Nick's Watering Pot, 146
Pendle, Fox's Well, 147
Preston, Avenham Park, 155
Preston, Our Lady's Well, 158
Sabden, Coffin Stone, 164
Slyne, St. Patrick's Well, 172
Tockholes, Hollinshead Hall, 179
Whalley, St. Mary's Well, 190
Wycoller, Wycoller Bridge and Clapper
   Bridge, 200

WITCHCRAFT

Barley, Lower Black Moss Reservoir, 24
Burnley, Local Legend, 50
Chipping, Churchyard, 58
Cliviger, Cliviger Gorge, 69
Goosnargh, Dun Cow Rib Farm, 95
Hurst Green, Stonyhurst College, 111
Lancaster, Gallows Hill, 117
Lancaster, Golden Lion, 117
Lancaster, Lancaster Castle, 119
Lancaster, Three Mariners, 120
Lytham, Witchwood, 128
Marton Moss, Witches and Wizard, 131
Newchurch in Pendle, Newchurch
   Church, 139
Newchurch in Pendle, Rossendale
   Wizard, 139
Parlick Pike, Old Nick's Watering Pot, 146
Pendle, Local Legend, 147
Pendle, Pendle Witches, 149
Poulton-Le-Fylde, Poulton Church, 154
Samlesbury, Samlesbury Hall, 164
Samlesbury, St. Leonard the Less
   Churchyard, 167
Trawden, Local Legend, 181
Walton-le-Dale, St. Leonard's Churchyard, 187
Weir, Local Legend, 189
West Bradford, Barn, 190
Whitewell, Saddle Bridge, 194
Woodplumpton, St. Anne's Churchyard, 196

APPENDIX

OS Map References and Postcodes

A

Accrington	SD7528	BB5 0
Adlington	SD6013	PR6 9
Anderton	SD6013	PR6 9
Appley Bridge	SD5209	WN6 9
Arkholme	SD5871	LA6 1
Ashton, near Preston	SD5230	PR2

B

Bacup	SD8622	OL13 8
Bamber Bridge	SD5626	PR5 6
Barley	SD8240	BB12 9
Barnoldswick	SD8746	BB18 5
Bashall Eaves	SD6943	BB7 3
Bickerstaffe	SD4404	L39 0
Bispham	SD3040	FY2 9
Blackburn	SD6827	BB11
Blacko	SD8541	BB9 6
Blackpool	SD3136	FY1 3
Bolton-by-Bowland	SD7849	BB7 4
Borwick	SD5273	LA6 1
Bretherton	SD4720	PR26 9
Briercliffe	SD8735	BB10
Brindle	SD5924	PR6 8
Broughton	SD5235	PR3 5
Brunshaw	SD8532	BB10 4
Burnley	SD8332	BB11 1
Burscough	SD4310	L40 7

C

Carleton	SD3339	FY6 7
Carnforth	SD4970	LA5 9
Caton	SD5364	LA2 9
Chaigley	D6837	BB7
Charnock Richard	SD5515	PR7 5
Chatburn	SD7644	BB7 4
Chipping	SD6243	PR3 2
Chorley	SD5817	PR7 1
Clayton-le-Moors	SD7431	BB5 5
Clayton-le-Woods	SD5622	PR25
Clitheroe	SD7441	BB7 1
Cliviger	SD8630	BB10
Clowbridge	SD8228	BB11 5
Cockerham	SD4652	LA2 0
Colne	SD8940	BB8 0
Coppull	SD5614	PR7 4
Crawshawbooth	SD8125	BB4 8
Croston	SD4819	PR26

D

Darwen	SD6922	BB3 3
Downham	SD7844	BB7 4

E

Eccleston	SD5117	PR7 5
Entwistle	SD7318	BL7
Euxton	SD5518	PR7 6
Extwistle	SD8735	BB10

F

Fair Snape Fell	SD5947	(None)
Fernyhalgh	SD5534	PR2 5
Fleetwood	SD3247	FY7 7
Foulridge	SD8842	BB8 7
Freckleton	SD4228	PR4 1
Fulwood	SD5431	PR2 8

G

Galgate	SD4855	LA2 0
Garstang	SD4945	PR3 1
Goosnargh	SD5536	PR3 2
Great Eccleston	SD4240	PR3 0
Great Mitton	SD7138	BB7 9
Greenhalgh	SD4035	PR4 3
Grindleton	SD7545	BB7 4

H

Halton	SD5064	LA2 6
Hapton	SD7931	BB11 5
Hardhorn	SD3538	FY6 8
Haslingden	SD7823	BB4 5
Heskin Green	SD5315	PR7 5
Heyhouses	SD3429	FY8 4
Heysham	SD4161	LA3 2
Higher Penwortham	SD5128	PR1 0
Hoghton	SD6126	PR5 0
Hornby	SD5868	LA2 8
Huncoat	SD7730	BB5 6
Hurst Green	SD6838	BB7 9
Hurstwood	SD8831	BB10 3

I

Inglewhite	SD5439	PR3 2

K

Kelbrook	SD9044	BB18 6
Kellamergh	SD4029	PR4 1
Kirkham	SD4232	PR4 2
Knowle Green	SD6338	PR3 2

L

Lancaster	SD4761	LA1 1
Laneshaw Bridge	SD9240	BB8 7
Larbreck	SD4040	PR3 0
Leyland	SD5422	PR25 3
Longridge	SD6037	PR3 3
Lostock Hall	SD5425	PR5 5
Lower Bartle	SD4933	PR4 0
Lytham	SD3527	FY8 4

M

Marton Moss	SD3333	FY4 4
Mawdesley	SD4914	L40 3
Medlar-with-Wesham	SD4135	PR4 3
Melling	SD5971	LA6 2
Mellor	SD6530	BB2 7
Mellor Brook	SD6431	BB2 7
Morecambe	SD4263	LA3 1

N

Nelson	SD8637	BB9 9
Newchurch in Pendle	SD8239	BB12 9
Newton in Bowland	SD6950	BB7 3

O

Old Langho	SD7035	BB6 8
Ormskirk	SD4108	L39 2
Osbaldeston	SD6431	BB2 7
Oswaldtwistle	SD7327	BB5 3

P

Padiham	SD7933	BB12 7
Parlick Pike	SD5945	(None)
Pendle	SD8041	(None)
Pilling	SD4048	PR3 6
Pleasington	SD6426	BB2 5
Poulton-le-Fylde	SD3439	FY6 7
Preesall	SD3647	FY6 0
Preston	SD5329	PR1 2

R

Rawtenstall	SD8124	BB4 8
Reedley	SD8435	BB10 2
Ribchester	SD6435	PR3 3
Rivington	SD6214	BL6 7
Rossendale	SD8123	(None)

S

Sabden	SD7737	BB7 9
Salwick	SD4763	PR4
Samlesbury	SD5930	PR5 0
Sawley	SD7746	BB7 4
Scotforth	SD4859	LA1 4
Silverdale	SD4675	LA5 0
Simonstone	SD7734	BB12 7
Singleton	SD3838	FY6 8
Slaidburn	SD7152	BB7 3
Slyne	SD4765	LA2 6
St. Annes	SD3128	FY8 2
St. Michael's on Wyre	SD4641	PR3 0
Staining	SD3436	FY3 0
Stalmine	SD3745	FY6 0
Stydd	SD6535	PR3 3

T

Thornton	SD3442	FY5 4
Thurnham	SD4654	LA2 0
Tockholes	SD6623	BB3 0
Torrisholme	SD4564	LA4 6
Trawden	SD9138	BB8 8
Tunstall	SD6073	LA6 2
Turton	SD7315	BL7 0

U

Ulnes Walton	SD5118	PR26 8
Upholland	SD5105	WN8 0

W

Walton-le-Dale	SD5527	PR5 4
Warton, Fylde	SD4128	PR4 1
Warton, near Carnforth	SD5072	LA5 9
Waterfoot	SD8321	BB4 7
Weeton	SD3834	PR4 3
Weir	SD8725	OL13 8
West Bradford	SD7444	BB7 4
Whalley	SD7336	BB7 9
Whitewell	SD6546	BB7 3
Winter Hill	SD6615	(None)
Wiswell Moor	SD7437	BB7 9
Withnell	SD6322	PR6 8
Woodplumpton	SD5034	PR4 0
Worsthorne	SD8732	BB10 3
Wrightington	SD5313	WN6 9
Wycoller	SD9339	BB8 8

AVE MARIA

FERNYHALGH–
LADYEWELL

COCKERHAM–THURNHAM HALL

WOODPLUMPTON—ST ANNE'S CHURCHYARD—
MARJORIE HILTON'S GRAVE

HEYSHAM—ST PETER'S CHURCH

SAMLESBURY HALL

LANCASTER—ASHTON HALL

HEYSHAM—ST PETER'S CHURCH—DETAIL

LANCASTER CASTLE

GREENHALGH CASTLE

HEYSHAM—THE BARROWS